I0763057

NATIONAL MONUMENT,
TO BE ERECTED AT
GETTYSBURG, PA.

REVISED REPORT

OF THE

SELECT COMMITTEE

RELATIVE TO THE

Soldiers' National Cemetery,

TOGETHER WITH THE

ACCOMPANYING DOCUMENTS,

AS REPORTED TO THE

HOUSE OF REPRESENTATIVES

OF THE

COMMONWEALTH OF PENNSYLVANIA.

"Wherosoever throughout the civilized world the accounts of this great warfare are read, and down to the latest period of recorded time, in the glorious annals of our common country there will be no brighter page than that which relates THE BATTLES OF GETTYSBURG."—EVERETT.

COMMONWEALTH OF PENNSYLVANIA.

[Extract from Governor CURTIN's Annual Message, January 7, 1864.]

After the battle of Gettysburg, in which loyal volunteers from eighteen States, including Pennsylvania, were engaged, it appeared to me proper that all those States should unite in establishing a cemetery, on the spot in which their soldiers who had fallen in that conflict, should be honorably interred. I accordingly appointed DAVID WILLS, Esq., of Gettysburg, my agent, and through him, a site was purchased at a cost of $2,475 87, and the conveyances made to the Commonwealth. On communicating with the authorities of the other States, they all readily agreed to become parties to the arrangement, and on the 19th day of November last, the cemetery was dedicated, with appropriate ceremonies, in the presence of the President of the United States, the Governors of the States concerned, and other high officers, State and National. On the 19th day of December, on the invitation of Mr. WILLS, commissioners representing the States interested in the cemetery, met in Harrisburg, and agreed upon a plan for its improvement and care in the future, and the apportionment of the sum of money required, to the several States, which is herewith communicated. The expenses attending the establishment of this cemetery, including the cost of the site and of removing the bodies of the slain, have thus far amounted to $5,209 38, and an appropriation will be required to pay these expenses, and to meet our portion of those attending its future maintenance. It will appear by the proceedings of the commissioners, that their due proportion of the expenses already incurred, are to be refunded by the States on whose account they were made. It is just to say, that Mr. WILLS has discharged his delicate and important duties with fidelity and to my entire satisfaction.

In the House of Representatives,
Thursday, January 19, 1865.

Resolved, That a committee of three members be appointed to revise the report on the Gettysburg Cemetery, and superintend the publication of ten thousand copies, nine thousand five hundred for the use of this House, and five hundred for the use of the Governor.

Ordered, That Messrs. Lee, Nelson and Slack be the said committee.

In the Senate, *March* 14, 1865.

Resolved, That five thousand copies of the report of the committee on the Gettysburg Cemetery be printed for the use of the Senate, and five hundred copies for the use of David Wills, State Agent at Gettysburg.

REPORT.

IN THE HOUSE OF REPRESENTATIVES,
HARRISBURG, *March* 23, 1865.

Mr. LEE, from the committee appointed under the following resolution, passed January 19, 1865, to wit:

"*Resolved,* That a committee of three members be appointed to revise the report of the Gettysburg Cemetery, and superintend the publication of ten thousand copies, nine thousand five hundred for the use of this House, and five hundred for the use of the Governor," made report:

That they have subjected said report to a thorough revision, and have made such alterations as, in their judgment, were necessary to perfect the work, and have made such arrangements as will secure to each member his due proportion, at as early a day as the nature of the work will permit it to be issued.

EDWARD G. LEE,
W. M. NELSON,
ALFRED SLACK,
Committee.

REPORT OF COMMITTEE

On Soldiers' National Cemetery, made January 7, 1864.

Mr. LEE, from the special committee, to whom was referred so much of the Governor's annual message to the Legislature of the Commonwealth of Pennsylvania, read January 7, 1864, as relates to the Gettysburg Cemetery, made report:

That they visited the grounds recently purchased by the State of Pennsylvania for the purpose of establishing a National Cemetery, in which to re-inter the bodies of our soldiers, who fell in the memorable three days' conflict at Gettysburg, and found in progress active and judicious efforts, under competent and constant supervision, to have all the bodies of the Union soldiers, known and unknown, transferred to this, their final resting place.

In view of the general interest manifested for this institution, your committee felt that they were charged with the responsible duty of preparing a detailed history of this cemetery and its purposes.

The intervention of obvious difficulties to the completion of this work, by your committee, in a satisfactory manner, suggested the propriety of invoking the services of DAVID WILLS, Esq., of Gettysburg, Commissioner for Pennsylvania, who, having in his possession all the facts necessary to an adequate description of the time, place and circumstances connected with this laudable enterprise, coupled with an intense and ardent devotion to its every detail, kindly consented to relieve their labors, by furnishing the following replete and deeply interesting history of the SOLDIERS' NATIONAL CEMETERY, which, together with the act of incorporation, approved by the Governor on the twenty-fifth day of March, A. D. one thousand eight hundred and sixty-four, your committee desire to present as embodying their report.

All of which is respectfully submitted.

(Signed)

EDWARD G. LEE,
L. B. LABAR,
T. J. BOYER,
ISAIAH WHITE,
H. B. BOWMAN.

REPORT OF DAVID WILLS,

[MADE TO THE COMMITTEE OF THE LEGISLATURE OF THE SESSION OF 1864.]

To the Honorable, the Committee of the House of Representatives of the Commonwealth of Pennsylvania, on the Soldiers' National Cemetery, at Gettysburg:

GENTLEMEN:—In obedience to your request, I have the honor to submit the following report on the subject of the SOLDIERS' NATIONAL CEMETERY, at Gettysburg:

The design of locating a place for the decent interment of the remains of our soldiers who fell in defence of the Union, in the battle of Gettysburg, was originated soon after that bloody conflict, in July last; but was not consummated by the purchase of the grounds for the purpose until August. A persistent effort was made by persons here, to have the soldiers buried in grounds controlled by the local cemetery association of this place. The plan proposed having the burials made at a stipulated price, to be paid the cemetery association. Failing in this project, these persons endeavored to connect the two cemeteries, so that they should both be in one enclosure, and all under the control, supervision, and management of the local cemetery association. As the agent of His Excellency, the Governor of Pennsylvania, I was in communication, by letter, and personally, for some time, with the representatives and citizens of other States, in reference to this proposed plan, and all were of the decided opinion that the Soldiers' Cemetery should be entirely distinct and disconnected from the local cemetery; that, to ensure success in obtaining concert of action among all the States, it must be made an independent cemetery, and the control and management of it be retained by the States interested. This whole matter was very thoroughly and impartially canvassed and discussed, and this conclusion arrived at and adopted. The grounds were subsequently laid out, and the burials made in view of the National character of the project.

His Excellency, Gov. CURTIN, having authorized me to buy grounds, and invite the other States interested to unite in the removal of the dead, and improving the grounds, I immediately endeavored to purchase land on Cemetery Hill, and, after much difficulty, succeeded in buying five different lots lying on Cemetery Hill, on the west side of the Baltimore turnpike, adjoining the local cemetery on the north and west. It is the ground on which the centre of our line of battle rested July 2d and 3d, and one of the most prominent and important positions on the whole battle field. The lots were purchased for different prices per acre, according to their location, but all at a very reasonable market price. Two lots were bought at the rate of $225 per acre; one for $200 per acre; one for $150 per acre, and one for $135 per acre. The whole embraces about seventeen acres, and for the exact area and amount in each purchase, I refer you to the deeds on file in the Auditor General's office.

The cemetery having assumed a National character, by being independent of any local controlling influences, the Governors of all the States having soldiers lying on this battle field, after much correspondence and conference through commissioners sent here for the purpose, committed their States to the project. I then made arrangements with Mr. William Saunders, an eminent landscape gardener, to lay out the grounds in State lots, apportioned in size according to the number of marked graves each State had on this battle field. This number was obtained by having a thorough search made for all the graves, and a complete list of the names accurately taken. The grounds were accordingly very neatly and appropriately laid out, and I refer you to the map of them.

To preserve their identity, I deemed it very important to have the removals of the dead made as soon as possible. The marks at the graves were but temporary; in many instances, a small rough board, on which the name was feintly written with a lead pencil. This would necessarily be effaced by the action of the weather, and the boards were also liable to be thrown down and lost. The graves which were unmarked were in many instances level with the surface of the earth, and the grass and weeds were growing over them; and in the forests, the fall of the leaves in the autumn would cover them so that they might be entirely lost. I, therefore, issued proposals for giving out the contract for disinterring, removing and burying in the National Cemetery, all the Union dead on this battle field. Thirty-four bids were handed in, varying, in amount, from $1 59 to $8. I awarded the work to F. W. Biesecker, the lowest bidder, for $1 59 per body. His duties are fully set forth in the specifications, which are embodied in the contract. I take pleasure in saying, that the work under this contract has been done with great care and to my entire satisfaction. This is owing in part to the great care and attention bestowed by Mr. Samuel Weaver, whom I employed to superintend the exhuming of the bodies. Through his untiring and faithful efforts, the bodies in many unmarked graves have been identified in various ways. Sometimes by letters, by papers, receipts, certificates, diaries, memorandum books, photographs, marks on the clothing, belts, or cartridge boxes, &c., have the names of the soldiers been discovered. Money, and other valuables, have frequently been found, which, where the residence of the friends is known, have been immediately sent to them. Those not returned to the friends are carefully packed up and marked, and every effort will be made to find the friends of the deceased and place these articles in their possession. Words would fail to describe the grateful relief that this work has brought to many a sorrowing household! A father, a brother, a son has been lost on this battle field, *supposed* to be killed, but no tidings whatever have the bereaved friends of him. Suddenly, in the progress of this work, his remains are discovered by sure marks, letters probably, photographs, &c., and they are deposited in a coffin with care, and buried in this very appropriate place, on the battle field where he fell, the SOLDIERS' NATIONAL CEMETERY. There his grave will be properly cared for and permanently marked. The friends, who have probably written me several letters of inquiry, are immediately informed of the discovery. What a relief from agonizing hope and despair such certain information brings!

After purchasing the grounds, I made application to the Secretary of War for coffins for the burial of these dead, and he at once approved of the application, and directed the Quartermaster General to furnish the number required for the purpose.

These cemetery grounds were solemnly dedicated to their present sacred purpose, by appropriate and imposing ceremonies, on Thursday, the 19th of November last. The public prints of that week contained full accounts of the proceedings. I refer you, also, to the accompanying proceedings, embraced in this volume.

I requested the Governors of the several States, having lots in the cemetery, to appoint commissioners to assemble at Harrisburg, on the 17th of December last, to adopt some uniform plan for the action of the Legislatures of the different States. Twelve States were represented, and the other five signified, in advance, their assent to any reasonable action of the convention. I herewith refer you to the report of the proceedings of the convention. The estimated expenses of finishing the cemetery, are $63,500, and it is proposed to divide this sum among the different States having lots in the cemetery, in the ratio of their representation in Congress.

The Legislatures of the other States are acting in this matter, and making the appropriations in the proportions as above indicated. Besides making this appropriation, an additional duty devolves upon the Legislature of Pennsylvania. For the management and care of the grounds, and the completion of the work, it is necessary to have a corporate body, and the State of Pennsylvania is requested, through her Legislature, to establish, by her letters patent, this corporation of "THE SOLDIERS' NATIONAL CEMETERY. This should be done without delay. It will necessarily require some time for the board of managers to meet and organize, and in the meantime the work which should be progressing is delayed. It is especially desirable that the Legislature act upon this matter at once, so that the organization may be perfected. Upon this board of managers, composed of one from each State having soldier-dead here, will devolve the completion of the project, and the future care of the grounds.

I herewith submit a list of the names of the soldiers buried in the Pennsylvania lot. The whole number is five hundred and one (501.) The total number buried in the cemetery, is thirty-five hundred and twelve (3,512.) I also submit a list giving the number buried in each State lot, and in the grounds set apart for the Regulars and the Unknown.

I also submit, herewith, for your satisfaction, the following interesting reports: First—that of Mr. William Saunders, the designer of the grounds. Second—the report of Samuel Weaver, the superintendent of the exhuming of the bodies. Third—the report of Joseph S. Townsend, the superintendent of interments in the cemetery, and the surveyor. I also transmit the names of persons upon whose bodies articles were found, referred to in Mr Weaver's report, containing a description of the articles obtained.

All of which is respectfully submitted.

DAVID WILLS,

Agent for A. G. Curtin, *Governor of Penn'a.*

Gettysburg, *March* 21, 1864.

SUPPLEMENTAL REPORT OF DAVID WILLS,

[MADE TO THE COMMITTEE OF THE LEGISLATURE OF 1865.]

To the Honorable, the Committee of the House of Representatives of the Commonwealth of Pennsylvania, appointed to revise the report of the Committee relative to the SOLDIERS' NATIONAL CEMETERY, *made March* 31, 1864.

GENTLEMEN:—At your suggestion, I take pleasure in submitting the following additional facts in reference to the SOLDIERS' NATIONAL CEMETERY.

In the month of April last, (1864,) the commissioners (one from each State) met and organized, in accordance with the provisions of the act of Assembly of this Commonwealth incorporating the SOLDIERS' NATIONAL CEMETERY, and elected DAVID WILLS, of Pennsylvania, President, and JOHN R. BARTLETT, of Rhode Island, Secretary.

Arrangements were then made for commencing the work of enclosing the grounds, and an Executive Committee was appointed, to whom was referred the details of the work.

The Board met again in June, and a large number of designs for a monument, to be erected in the Cemetery, was submitted to them. These designs were obtained from the best artists in the country, by a committee appointed for that purpose, who advertised for them through the press. After mature deliberation, the board adopted the design proposed by J. G. BATTERSON, of Hartford, Connecticut. I herewith submit a lithograph, together with an artistic description of the adopted design. The board has not yet entered into a contract for the construction of this monument, but expect to do so during this year.

The enclosure around the cemetery grounds is nearly completed. It consists of a well built stone wall, surmounted with heavy dressed capping stone. This wall extends along the south, west and north sides of the grounds. The division fence between the SOLDIERS' NATIONAL CEMETERY and the local cemetery, is of iron, and is already put up complete. The fron fence and gate way is of ornamental iron work, and ready to put up, as soon as the weather will admit of it. The gate lodge is also built.

The grounds have been graded and prepared for the planting of the trees, in part, this spring. They cannot all be planted, until the work of constructing the monument and headstones is finished. A contract has been entered into for putting up the headstones, and the work has been commenced. It is a large contract, costing over $20,000 00, and will take a year to complete. When finished, it will make a most permanent and durable piece of work. The report of WILLIAM SAUNDERS, accompanying my report made to the committee last winter, explains the manner of putting up these headstones.

The amount of money drawn from the different States, up to the 30th of last November, was $28,045 95, and the amount expended to the same date, was $23,851 09. A detailed report of the receipts and expenditures was made by the Board, and a copy thereof sent to each of the Governors of the several States, represented in the Cemetery. I refer you to this report, on file in the Executive Chamber, for further details.

I herewith furnish you with a complete list of the names of the dead, buried in the SOLDIERS' NATIONAL CEMETERY, so far as the bodies were identified. After a laborious correspondence, and through the aid of the different members of the Board, I have made many corrections in the spelling of the names, and in the number of the regiment and letter of the company of the deceased soldier; but there are doubtless still some inaccuracies in the list. I respectfully suggest that you have this whole list printed in your report. These men came here from the east and from the west, stood side by side, and fought and fell in one common cause and for one common country, irrespective of State organizations or geographical lines, and their dust is now in common, mouldering together on this National Battle Field. Then let their names all be published together in your report, and make one record. Well was it said by the lamented EVERETT, as he stood over these honored graves, "All time is the millenium of their glory." Their names and the record of their deeds, will make one of the brightest pages of the history of this great struggle; and they are worthy of all being written in letters of gold.

DAVID WILLS,
Commissioner for Pennsylvania.

GETTYSBURG, *March* 6, 1865.

MEMBERS

Of the Board of Managers of the SOLDIERS' NATIONAL CEMETERY, *for* 1865.

B. W. NORRIS, Maine.
IRA PERLEY, New Hampshire.
PAUL DILLINGHAM, Vermont.
HENRY EDWARDS, Massachusetts.
JOHN R. BARTLETT, Rhode Island.
A. G. HAMMOND, Connecticut.
R. H. M'CURDY, New York.
LEVI SCOBEY, New Jersey.
DAVID WILLS, Pennsylvania.
WILLIAM TOWNSEND, Delaware.
B. DEFORD, Maryland.
C. D. HUBBARD, West Virginia.
GORDON LOFLAND, Ohio.
J. G. STEPHENSON, Indiana.
C. E. CARR, Illinois.
T. W. FERRY, Michigan.
W. Y. SELLECK, Wisconsin.
ALEXANDER RAMSEY, Minnesota.

OFFICERS.

President, DAVID WILLS.
Secretary, JOHN R. BARTLETT.
Treasurer, S. R. RUSSELL.

SPECIFICATIONS

For proposals invited to be handed in at my office in Gettysburg, up to the 22d inst., at 12 o'clock, noon, for the two contracts referred to in the advertisement of this date, (*Oct.* 15, 1863.)

First.—For the exhuming and removal to the SOLDIERS' NATIONAL CEMETERY, of the dead of the Union army, buried on the Gettysburg battle field, and at the several hospitals in the vicinity:—

The party taking this contract shall receive the coffins at the railroad station, in Gettysburg, and only take them to the field as fast as used each day.

He shall go upon the premises where the dead are buried, under the direction of the person having the superintendence—doing as little damage as possible—and where an enclosure is thrown open, he shall re-place it. He shall open up the grave or trench where the dead are buried, and carefully take out the remains and place them in a coffin, and screw down the lid tight, and nail the head-board, where the grave has been marked, carefully on the lid of the coffin. He shall then re-place all blankets, &c., that may have been taken out of the grave and not put around the body, back in the grave, and close it up, neatly leveling it over.

He shall transport the remains thus secured to the grounds selected for their burial, on the south side of the borough of Gettysburg, and deposit them at such a place on the grounds as may be designated by the person having the superintendence of the removals and re-interments.

He shall remove as many bodies to the grounds per day as shall be ordered by the person in charge, not exceeding one hundred bodies per day.

He shall exhume all bodies designated by the person in charge, and none others; and when ordered, he shall open up graves and trenches for personal inspection of the remains, for the purpose of ascertaining whether they are bodies of Union soldiers, and close them over again when ordered to do so.

He shall stipulate the price per body, at which he will contract to perform the work as above set forth. Payment will be made on Saturday evening of every week for the full amount of the work done.

Bonds will be required in the sum of three thousand dollars for the faithful performance of the contract, with two or more sureties, to be approved by DAVID WILLS.

He will commence the work on the 26th of October, inst., privilege being reserved to order a postponement of the time to a day not later than Nov.

1st, next. The right is also reserved to order a total suspension of the work at the time of the consecration of the grounds, and on Thanksgiving day.

Second.—For the digging of the graves in the cemetery, putting in the bodies, building a stone foundation for the headstones, and burying the bodies :—

The graves shall be dug where designated by the superintendent in charge. They shall be dug in trenches, and the coffins placed in them side by side, of the number in each trench designated by the plot of the grounds. They shall be three feet in depth from the surface of the ground, and of the length of the coffin. At the head of each trench, there shall be an offset dug in the earth of the width of twenty inches, and of the depth of two feet from the surface of the ground. On this offset a stone wall, of dry masonry, shall be substantially built of stone found on the ground, at such places as may be designated by the person in charge, eighteen inches in height, or within six inches of the surface of the ground.

The coffins shall then be placed in the grave, side by side, as ordered by the superintendent—the head-board of each one nailed upright against the head of the coffin, and of sufficient height above the ground not to conceal the lettering when the grave is filled up. The grave must then be filled up a sufficient height, in the opinion of the superintendent, to prevent settling below the surface.

He shall bury as many per day as may be brought to the cemetery, not to exceed one hundred bodies; and no bodies shall be left unburied over night.

The work shall be commenced on the 26th of October, inst., privilege being reserved to order a postponement of the time to a day not later than November 1st, next. The right is also reserved to order a total suspension of the work at the time of the consecration of the grounds, and on Thanksgiving day.

The person proposing to take this contract shall stipulate the price per body at which he will contract to perform the work as above set forth.—Payment will be made on Saturday evening of every week, for the full amount of the work done.

Bonds will be required in the sum of three thousand dollars for the faithful performance of the contract, with two or more sureties, to be approved of by DAVID WILLS.

DAVID WILLS,
Agent for A. G. CURTIN, *Gov. of Penn'a.*

GETTYSBURG, *October* 15, 1863.

NOTE.—The two contracts above referred to were united in one, at $1 59 for the whole.

SOLDIERS' NATIONAL CEMETERY.

HARRISBURG, *December* 17, 1863.

The Commissioners appointed by the Governors of the different States, which have soldiers buried in the SOLDIERS' NATIONAL CEMETERY, at Gettysburg, Pa., met at the Jones House, in Harrisburg, Pa., at 3 o'clock, P. M., on the 17th of December, 1863.

The following named Commissioners were present, viz:

Hon. B. W. NORRIS, of Maine.
Hon. L. B. MASON, of New Hampshire.
Mr. HENRY EDWARDS, of Massachusetts.
Mr. ALFRED COIT, of Connecticut.
Hon. LEVI SCOBEY, of New Jersey.
Mr. DAVID WILLS, of Pennsylvania.
Col. JAMES WORRALL, of Pennsylvania.
Col. JOHN S. BERRY, of Maryland.
Mr. L. W. BROWN, of Ohio.
Col. GORDON LOFLAND, of Ohio.
Col. JOHN G. STEPHENSON, of Indiana.
Mr. W. Y. SELLECK, of Wisconsin.

On motion of Col. LOFLAND, of Ohio, Mr. DAVID WILLS, of Pennsylvania, was elected Chairman of the Convention.

On motion of Col. STEPHENSON, of Indiana, Mr. W. Y. SELLECK, of Wisconsin, was elected Secretary of the Convention.

After some discussion by the members of the Convention, Col. STEPHENSON, of Indiana, moved that a committee of four, of which the President of this Convention be one, be appointed for the purpose of preparing and putting in appropriate shape the details of the plan in reference to the SOLDIERS' NATIONAL CEMETERY, at Gettysburg, Pa., to be presented to the Convention for their action, which was carried. The committee was appointed as follows:

Chairman, Col. JOHN G. STEPHENSON, of Indiana; Mr. HENRY EDWARDS, of Massachusetts, Hon. LEVI SCOBEY, of New Jersey, Mr. DAVID WILLS, of Pennsylvania.

On motion of Mr. ALFRED COIT, of Connecticut, the Convention took a recess to await the action of the committee.

The Convention met again at 5 o'clock, P. M., to hear the report of the committee.

The committee made the following report:

WHEREAS, In accordance with an invitation from DAVID WILLS, Esq., agent for His Excellency, A. G. CURTIN, Governor of Pennsylvania, the Governors of the several States appointed Commissioners, who met at Harrisburg, December 17, 1863, to represent the States in convention, for the purpose of making arrangements for finishing the SOLDIERS' NATIONAL CEMETERY; therefore, be it

Resolved, By the said commissioners, in convention assembled, that the following be submitted to the different States interested in the "SOLDIERS' NATIONAL CEMETERY," through their respective Governors:

First. That the Commonwealth of Pennsylvania shall hold the title to the land which she has purchased at Gettysburg for the SOLDIERS' NATIONAL CEMETERY, in trust for States having soldiers buried in said cemetery, in perpetuity, for the purpose to which it is now applied.

Second That the Legislature of the Commonwealth of Pennsylvania be requested to create a corporation, to be managed by trustees, one to be appointed by each of the Governors of the States of Maine, New Hampshire, Vermont, Massachusetts, Rhode Island, Connecticut, New York, New Jersey, Pennsylvania, Maryland, Delaware, West Virginia, Ohio, Indiana, Illinois, Michigan, Wisconsin, Minnesota, and of such other States as may hereafter desire to be represented in this corporation, which trustees shall at their first meeting, be divided into three classes. The term of office of the first class to expire on the first day of January, 1865. The second class on the first day of January, 1866. The third class on the first day of January, 1867. The vacancies thus occurring to be filled by the several Governors, and the persons thus appointed to fill such vacancies, to hold their office for the term of three years. This corporation to have exclusive control of the SOLDIERS' NATIONAL CEMETERY.

Third. The following is the estimated expense of finishing the cemetery:

Enclosing grounds	$15,000 00
Burial expenses and superintending	6,000 00
Headstones	10,000 00
Laying out grounds and planting trees	5,000 00
Lodge	2,500 00
Monument	25,000 00
Total	63,500 00

Fourth. That the several States be asked to appropriate a sum of money, to be determined by a division of the estimated expenses according to representation in Congress, to be expended in defraying the cost of removing and re-interring the dead, and finishing the cemetery, under directions of the cemetery corporation.

Fifth. When the cemetery shall have been finished, the grounds are to be kept in order, the house and enclosure in repair, out of a fund created by annual appropriations made by the States which may be represented in the cemetery corporation, in proportion to their representation in Congress.

On motion of Col. BERRY, of Maryland, the report of the committee was accepted, and the committee discharged.

It was moved by Col. BERRY, of Maryland, that the report of the committee be considered *seriatim*, which was concurred in, and the report was then adopted in detail.

Letters from the Governors of the following States were received by Mr. WILLS, chairman of the convention, which were not represented by commissioners, expressing their disposition to approve any reasonable action of the convention in reference to the completion of the cemetery at Gettysburg, Pa., viz:

Hon. HORATIO SEYMOUR, of New York.

Hon. AUSTIN BLAIR, of Michigan.

Hon. JAMES Y. SMITH, of Rhode Island.

Hon. WILLIAM CANNON, of Delaware.

Hon. HENRY G. SWIFT, of Minnesota.

On motion of Mr. SCOBEY, of New Jersey, the following committee was appointed by the chairman, with the view to procure designs of a monument to be erected in the cemetery:

Hon. LEVI SCOBEY, of New Jersey.

Hon. B. W. MORRIS, of Maine.

Mr. D. W. BROWN, of Ohio.

Col. J. G. STEPHENSON, of Indiana.

Col. JOHN S. BERRY, of Maryland.

On motion of Mr. ALFRED COIT, of Connecticut, the plans and designs of the SOLDIERS' NATIONAL CEMETERY, as laid out and designed by Mr. WILLIAM SAUNDERS, were adopted by the convention.

A motion was made by Mr. COIT, of Connecticut, returning thanks to Mr. WILLIAM SAUNDERS, for the designs and drawings furnished gratuitously for the SOLDIERS' NATIONAL CEMETERY, at Gettysburg, Pa.; which was unanimously adopted.

Mr. BROWN, of Ohio, offered the following, which was adopted:

Resolved, That Mr. WILLIAM SAUNDERS be authorized to furnish forty photographs of the plan of the SOLDIERS' NATIONAL CEMETERY, for the use of the States having soldiers buried therein.

DAVID WILLS, *President.*

W. Y. SELLECK, *Secretary.*

LIST OF NAMES

OF SOLDIERS BURIED IN THE SOLDIERS' NATIONAL CEMETERY, GETTYSBURG, PA.

PENNSYLVANIA.

SECTION A.

No. of grave.	Names.	Comp'y.	Regiment.
1	Robert Lockhart..................	K......	29th Regiment, P. V.
2	Theodore Saylor.................	C......	72d Regiment, P. V.
3	Lieut. J. D. Gordon.............	B......	56th Regiment, P. V.
4	Alexander Creighton............	F......	148th Regiment, P. V.
5	Serg. R. H. Cowpland.........	....	121st Regiment, P. V.
6	J. J. Finnefrock.		
7	Samuel Finnefrock.		
8	Corp. C. Walters.................	C......	142d Regiment, P. V.
9	Unknown.........................	....	149th Regiment, P. V.
10	Unknown..........................	....	149th Regiment, P. V.
11	Corp. J. S. Gutelius............	D......	150th Regiment, P. V.
12	Nathan H ———...............	A.....	149th Regiment, P. V.
13	Unknown..........................	F......	149th Regiment, P. V.
14	F. E. Northorp	....	150th Regiment, P. V.
15	Unknown..........................	....	149th Regiment, P. V.
16	Unknown..........................		
17	William H. Harman............	I.......	149th Regiment, P. V.
18	Unknown..........................	....	149th Regiment, P. V.
19	Corp. James Logan............	G......	149th Regiment, P. V.
20	Robert M'Guire	F......	53d Regiment, P. V.
21	Serg. Daniel Harrington......	F......	53d Regiment, P. V.

Pennsylvania.—SECTION A—*Continued.*

No. of grave.	Names.	Comp'y	Regiment.
22	C. Herbster	C	69th Regiment, P. V.
23	Franklin Myers	D	99th Regiment, P. V.
24	Thomas Hand	K	99th Regiment, P. V.
25	Josiah Butterworth	E	114th Regiment, P. V.
26	Thomas Burns	B	2d Regiment, P. R. C.
27	Thomas M. Savage	H	2d Regiment, P. R. C.
28	Color Serg. John Greenwood	I	109th Regiment, P. V.
29	J. Bainbridge	F	147th Regiment, P. V.
30	G. Deisroth	F	147th Regiment, P. V.
31	Corp. Abraham Crawley	A	68th Regiment, P. V.
32	Serg. John Wogan	G	69th Regiment, P. V.
33	James M'Intyre	G	69th Regiment, P. V.
34	James Clary	G	69th Regiment, P. V.
35	James Coyle	G	69th Regiment, P. V.
36	James Rice	G	69th Regiment, P. V.
37	William Kiker	K	72d Regiment, P. V.
38	John Hope	H	71st Regiment, P. V.
39	Nelson Reaser	B	151st Regiment, P. V.
40	Robert Lesher	D	71st Regiment, P. V.
41	Washington Lininger	B	145th Regiment, P. V.
42	William Conley		140th Regiment, P. V.
43	Lieut. G. H. Finch	E	145th Regiment, P. V.
44	Isaac E. Dorman	A	145th Regiment, P. V.
45	John Stockton	I	71st Regiment, P. V.
46	Robert W. Bell	I	56th Regiment, P. V.
47	Unknown	B	149th Regiment, P. V.
48	John E. White	D	53d Regiment, P. V.

Pennsylvania.—SECTION A—*Continued.*

No. of grave.	Names.	Comp'y.	Regiment.
49	Matthew Smith	G	1st Reg't California brig.
50	Lieut. Michael Mullin	G	69th Regiment, P. V.
51	Samuel W. Barnet	H	140th Regiment, P. V.
52	J. Rich	H	106th Regiment, P. V.
53	Frederick Gillhouse.		
54	R. J. Akan	I	145th Regiment, P. V.
55	John M'Casland	D	72d Regiment, P. V.
56	Harrison Long	I	148th Regiment, P. V.
57	John Kunkle	E	148th Regiment, P. V.
58	John Weidner	B	68th Regiment, P. V.
59	Thomas B. M'Cullough	I	148th Regiment, P. V.
60	Jeremiah Dermandy	G	19th Regiment, P. V.
61	William Munsen		1st Penn'a Artillery.
62	Charles Carmer	A	57th Regiment, P. V.
63	Corp. Martin Berry	D	140th Regiment, P. V.
64	Absalom Link	G	64th Artillery.
65	Serg. J. Hunter	B	57th Regiment, P. V.
66	Lawrence Bennet	B	141st Regiment, P. V.
67	J. Rhodes	C	105th Regiment, P. V.
68	Unknown.		
69	George Howard	I	111th Regiment, P. V.
70	Serg. Francis M. Burley	A	110th Regiment, P. V.
71	Corp. George W. Ingraham	A	68th Regiment, P. V.
72	Corp. David Stoup	E	63d Regiment, P. V.
73	John Devon	F	26th Regiment, P. V.
74	William Callan	C	26th Regiment, P. V.
75	J. Hayman	A	26th Regiment, P. V.

Pennsylvania.—SECTION A—*Continued.*

No. of grave.	Names.	Comp'y.	Regiment.
76	William H. Knichenbecher....	K......	141st Regiment, P. V.
77	Corp. W. Gordon................	I.......	26th Regiment, P. V.
78	John C. Downing................	C......	57th Regiment, P. V.
79	J. J. Wood........................	I.......	114th Regiment, P. V.
80	Serg. Vonderfeer	H......	71st Regiment, P. V.
81	A. Delinger........................	K......	71st Regiment, P. V.
82	Joseph A. Furgeson............	A......	139th Regiment, P. V.
83	Benjamin Hassiler.....	D......	93d Regiment, P. V.
84	James Kay...	E	91st Regiment, P. V.
85	G. W. Stalker.....................	I.......	83d Regiment, P. V.
86	Lieut. P. Morris..................	D......	62d Regiment, P. V.
87	C. D. Coyle........................	D......	83d Regiment, P. V.
88	Stephen Kelly.....................	E	91st Regiment, P. V.
89	T. P. Swoop........................	H	111th Regiment, P. V.
90	Unknown............................	....	26th Regiment, P. V.
91	D. Hanna..................	A	29th Regiment, P. V.
92	Patrick Fury.......................	F	115th Regiment, P. V.
93	Benjamin Slavach....	....	153d Regiment, P. V.
94	Corp. Uriah M'Cracken........	G......	153d Regiment, P. V.
95	James Irving.......................	G......	73d Regiment, P. V.
96	John Reimel.......................	H	153d Regiment, P. V.
97	Fritz Smittle......................	H.....	74th Regiment, P. V.
98	Emil Preifer.	E......	27th Regiment, P. V.

Pennsylvania.—SECTION B.

No. of grave.	Names.	Comp'y.	Regiment.
1	Capt. A. J. Sofield..............	A.....	149th Regiment, P. V.
2	Unknown..................	....	149th Regiment, P. V.
3	Unknown..........................	....	149th Regiment, P. V.
4	Unknown..........................	....	149th Regiment, P. V.
5	George Seip.......................	....	148th Regiment, P. V.
6	Unknown..........................	....	149th Regiment, P. V.
7	Unknown Corporal..............	....	149th Regiment, P. V.
8	Unknown..........................	....	149th Regiment, P. V.
9	Unknown.........	....	149th Regiment, P. V.
10	D. G..........	....	149th Regiment, P. V.
11	Unknown..........................	....	149th Regiment, P. V.
12	Unknown.......	....	149th Regiment, P. V.
13	Unknown	....	149th Regiment, P. V.
14	Unknown..........................	....	149th Regiment, P. V.
15	David C. Kline..................	H.....	149th Regiment, P. V.
16	Sergt. Philip Peckens...........	F......	141st Regiment, P. V.
17	Robert Morrison.................	A......	69th Regiment, P. V.
18	Corp. Samuel Hayburn.........	B......	106th Regiment, P. V.
19	Samuel R. Garvin	E......	72d Regiment, P. V.
20	John M'Hugh.....................	K.....	72d Regiment, P. V.
21	Ira Corbin.........................	D.....	145th Regiment, P. V.
22	H. S. Thomas	I.......	145th Regiment, P. V.
23	S. Taylor...........................	G.....	145th Regiment, P. V.
24	S. Shoemaker.		
25	Corp. William H. Myers.......	E......	62d Regiment, P. V.
26	Major W. G. Lowry.............	....	26th Regiment, P. V.
27	James Hill.........................	I.......	142d Regiment, P. V.

Pennsylvania.—SECTION B—*Continued.*

No. of grave.	Names.	Comp'y.	Regiment.
28	Thomas D. Allen................	A.....	157t Re iment, P. V.
29	Patrick Hayes..................	D......	81st egi ent, P. V.
30	Charles M'Carty	K......	72d R gim nt, P. V
31	Joseph Newton..................	D......	81st Re im nt, P. V.
32	Alexander Mills	E......	72d Reg men t,P. V.
33	D. A. Ammerman..............	B......	148th Re ime t, P. V.
34	James S. Lynn..................	G......	140th Reg men P. V.
35	William Van Buskirk...........	K......	142d Regiment, P. V.
36	Henry A. Comwell.............	A......	121st Regiment, P. V.
37	George Young..................	F......	150th Regiment, P. V.
38	Albert Dustun....................	....	75th Regiment, P. V.
39	Sergt. Almond M. Chesbro....	G......	53d Regiment, P. V.
40	Joseph Kile........................	G	53d Regiment, P. V.
41	E. A. Allen........................	I.......	145th Regiment, P. V.
42	Richard Miller....................	C......	140th Regiment, P. V.
43	M. Charrity........................	A.....	71st Regiment, P. V.
44	Louis Dille........................	D.....	140th Regiment, P. V.
45	Ethiel A. Wood..................	B......	141st Regiment, P. V.
46	Serg. Major Joseph G. Fell...	....	141st Regiment, P. V.
47	Robert Michaels..................	A......	145th Regiment, P. V.
48	Petèr Hilt...........................	G......	68th Regiment, P. V.
49	Ord. Sergt. Herrick.............	H.....	110th Regiment, P. V.
50	J. W. Guthrie.....................	B......	105th Regiment, P. V.
51	Moses Miller......................	B......	110th Regiment, P. V.
52	George Rowand..................	K......	26th Regiment, P. V.
53	George Osman	C......	148th Regiment, P. V.
54	Sergt. Peter Hilgers	D......	73d Regiment, P. V.

Pennsylvania.—Section B—*Continued.*

No. of grave.	Names.	Comp'y.	Regiment.
55	Frederick Heinley	K	74th Regiment, P. V.
56	W. Cragle	D	143d Regiment, P. V.
57	Corp. B. F. Ulrich	B	153d Regiment, P. V.
58	Charles Clyde	I	150th Regiment, P. V.
59	Jacob Mauch	I	150th Regiment, P. V.
60	Corp. William Holmes	G	150th Regiment, P. V.
61	William S. Stamm	G	150th Regiment, P. V.
62	J. Jones	A	142d Regiment, P. V.
63	Samuel Cramer	B	142d Regiment, P. V.
64	John W. Crusan	B	56th Regiment, P. V.
65	Solomon Shirk	B	107th Regiment, P. V.
66	James Lukens	E	150th Regiment, P. V.
67	M. Kelley	E	106th Regiment, P. V.
68	Serg. John O. Lorner	G	69th Regiment, P. V.
69	John Harrington	K	69th Regiment, P. V.
70	James Keatings	H	90th Regiment, P. V.
71	Isaac Jenkins	G	107th Regiment, P. V.
72	J. Ruppins	B	107th Regiment, P. V.
73	William Beaumont	A	88th Regiment, P. V.
74	James Amsley	H	107th Regiment, P. V.
75	J. N. Burr		147th Regiment, P. V.
76	James W. Taft	D	142d Regiment, P. V.
77	Joseph Montange	D	143d Regiment, P. V.
78	Alfred Boyden	A	149th Regiment, P. V.
79	Unknown.		
80	Charles E. Webster	C	26th Regiment, P. V.
81	J. H. Rendools		68th Regiment, P. V.

Pennsylvania.—Section B—*Continued.*

No. of grave.	Names.	Comp'y.	Regiment.
82	Alonzo M'Call	B	10th Regiment, P. R. C.
83	Ord. Serg. J. W. Molineaux	B	91st Regiment, P. V.
84	Unknown.		
85	Unknown.		
86	James S. Rutter	B	1st Regiment, P. R. C.
87	Unknown P. V.		
88	B. E. True	B	83d Regiment, P. V.
89	Unknown.		
90	Unknown.		
91	1st Serg. T. J. Belton	B	Bucktail Regiment.
92	Unknown.		
93	Unknown.		
94	James Wallace	G	26th Regiment, P. V.

Section C.

No. of grave.	Names.	Comp'y.	Regiment.
1	Unknown		149th Regiment, P. V.
2	Unknown		149th Regiment, P. V.
3	Unknown		149th Regiment, P. V.
4	Unknown		149th Regiment, P. V.
5	Unknown		149th Regiment, P. V.
6	Unknown		149th Regiment, P. V.
7	Unknown		149th Regiment, P. V.
8	Unknown		149th Regiment, P. V.
9	Unknown		149th Regiment, P. V.
10	Unknown		149th Regiment, P. V.
11	Unknown		149th Regiment, P. V.

Pennsylvania.—SECTION C—*Continued.*

No. of grave.	Names.	Comp'y.	Regiment.
12	Unknown		149th Regiment, P. V.
13	H. M. Kinsel	H	110th Regiment, P. V.
14	Charles T. Gardner	H	111th Regiment, P. V.
15	Hiram Woodruff	G	1st Bucktail Regiment.
16	P. O'Brian	A	69th Regiment, P. V.
17	John Hurley	H	69th Regiment, P. V.
18	George Dunkinfield	I	72d Regiment, P. V.
19	William Evans	I	71st Regiment, P. V.
20	David Stainbrook	E	71st Regiment, P. V.
21	William W. Clark	A	72d Regiment, P. V.
22	William Brown	D	71st Regiment, P. V.
23	Robert L. Platt	C	149th Regiment, P. V.
24	D. Bumgardner	A	141st Regiment, P. V.
25	George Hiles	C	68th Regiment, P. V.
26	Serg. John Loughery	E	26th Regiment, P. V.
27	G. T. Bishop	I	141st Regiment, P. V.
28	Corp. Robert Thompson	I	83d Regiment, P. V.
29	Serg. J. Myers	G	62d Regiment, P. V.
30	Joseph Sherran	F	62d Regiment, P. V.
31	J. Simonson	I	28th Regiment, P. V.
32	Gideon F. Borger	H	153d Regiment, P. V.
33	Gotfried Hamman		74th Regiment, P. V.
34	William L. Miller	E	153d Regiment, P. V.
35	2d Lt. John O'H. Woods	D	11th Regiment, P. R. C.
36	Serg. William Reynolds	I	142d Regiment, P. V.
37	Amos P. Sweet	H	150th Regiment, P. V.
38	Serg. Lorenzo Hodges	G	150th Regiment, P. V.

Pennsylvania.—SECTION C—*Continued.*

No. of grave.	Names.	Comp'y.	Regiment.
39	1st Lieut. F. Keimpel.....	E......	27th Regiment, P. V.
40	Unknown.		
41	James O'Neil......................	B......	69th Regiment, P. V.
42	Lieut. William H. Smith.......	B......	106th Regiment, P. V.
43	Unknown—Orderly Sergeant.		
44	Serg. James M. Shea	B......	69th Regiment, P. V.
45	F. Gallagher.......................	B......	69th Regiment, P. V.
46	John Heneison	C......	153d Regiment, P. V.
47	Serg. E. N. Somercamp.......	I......	29th Regiment, P. V.
48	Unknown.		
49	William Douglass...............	B	155th Regiment, P. V.
50	George W. Wilson...............	I......	155th Regiment, P. V.
51	Patrick J. O'Connor............	D......	91st Regiment, P. V.
52	E. Berlin...........................	G......	83d Regiment, P. V.
53	Unknown.		
54	Robert Griffin.....................	A	83d Regiment, P. V.
55	Unknown.		
56	Unknown, (with two gold ear	rings.)	
57	Unknown.		
58	Unknown—Corporal.		
59	Unknown.		
60	L. F.........	E......	53d Regiment, P. V.
61	Unknown.		
62	Unknown.		
63	Unknown—Sergeant.		
64	Ord. Serg. M. G. Isett.........	C	53d Regiment, P. V.
65	Unknown.		

Pennsylvania.—SECTION C—*Continued.*

No. of grave.	Names.	Comp'y.	Regiment.
66	Unknown.		
67	Unknown.		
68	Unknown.		
69	Unknown.		
70	Unknown Ord. Sergeant, (with knife and screw driver.)		
71	Unknown, (with medal, hymn book, &c.		
72	Unknown, (with knife and pencil.)		
73	John K. Inery	C	2d Regiment, P. R. C.
74	Isaac Eaton	D	10th Regiment, P. R. C.
75	Patrick Hunt	F	99th Regiment, P. V.
76	William Danchy	H	1st Regiment, P. R. C.
77	Thomas Shields	H	99th Regiment, P. V.
78	John Lusk	I	1st Regiment, P. R. C.
79	J. Kleppinger	D	153d Regiment, P. V.
80	Lieut. William H. Beaver	D	153d Regiment, P. V.
81	J. Quinn	H	99th Regiment, P. V.
82	William Thomas	E	110th Regiment, P. V.
83	D. Hemphill	E	72d Regiment, P. V.
84	H. Purdy	C	Hampton's Battery.
85	James E. Beals	H	148th Regiment, P. V.
86	F. Bordenstedt	A	69th Regiment, P. V.
87	William J. Strause	H	151st Regiment, P. V.
88	Serg. James Parks	C	139th Regiment, P. V.
89	James Kelly	C	69th Regiment, P. V.
90	Jacob Frey	C	105th Regiment, P. V.

Pennsylvania.—SECTION D.

No. of grave.	Names.	Comp'y.	Regiment.
1	Unknown		149th Regiment, P. V.
2	Unknown		149th Regiment, P. V.
3	Calvin Potter	H	149th Regiment, P. V.
4	Unknown		149th Regiment, P. V.
5	Unknown		149th Regiment, P. V.
6	Corp. Samuel M. Caldwell	D	118th Regiment, P. V.
7	Frederick Shoner	E	72d Regiment, P. V.
8	Serg. Jeremiah Boyle	H	69th Regiment, P. V.
9	George Herpich	H	71st Regiment, P. V.
10	Corp. James M'Manus	D	69th Regiment, P. V.
11	James Gallagher	H	71st Regiment, P. V.
12	Serg. J. Gallagher	D	69th Regiment, P. V.
13	S. S. Odare	F	71st Regiment, P. V.
14	Corp. William Shultz	I	71st Regiment, P. V.
15	William Simpson	D	145th Regiment, P. V.
16	Anthony Stark	G	106th Regiment, P. V.
17	Charles Trisket	G	140th Regiment, P. V.
18	Charles F. Loby	I	118th Regiment, P. V.
19	Unknown, (with three ambrotypes.)		
20	Unknown.		
21	Unknown.		
22	Unknown.		
23	Unknown.		
24	G. H. Allen	C	59th Regiment, P. V.
25	Charles M. Connel	K	11th Regiment, P. V.
26	John Aker.		
27	Unknown		26th Regiment, P. V.

Pennsylvania.—SECTION D—*Continued.*

No. of grave.	Names.	Comp'y.	Regiment.
28	Jacob Keirsh	....	Hampton's Battery.
29	Unknown, (with silver watch.)		
30	J. Graves	C	1st Regiment, P. V.
31	Unknown, (with an order, signed John Kramer,)	....	6th Regiment, P. V.
32	Unknown, (with rings, purse, pin box, &c.)		
33	Unknown, (with books, and two letters from Mary Ann.)		
34	Unknown, (with $5 in Confederate money.)		
35	Unknown, (with inkstand, cross, book, &c.		
36	George Moyer	F	2d Regiment, P. R. C.
37	Cordillo Collins	D	1st Regiment, P. R. C.
38	A. J. Bittinger	C	11th Regiment, P. R. C.
39	Milton Campbell	C	11th Regiment, P. R. C.
40	Samuel Zeckman	E	6th Regiment, P. R. C.
41	A. S. Davis	G	1st Penn'a Rifles.
42	George Stewart	E	2d Regiment, P. R. C.
43	Serg. Robert Sensenmyer	E	2d Regiment, P. R. C.
44	F. Smith	I	20th Regiment, P. V.
45	Unknown.		
46	James Binker	B	106th Regiment, P. V.
47	Henry W. Beegel	H	110th Regiment, P. V.
48	James S. Puryne	....	Battery F, 1st Artillery.
49	O. S. Campbell	K	111th Regiment, P. V.
50	J. Watson	I	29th Regiment, P. V.
51	Thomas Acton	B	29th Regiment, P. V.
52	James Morrow	I	29th Regiment, P. V.
53	Corp. James D. Butcher	D	28th Regiment, P. V.
54	John Richardson	B	111th Regiment, P. V.

Pennsylvania.—SECTION D—*Continued.*

No. of grave.	Names.	Comp'y.	Regiment.
55	Charles Miller........	B......	111th Regiment, P. V.
56	G. B. Wireman..........	E......	107th Regiment, P. V.
57	Corp. John S. Pomeroy.		
58	T. Miller..........................	....	Battery G, 1st Art., P. R. C.
59	S. D. Campbell......................	A......	142d Regiment, P. V.
60	John Metz........................	A......	68th Regiment, P. V.
61	E. T. Green......................	E......	14th Regiment, P. V.
62	S. N. Warner	H......	83d Regiment, P. V.
63	A. P. M'Clarey..................	B......	63d Regiment, P. V.
64	N. P. Govan......................	C......	150th Regiment, P. V.
65	Elisha Bond...	....	27th Regiment, P. V.
66	I. Beider..........................	F.....	1st Regiment, P. V.
67	N. M'Witkin......................	A......	15th Regiment, P. V.
68	Corp. Hugh Farley..............	H......	57th Regiment, P. V.
69	H. H. Hay........................	A......	145th Regiment, P. V.
70	Mager Sorber......................	B......	143d Regiment, P. V.
71	Mark Beary........................	D......	1st Regiment, P. V.
72	John Harvey......................	A......	69th Regiment, P. V.
73	Joseph Werst..........	C......	153d Regiment, P. V.
74	John Boyer, (with ambrotype and letter.)		
75	S. M. Little........................	F......	62d Regiment, P. V.
76	William H. Dunn...............	F......	62d Regiment, P. V.
77	J. A. Walker......................	D......	62d Regiment, P. V.
78	Richard Loudman...............	H......	62d Regiment, P. V.
79	T. R. Woods......................	A......	62d Regiment, P. V.
80	John Mathers	L......	62d Regiment, P. V.
81	George M'Intosh.................	L......	62d Regiment, P. V.

Pennsylvania.—Section D—*Continued.*

No. of grave.	Names.	Comp'y.	Regiment.
82	Serg. J. S. Osborn..........	I.......	62d Regiment, P. V.
83	E. M'Mahon	I.......	140th Regiment, P. V.
84	John Buckley......................	B......	140th Regiment, P. V.
85	John Long..........................	D......	62d Regiment, P. V.

Section E.

No. of grave.	Names.	Comp'y.	Regiment.
1	Reuben Miller......................	K......	1st Regiment, P. V.
2	Jacob Christ........................	D......	56th Regiment, P. V.
3	Robert Johnson..........	G......	28th Regiment, P. V.
4	Auton Frank.		
5	John W. Buchanan.............	A......	1st Regiment, P. R. C.
6	N. Townsend........................	C......	1st Regiment, P. R. C.
7	W. H. Burrel.......................	F......	148th Regiment, P. V.
8	William Orr..........................	I.......	62d Regiment, P. V.
9	Serg. K. Doty.......................	F......	105th Regiment, P. V.
10	David Winning.....................	D......	18th Cavalry.
11	Jacob Harvey.......................	M......	18th Cavalry.
12	William Crawford.................	C......	18th Cavalry.
13	W. N. Williams.........	K......	143d Regiment, P. V.
14	Jacob Zimmerman................	I.......	151st Regiment, P. V.
15	A. H. Fish............................	I.......	150th Regiment, P. V.
16	A. Lees	A......	150th Regiment, P. V.
17	Wilson Miller	....	90th Regiment, P. V.
18	J. Stroble..............................	I.......	11th Regiment, P. V.
19	C. B. Ling............................	B... ..	56th Regiment, P. V.
20	Wendle Dorn........................	I.......	139th Regiment, P. V.

Pennsylvania.—Section E—*Continued.*

No. of grave.	Names.	Comp'y.	Regiment.
21	Unknown..........................	....	148th Regiment, P. V.
22	Samuel Dearmott................	C......	62d Regiment, P. V.
23	John Stottard......................	A......	110th Regiment, P. V.
24	Francis Merrian Hansel.........	E......	140th Regiment, P. V.
25	Ord. Serg. Joseph H. Core...	A......	110th Regiment, P. V.
26	J. D. Campbell....................	C......	140th Regiment, P. V.
27	T. J. Carpenter....................	K......	140th Regiment, P. V.
28	Tobias Jones, (removed)	B......	153d Regiment, P. V.
29	Unknown.		
30	Jesse Coburn.......................	C......	142d Regiment, P. V.
31	John W. M'Kinney	K......	1st Regiment, P. R. C.
32	Ord. Serg. H. M'Carty.........	K......	114th Regiment, P. V.
33	Unknown.		
34	Unknown Zouave.		
35	Unknown.		
36	Unknown Zouave.		
37	Unknown.		
38	Unknown.		
39	John Walker.......................	C......	110th Regiment, P. V.
40	Unknown.		
41	William Crowl	K......	141st Regiment, P. V.
42	Robert Robinson..................	L......	4th Regiment, Cavalry.
43	Guy Southwick....................	L......	16th Regiment, Cavalry.
44	John G. Coyle, with diary & $6,	C	75th Regiment, P. V.
45	F. Hubbard, with ambrotype..		
46	Unknown.		
47	William Vosburg..	....	2d Div. 2d Corps, (Buford's) [Cavalry.

Pennsylvania.—SECTION E—*Continued.*

No of grave.	Names.	Comp'y	Regiment.
48	Unknown P. V.		
49	G. Wm. ——........................	A......	With knife and comb.
50	Unknown.		
51	Serg. George O. Fell............	B......	143d Regiment, P. V.
52	Supposed P. V.		
53	Supposed P. V.		
54	Supposed Serg., (with letters.)		
55	Supposed P. V.		
56	Supposed P. V.		
57	Supposed P. V.		
58	Unknown Ord. Sergeant.		
59	Supposed P. V.		
60	Supposed P. V.		
61	Supposed P. V.		
62	Supposed P. V.		
63	Supposed P. V.		
64	Supposed P. V.		
65	Unknown P. V.		
66	Corp., unknown, P. V.		
67	Serg., unknown, P. V.		
68	Unknown P. V.		
69	Unknown P. V.		
70	Unknown, (with swawl pin.)		
71	Unknown.		
72	Unknown.		
73	Sergeant, supposed P. V.		
74	Supposed P. V.		

Pennsylvania.—SECTION E—*Continued.*

No. of grave.	Names.	Comp'y.	Regiment.
75	Supposed P. V.		
76	Supposed P. V.		
77	Supposed P. V.		
78	Supposed P. V.		
79	Supposed P. V.		
80	Supposed P. V.		
81	2d Lieut. John F. Cox.........	I	57th Regiment, P. V.

SECTION F.

No. of grave.	Names.	Comp'y.	Regiment.
1	Unknown.		
2	Unknown P. V.		
3	Supposed P. V.		
4	Supposed V. V.		
5	Supposed P. V.		
6	Supposed P. V.		
7	Supposed P. V.		
8	——— Barr......................	B......	105th Regiment, P. V.
9	Unknown Zouave.		
10	Unknown Zouave.		
11	Unknown Zouave.		
12	Unknown Zouave, (burned in destruction of Sherfy's barn.)		
13	Unknown Zouave, (burned in destruction of Sherfy's barn.)		
14	Unknown Zouave, (burned in destruction of Sherfy's barn.)		
15	Unknown Zouave.		
16	——— Oxford.		
17	William M'Grew................	K......	1st Regiment, P. R. C.

Pennsylvania.—Section F—*Continued.*

No. of grave.	Names.	Comp'y.	Regiment.
18	Unknown Sergeant, P. V.		
19	Charles Martin	C	107th Regiment, P. V.
20	Unknown, P. V.		
21	A. K. Coolbaugh	C	141st Regiment, P. V.
22	Joshua M. Hider	I	106th Regiment, P. V.
23	Unknown Sergeant, P. V		
24	Matthew Johnston	H	11th Regiment, P. V.
25	Unknown Zouave, P. V.		
26	G. M. S., with knife and comb.		
27	Jos. Conner, Carner or Carver,	C	148th Regiment, P. V.
28	John M'Nutt	G	140th Regiment, P. V.
29	Francis A. Osborne	E	16th Cavalry.
30	Unknown.		
31	Unknown.		
32	George Cogswell	A	156th Regiment, P. V.
33	John Bunn	C	26th Regiment, P. V.
34	William Kelley	A	126th Regiment, P. V.
35	Unknown P. V., with knife and	spoon.	
36	Supposed P. V.		
37	S. Brookmeyer.		
38	J. Little	B	26th Regiment, P. V.
39	Unknown P. V.		
40	Unknown, 2 knives and comb.		
41	Corp. Peter M'Mahon	E	26th Regiment, P. V.
42	Charles Kelly, with letter, &c.		
43	E. H. Brown	K	26th Regiment, P. V.
44	Supposed P. V.		

Pennsylvania.—SECTION F—*Continued.*

No. of grave.	Names.	Comp'y.	Regiment.
45	Supposed P. V.		
46	John Zouwell, letter.		
47	Supposed P. V.		
48	William M'Neil...................	I......	26th Regiment, P. V.
49	Supposed P. V.		
50	Supposed P. V.		
51	Corp. Samuel Fitzinger.........	B......	106th Regiment, P. V.
52	Supposed P. V.		
53	H. C. Tafel	I......	62d Regiment, P. V.
54	Supposed P. V.		
55	David W. Boyd..................	G......	140th Regiment, P. V.
56	Supposed P. V., (small man with large black whiskers.)		
57	Supposed P. V.		
58	Supposed P. V.		
59	Supposed P. V.		
60	Supposed P. V.		
61	Harry Evans	B......	88th Regiment, P. V.
62	Supposed P. V.		
63	Supposed P. V.		
64	Supposed P. V.		
65	Supposed P. V.		
66	G. Mickle............................	C......	72d Regiment, P. V.
67	Supposed P. V.		
68	Supposed P. V.		
69	Unknown.		
70	Unknown.		
71	Unknown.		

Pennsylvania.—SECTION F—*Continued.*

No. of grave.	Names.	Comp'y.	Regiment.
72	Unknown.		
73	Unknown.		
74	Unknown.		
75	S. B. Stewart	F......	2d Regiment, P. R. C.
76	——— Welsh		
77	Unknown.		
78	Walter S. Briggs, Adjutant ...	....	27th Regiment, P. V.

TOTAL, 526.

MAINE.

SECTION A.

No. of grave.	Names.	Comp'y.	Regiment.
1	Corp. Frank. Devereux..........	K......	16th Regiment, M. V.
2	Unknown	....	16th Regiment, M. V.
3	George D. Marston	I.......	16th Regiment, M. V.
4	Unknown—Supposed..............	....	16th Regiment, M. V.
5	E. Bishop.		
6	W. H. Lowe.........................	E......	19th Regiment, M. V.
7	Alfred P. Watterman..............	D......	19th Regiment, M. V.
8	Serg. Alex. W. Lord............	C	19th Regiment, M. V.
9	Serg. William E. Barrows	I.......	19th Regiment, M. V.
10	Unknown.....	....	19th Regiment, M. V.
11	Serg. Chandler F. Perry.......	I.......	19th Regiment, M. V.
12	Louira A. Kelley	D......	19th Regiment, M. V.

Maine.—Section A—*Continued.*

No. of grave.	Names.	Comp'y.	Regiment.
13	Unknown	....	19th Regiment, M. V.
14	Charles W. Collins.....	A......	19th Regiment, M. V.
15	Corp. Austin Hanson............	F......	17th Regiment, M. V.
16	Isaiah V. Eaton...................	D......	4th Regiment, M. V.
17	Frank. Fairbrother..............	G......	16th Regiment, M. V.
18	Robert T. Newell................	D......	19th Regiment, M. V.

Section B.

No. of grave.	Names.	Comp'y.	Regiment.
1	Samuel L. Dwelley......	D......	17th Regiment, M. V.
2	Frank. Coffin......................	B......	19th Regiment, M. V.
3	James T. Neal	K......	19th Regiment, M. V.
4	Loring C. Oliver..................	K......	19th Regiment, M. V.
5	Samuel B. Shea.	K......	19th Regiment, M. V.
6	Corp. Hollis F. Arnold.........	H......	19th Regiment, M. V.
7	Sergt. Jesse A. Dorman........	H......	19th Regiment, M. V.
8	George E. Hodgdon..............	C......	19th Regiment, M. V.
9	Charles J. Carroll................	G......	19th Regiment, M. V.
10	Ruel Nickerson....................	E......	19th Regiment, M. V.
11	Henshai C. Thomas.............	D......	19th Regiment, M. V.
12	John F. Carey	I......	19th Regiment, M. V.
13	Moses D. Emery..................	B......	17th Regiment, M. V.
14	Fessenden M. Mills.............	C......	17th Regiment, M. V.
15	Joseph A. Roach..................	D......	3d Regiment, M. V.
16	Allen H. Sprague................	E......	3d Regiment, M. V.
17	John S. Gray.......................	D......	4th Regiment, M. V.

Maine.—Section C.

No. of grave.	Names.	Comp'y.	Regiment.
1	George F. Johnson...............	K......	4th Regiment, M. V.
2	—— ——ickels.....................	G......	
3	Corp. George W. Jones.........	B......	7th Regiment, M. V.
4	Eben S. Allen, Ord. Sergt.....	D......	3d Regiment, M. V.
5	Ira L. Martin	H......	11th Regiment, M. V.
6	John F. Shuman.................	K......	4th Regiment, M. V.
7	Unknown..........................	....	3d Regiment, M. V.
8	Corp. Bernard Hogan...........	D......	17th Regiment, M. V.
9	Lieut. George M. Bragg.......	F......	4th Regiment, M. V.
10	1st Sergt. Thomas T. Rideout,	F......	19th Regiment, M. V.
11	James Robbins	D......	19th Regiment, M. V.
12	Sergt. Enoch C. Dow...........	E......	19th Regiment, M. V.
13	Sergt. W. S. Jordon............	G......	20th Regiment, M. V.
14	Frank B. Curtis..................	F......	20th Regiment, M. V.
15	Elfin J. Foss.......................	F......	20th Regiment, M. V.
16	Lieut. W. L. Kendall...........	G......	20th Regiment, M. V.

Section D.

No. of grave.	Names.	Comp'y.	Regiment.
1	Samuel O. Hatch...............	K.....	17th Regiment, M. V.
2	1st Sergt. Isaac N. Lathrop...	H......	20th Regiment, M. V.
3	Benjamin W. Grant.............	F......	20th Regiment, M. V.
4	Corp. Samuel C. Davis.........	B......	17th Regiment, M. V.
5	Royal Rand....	H......	17th Regiment, M. V.
6	Charles E. Herriman	E......	19th Regiment, M. V.
7	George H. Willey................	H......	19th Regiment, M. V.
8	Wm. H. Huntingdon.......	B......	16th Regiment, M. V.

Maine.—SECTION D—*Continued.*

No. of grave.	Names.	Comp'y.	Regiment.
9	Harrison Pullen	G......	16th Regiment, M. V.
10	Edward Cunningham............	L......	1st Cavalry.
11	M. Quint	B......	17th Regiment, M. V.
12	Alsbury Luce	F......	3d Regiment, M. V.
13	Corp. Eben Farrington.........	H......	3d Regiment, M. V.
14	Unknown............................	....	20th Regiment, M. V.

SECTION E.

No. of grave.	Names.	Comp'y.	Regiment.
1	Unknown............................	....	20th Regiment, M. V.
2	Goodwin S. Ireland............	H.....	20th Regiment, M. V.
3	Unknown.....	....	20th Regiment, M. V.
4	Orrin Walker......................	K......	20th Regiment, M. V.
5	Unknown	....	20th Regiment, M. V.
6	Unknown	....	20th Regiment, M. V.
7	Unknown	....	20th Regiment, M. V.
8	Corp. Wm. S. Hodgdon........	F	20th Regiment, M. V.
9	Corp. Mellville C. Day.........	G......	20th Regiment, M. V.
10	1st Serg. Charles W. Steel....	H	20th Regiment, M. V.
11	Unknown	....	20th Regiment, M. V.
12	Unknown	....	20th Regiment, M. V.
13	Unknown	....	20th Regiment, M. V.
14	Unknown	....	20th Regiment, M. V.

Maine.—Section F.

No. of grave.	Names.	Comp'y.	Regiment.
1	Capt. G. D. Smith	I	19th Regiment, M. V.
2	Joseph D. Simpson	A	20th Regiment, M. V.
3	Moses Davis	C	20th Regiment, M. V.
4	Samuel C. Brookings	H	19th Regiment, M. V.
5	Corp. W. K.		20th Regiment, M. V.
6	Ord. Serg. Geo. S. Noyes	K	20th Regiment, M. V.
7	Unknown		20th Regiment, M. V.
8	Michael Rariden	K	4th Regiment, M. V.
9	Sullivan Luce		5th Battery, M. V.
10	W. H. Smith	K	7th Regiment, M. V.
11	Wm. H. Day	F	17th Regiment, M. V.
12	R. Finch	E	17th Regiment, M. V.
13	Crosby R. Brookings	G	4th Regiment, M. V.

Section G.

No. of grave.	Names.	Comp'y.	Regiment.
1	Albion B. Mills	E	16th Regiment, M. V.
2	Corp. John Merriam	D	19th Regiment, M. V.
3	Abijah Crosby	C	19th Regiment, M. V.
4	Corp. Richard Sculley	K	7th Regiment, M. V.
5	Corp. A. H. Cole		3d Regiment, M. V.
6	John W. Jones	B	3d Regiment, M. V.
7	Serg. Major Henry S. Small		3d Regiment, M. V.
8	Corp. J. L. Little	A	3d Regiment, M. V.
9	Calvin H. Burdin	I	3d Regiment, M. V.
10	Capt. John C. Keen	K	3d Regiment, P. V.

Maine.—SECTION G—*Continued.*

No. of grave.	Names.	Comp'y.	Regiment.
11	Serg. Nelson W. Jones.........	I.......	3d Regiment, M. V.
12	J. Bartlett.		

TOTAL, 104.

NEW HAMPSHIRE.

SECTION A.

No. of grave.	Names.	Comp'y.	Regiment.
1	William H. Spring...............	A.....	2d Regiment, N. H. V.
2	Charles A. Moore...............	C	2d Regiment, N. H. V.
3	E. J. Plummer....................	A.....	2d Regiment, N. H. V.
4	Stephen H. Palmer...............	I.......	2d Regiment, N. H. V.
5	Charles V. Buzzell..............	E......	12th Regiment, N. H. V.
6	Roland Taylor......................	G......	5th Regiment, N. H. V.
7	S. R. Green.........................	A......	5th Regiment, N. H. V.
8	John Henderson...................	F......	2d Regiment, N. H. V.
9	Serg. G. A. Jones................	E......	2d Regiment, N. H. V.
10	George S. Vittum................	F......	2d Regiment, N. H. V.
11	Lieut. E. Dascomb..............	G......	2d Regiment, N. H. V.
12	Charles W. Taylor...............	D......	2d Regiment, N. H. V.
13	Cornelius Cleary..................	....	2d Regiment, N. H. V.
14	James S. Hawkins	C......	12th Regiment, N. H. V.
15	John Totten.........................	A......	2d Regiment, N. H. V.
16	Joseph M. Chesley...............	E......	2d Regiment, N. H. V.
17	Unknown	....	2d Regiment, N. H. V.
18	Unknown.		

New Hampshire.—SECTION B.

No. of grave.	Names.	Comp'y.	Regiment.
1	Unknown.		
2	Unknown.		
3	Unknown.		
4	Unknown.		
5	Unknown.		
6	Unknown.		
7	Unknown, (with red chin whiskers)		2d Regiment, N. H. V.
8	Unknown		2d Regiment, N. H. V.
9	Unknown.		
10	Unknown		2d Regiment, N. H. V.
11	Unknown		2d Regiment, N. H. V.
12	Unknown.		
13	Unknown.		
14	Unknown.		
15	Unknown.		
16	Unknown.		

SECTION C.

No. of grave.	Names.	Comp'y.	Regiment.
1	Unknown.		
2	Unknown.		
3	Unknown.		
4	Unknown		2d Regiment, N. H. V.
5	Unknown		2d Regiment, N. H. V.
6	Unknown		2d Regiment, N. H. V.
7	John Taylor	E	12th Regiment, N. H. V.
8	Kendall H. Cofren		2d Regiment, N. H. V.

New Hampshire.—SECTION C—*Continued.*

No. of grave.	Names.	Comp'y.	Regiment.
9	Joseph Bond, Jr.	E.	5th Regiment, N. H. V.
10	Oscar D. Allen	E.	5th Regiment, N. H. V.
11	Supposed.		
12	Supposed.		
13	Charles T. Kelley	H.	12th Regiment, N. H. V.
14	Unknown.		
15	Bartlett Brown	E.	

TOTAL, 49.

VERMONT.

SECTION A.

No. of grave.	Names.	Comp'y.	Regiment.
1	Unknown		V. M. M.
2	Joseph Ashley	C.	16th Regiment, V. V.
3	Charles W. Ross	G.	14th Regiment, V. V.
4	Corp. Charles E. Mead	G.	14th Regiment, V. V.
5	Unknown		14th Regiment, V. V.
6	Unknown		14th Regiment, V. V.
7	Unknown		14th Regiment, V. V.
8	Martin J. Cook	D.	16th Regiment, V. V.
9	Joseph M. Martin	D.	16th Regiment, V. V.
10	William E. Green	G.	14th Regiment, V. V.
11	Unknown		14th Regiment, V. V.
12	Unknown		14th Regiment, V. V.

Vermont.—Section A—*Continued.*

No. of grave.	Names.	Comp'y.	Regiment.
13	Dyer Rogers	D	14th Regiment, V. V.
14	Unknown		14th Regiment, V. V.
15	Albert A. Walker	D	14th Regiment, V. V.
16	Corp. Charles Morse, Jr	A	16th Regiment, V. V.
17	Garrett L. Roseboom	D	14th Regiment, V. V.
18	Ira Emery, Jr., (removed)	A	16th Regiment, V. V.
19	William O. Doubleday	H	14th Regiment, V. V.
20	Andrew E. Osgood	H	13th Regiment, V. V.
21	Corp. George L. Baldwin	F	14th Regiment, V. V.
22	G. F. Simmons		13th Regiment, V. V.
23	Sylvanus A. Winship	C	16th Regiment, V. V.
24	Sergt. Moses P. Baldwin	C	16th Regiment, V. V.
25	Sergt. Major Henry H. Smith,		13th Regiment, V. V.
26	Corp. Ira E. Sperry	L	1st Cavalry.
27	John L. Marshall	K	4th Regiment, V. V.
28	Sergt. Thomas Blake	A	13th Regiment, V. V.
29	Corp. Michael M'Enerny	A	13th Regiment, V. V.

Section B.

No. of grave.	Names.	Comp'y.	Regiment.
1	Lieut. William H. Hamilton	I	14th Regiment, V. V.
2	William G. Jeffrey	A	1st Regiment, V. V.
3	W. Fletcher	D	13th Regiment, V. V.
4	William March	D	13th Regiment, V. V.
5	Orson S. Carr	E	13th Regiment, V. V.
6	Pliny F. White	E	14th Regiment, V. V.
7	Antoine Ash	C	2d Regiment, V. V.
8	Charles W. Whitney	E	13th Regiment, V. V.

Vermont.—Section B—*Continued.*

No. of grave.	Names.	Comp'y.	Regiment.
9	Benjamin N. Wright............	I.......	13th Regiment, V. V.
10	Lester L. Baird, (with $3 35,)	H.....	14th Regiment, V. V.
11	Richard C. Archer...............	B......	14th Regiment, V. V.
12	Corp. Henry C. White..........	E......	16th Regiment, V. V.
13	Zenal C. Lamb.....................	C......	16th Regiment, V. V.
14	John Dyer..........................	D......	16th Regiment, V. V.
15	Unknown..............................	....	1st Cavalry.
16	Unknown.		
17	Unknown..............................	....	1st Cavalry.
18	Corporal ——— Warren.......	....	1st Cavalry.
19	Rufus D. Thompson.............	L......	1st Cavalry.
20	Supposed, Charles Curley.....	....	1st Musician.
21	Joel J. Smith.......................	C......	1st Cavalry.
22	Unknown..............................	....	1st Cavalry.
23	Unknown..............................	....	1st Cavalry.
24	Unknown..............................	....	1st Cavalry.
25	Unknown.		
26	Unknown.		
27	Willard M. Pierce	I.......	16th Regiment, V. V.

Section C.

No. of grave.	Names.	Comp'y.	Regiment.
1	Unknown.		
2	Unknown..............................	....	M. M.
3	Unknown..............................	....	M. M.
4	Edmond P. Davis................	H.....	16th Regiment, V. V.
5	Phillip Howard.....	A......	16th Regiment, V. V.

Total, 61.

MASSACHUSETTS.

SECTION A.

No. of grave.	Names.	Comp'y.	Regiment.
1	Arthur Murphy		9th Battery.
2	John W. Verity		5th Battery.
3	Edward Frothingham		5th Battery.
4	John Crasson		9th Battery.
5	Henry C. Burrill	H	20th Regiment, M. V.
6	Thomas Kelly	A	20th Regiment, M. V.
7	George Lucas	D	20th Regiment, M. V.
8	Alios Kraft	C	20th Regiment, M. V.
9	T. R. Gallivan	F	20th Regiment, M. V.
10	M. Kinarch	H	20th Regiment, M. V.
11	E. Barry	G	20th Regiment, M. V.
12	Serg. George Jæckel	B	20th Regiment, M. V.
13	Patrick O'Keefe	F	20th Regiment, M. V.
14	Thomas Downey	E	20th Regiment, M. V.
15	Corp. James Somerville	E	20th Regiment, M. V.
16	William Inch	D	20th Regiment, M. V.
17	Augustus Deitling	C	20th Regiment, M. V.
18	Sergt. George F. Cate	A	20th Regiment, M. V.
19	Clemens Wiessensee	B	20th Regiment, M. V.
20	Patrick Quinlin	F	20th Regiment, M. V.
21	G. C. Plant	A	20th Regiment, M. V.
22	Hugh Blain	H	20th Regiment, M. V.
23	Patrick Manning	D	20th Regiment, M. V.
24	John M'Clarence	F	20th Regiment, M. V.
25	John Dippolt	B	20th Regiment, M. V.

Massachusetts.—SECTION A—*Continued.*

No. of grave.	Names.	Comp'y.	Regiment.
26	Hiram B. Howard..............	D......	20th Regiment, M. V.
27	Eugene M'Laughlin............	F......	20th Regiment, M. V.
28	Corp. John Burke...............	K......	20th Regiment, M. V.
29	Alexander Aiken	D......	20th Regiment, M. V.
30	James Lane........................	F......	20th Regiment, M. V.
31	George F. Fales, of Boston...	D......	Excelsior, of N. Y.
32	George S. Wise...................	D......	13th Regiment, M. V.
33	Michael Laughlin	K......	13th Regiment, M. V.
34	Edwin Field.......................	B......	13th Regiment, M. V.
35	John M. Brock	H......	13th Regiment, M. V.
36	Frank A. Gould	K......	13th Regiment, M. V.
37	Corp. Prince A. Dunton.......	H......	13th Regiment, M. V.
38	John Flye	K......	13th Regiment, M. V.
39	Sergt. Edgar A. Fiske.........	E......	13th Regiment, M. V.

SECTION B.

No. of grave.	Names.	Comp'y.	Regiment.
1	Charles Traynor.................	I......	2d Regiment, M. V.
2	William T. Bullard..............	A......	2d Regiment, M. V.
3	John Joy	H......	2d Regiment, M. V.
4	Philo H. Peck...	G......	2d Regiment, M. V.
5	Stephen Cody....................	I......	2d Regiment, M. V.
6	Richard Seavers.................	I......	2d Regiment, M. V.
7	George Bailey............	I......	2d Regiment, M. V.
8	Andrew Nelson..................	D......	2d Regiment, M. V.
9	John Deer.........................	D......	2d Regiment, M. V.
10	Corp. Gordon S. Wilson.......	G......	2d Regiment, M. V.

Massachusetts.—Section B—*Continued.*

No. of grave.	Names.	Comp'y.	Regiment.
11	Joseph Furbur	G	2d Regiment, M. V.
12	Rupert J. Saddler, Col. Corp.,	D	2d Regiment, M. V.
13	Frederick Maynard	D	2d Regiment, M. V.
14	Patrick Hoey	A	2d Regiment, M. V.
15	Sergt. Leavitt C. Durgin	A	2d Regiment, M. V.
16	Corp. William Marshall	C	2d Regiment, M. V.
17	Corp. Ruel Whittier	B	2d Regiment, M. V.
18	James T. Edmands	I	2d Regiment, M. V.
19	John E. Farrington	H	2d Regiment, M. V.
20	Peter Conlan	B	2d Regiment, M. V.
21	Sidney S. Prouty	A	2d Regiment, M. V.
22	F. Goetz	C	2d Regiment, M. V.
23	Corp. Theodore S. Butters	I	2d Regiment, M. V.
24	David B. Brown	I	2d Regiment, M. V.
25	William H. Ela	D	2d Regiment, M. V.
26	James A. Chase	C	2d Regiment, M. V.
27	Charles Keirnan	F	2d Regiment, M. V.
28	And. Moore	F	1st Regiment, M. V.
29	Lieut. Henry Hartley	E	1st Regiment, M. V.
30	Frederick S. Kettel	E	1st Regiment, M. V.
31	George Golden	B	1st Regiment, M. V.
32	David H. Eaton	B	1st Regiment, M. V.
33	Jacob Kesland	B	1st Regiment, M. V.
34	Sergt. Edward J. M'Ginnis	C	1st Regiment, M. V.
35	J. Matthews	B	1st Regiment, M. V.
36	Sergt. William Kelren	E	1st Regiment, M. V.
37	Corp. Henry Evans	A	1st Regiment, M. V.

Massachusetts.—SECTION C.

No. of grave.	Names.	Comp'y.	Regiment.
1	J. L. Johnson	K	11th Regiment, M. V.
2	Joseph Marshall	K	11th Regiment, M. V.
3	James E. Butler	D	11th Regiment, M. V.
4	Michael Doherty	A	11th Regiment, M. V.
5	Lucius Staples	A	11th Regiment, M. V.
6	Corp. Edwin F. Trufant	F	11th Regiment, M. V.
7	Corp. C. R. T. Knowlton	H	11th Regiment, M. V.
8	Sergt. William Sawtell	E	11th Regiment, M. V.
9	J. S. Rice	K	11th Regiment, M. V.
10	Sumner A. Davis	K	11th Regiment, M. V.
11	Francis T. Flint	H	11th Regiment, M. V.
12	John Brodie.		
13	Sergt. William Carr	I	12th Regiment, M. V.
14	George F. Lewis	H	12th Regiment, M. V.
15	Hardy P. Murray	K	12th Regiment, M. V.
16	Corp. T. H. Fenelon	G	32d Regiment, M. V.
17	William D. Hudson	H	32d Regiment, M. V.
18	Barney Clark	G	32d Regiment, M. V.
19	Sergt. James M. Haskell	A	32d Regiment, M. V.
20	Alvin W. Lamb	A	32d Regiment, M. V.
21	William F. Baldwin	B	32d Regiment, M. V.
22	Henry T. Wade	E	32d Regiment, M. V.
23	Corp. William L. Gillman	K	32d Regiment, M. V.
24	Daniel Stoddard	F	32d Regiment, M. V.
25	Corp. Nathaniel Mayo	F	32d Regiment, M. V.
26	T. J. Healey	G	32d Regiment, M. V.
27	James H. Leavens	I	32d Regiment, M. V.

Massachusetts.—SECTION C—*Continued.*

No. of grave.	Names.	Comp'y.	Regiment.
28	Sergt. Gorham Coffin	A	19th Regiment, M. V.
29	Sergt. Joseph Ford	K	19th Regiment, M. V.
30	Edward Roche	E	19th Regiment, M. V.
31	Corp. Thomas W. Tuttle	I	19th Regiment, M. V.
32	Jeremiah Wells	H	19th Regiment, M. V.
33	Charles Gurney	E	37th Regiment, M. V.
34	E. Bassamunson	B	37th Regiment, M. V.
35	Elisha Covill	E	37th Regiment, M. V.

SECTION D.

No. of grave.	Names.	Comp'y.	Regiment.
1	Sergt. Henry C. Ball	F	15th Regiment, M. V.
2	John Marsh	B	15th Regiment, M. V.
3	Michael Flinn	G	15th Regiment, M. V.
4	O. Stevens	D	15th Regiment, M. V.
5	Geo. W. Cross	E	15th Regiment, M. V.
6	Joseph Bardsley	I	15th Regiment, M. V.
7	Francis Santum	I	15th Regiment, M V.
8	Francis A. Lewis	A	15th Regiment, M V.
9	George E. Burns	G	15th Regiment, M. V.
10	George L. Bass	B	15th Regiment, M. V.
11	Sergt. Edward B. Rollins	A	15th Regiment, M. V.
12	John Grady	I	15th Regiment, M. V.
13	N. B. Bicknell	C	11th Regiment, M. V.
14	Pierce Harvey		15th Regiment, M. V.
15	G. Lambert	F	15th Regiment, M. V.
16	Calvin S. Field	B	22d Regiment, M. V.

Massachusetts.—SECTION D—*Continued.*

No. of grave.	Names.	Comp'y.	Regiment.
17	John Hickey	C	28th Regiment, M. V.
18	John Caswell	G	28th Regiment, M. V.
19	Sergt. Edward Mooney	D	28th Regiment, M. V.
20	Joseph Beal	I	33d Regiment, M. V.
21	C. H. Pierce	E	33d Regiment, M. V.
22	Unknown.		
23	Geo. Hills, of New Bedford.		
24	Corp. Patrick Scannell	B	19th Regiment, M. V.
25	Sergt. Alonzo J. Babcock	H	2d Regiment, M. V.
26	Corp. Jules B. Allen	D	33d Regiment, M. V.
27	Calvin Howe	I	33d Regiment, M. V.
28	E. Howe	H	33d Regiment, M. V.
29	Jeremiah Danforth	C	19th Regiment, M. V.
30	Charles A. Trask	K	13th Regiment, M. V.
31	Charles H. Wellington	K	13th Regiment, M. V.
32	Daniel Holland	D	19th Regiment, M. V.
33	P. W. Price	C	28th Regiment, M. V.
34	George Lawton	H	16th Regiment, M. V.
35	J. Coakley	A	19th Regiment, M. V.

SECTION E.

No. of grave.	Names.	Comp'y.	Regiment.
1	G. P. Roundey, Massachusetts.		
2	J. B. Nincent	G	22d Regiment, M. V.
3	Unknown.		
4	James Crampton	K	3d Regiment, M. V.
5	John F. Moore	K	22d Regiment, M. V.

Massachusetts.—Section E—*Continued.*

No. of grave.	Names.	Comp'y.	Regiment.
6	C. H. Reed........................	H.....	15th Regiment, M. V.
7	John T. Bixby......................	H.....	15th Regiment, M. V.
8	S. Hindeman.......................	....	15th Regiment, M. V.
9	G. F. Leonard......................	....	13th Regiment, M. V.

Section F.

No. of grave.	Names.	Comp'y.	Regiment.
1	1st Lieut. Sumner Paine.......	....	20th Regiment, M. V.
2	Lieut. J. H. Parkins	E.....	37th Regiment, M. V.
3	Lieut. Sherman S. Robinson..	....	19th Regiment, M. V.

Total, 158.

RHODE ISLAND.

SECTION A.

No. of grave.	Names.	Battery.	Regiment.
1	Ira Bennett*	B	1st Regiment, R. I. Art.
2	David B. King	B	1st Regiment, R. I. Art.
3	John Zimmila	A	1st Regiment, R. I. Art.
4	Ernest Simpson	E	1st Regiment, R. I. Art.
5	John Greene	B	1st Regiment, R. I. Art.
6	John Higgins	A	1st Regiment, R. I. Art.
7	Alvin Hilton†	E	1st Regiment, R. I. Art.
8	Francis H. Martin‡	E	1st Regiment, R. I. Art.
9	Patrick Lonnegan	A	1st Regiment, R. I. Art.
10	Charles Powers	Co C.	2d Regiment, R. I. V.

SECTION B.

No. of grave.	Names.	Battery.	Regiment.
1	William Beard	E	1st Regiment, R. I. Art.
2	Corp. Henry H. Ballou	B	1st Regiment, R. I. Art.

TOTAL, 12.

* Temporarily transferred from the 19th Maine Regiment of Infantry.
† Was temporarily attached to this Battery, from 20th Regiment, Indiana Volunteers.
‡ Was temporarily attached to this Battery, from 99th Pennsylvania Volunteers.

CONNECTICUT.

SECTION A.

No. of grave.	Names.	Comp'y.	Regiment.
1	Corp. William E. Wilson.......	D......	27th Regiment, C. V.
2	Corp. Joseph Puffer............	I.......	14th Regiment, C. V.
3	William D. Marsh................	G......	14th Regiment, C. V.
4	Moses G. Clement................	G......	14th Regiment, C. V.
5	S. Carter	A......	15th Regiment, C. V.
6	Edward B. Farr	F......	27th Regiment, C. V.
7	Michael Confrey..................	F......	27th Regiment, C. V.
8	John D. Perry......................	F......	20th Regiment, C. V.
9	Bernard Mulvey..................	I.......	20th Regiment, C. V.
10	Frank J. Benson..................	C......	17th Regiment, C. V.
11	Joseph Whitlock..................	C......	17th Regiment, C. V.

SECTION B

No. of grave.	Names.	Comp'y.	Regiment.
1	Alfred H. Dibble................	G......	14th Regiment, C. V.
2	Nelson Hodge................. ..	I.......	14th Regiment, C. V.
3	James Cassidy.........	C......	20th Regiment, C. V.
4	Corp. Joel C. Dickerman	I.......	20th Regiment, C. V.
5	Charles H. Roberts.............	F......	20th Regiment, C. V.
6	Daniel H. Prudy................	C.....	17th Regiment, C. V.
7	James Flynn......................	E......	17th Regiment, C. V.
8	Corp. ——— Williams	D......	20th Regiment, C. V.
9	John W. Metcalf................	F......	17th Regiment, C. V.
10	William Cannells.		

Connecticut.—SECTION C.

No. of grave.	Names.	Comp'y.	Regiment.
1	Patrick Dunn........................	D......	27th Regiment, C. V.

TOTAL, 22.

NEW YORK.

SECTION A.

No. of grave.	Names.	Comp'y.	Regiment.
1	L. Vangorder	E......	20th Regiment, N. Y. S. M.
2	G. H. Babcock....................	E......	20th Regiment, N. Y. S. M.
3	——— Easter.......................	K......	14th Regiment, N. Y. S. M.
4	E. B. Miller........................	D......	146th Regiment, N. Y. V.
5	William Millard..................	F......	14th Regiment, N. Y. S. M.
6	Unknown.............................	....	14th Regiment, N. Y. S. M.
7	Unknown.............................	....	14th Regiment, N. Y. S. M.
8	Unknown.............	....	14th Regiment, N. Y. S. M.
9	Unknown.....	....	14th Regiment, N. Y. S. M.
10	Unknown.............................	....	14th Regiment, N. Y. S. M.
11	Unknown........	....	14th Regiment, N. Y. S. M.
12	Unknown.............................	....	14th Regiment, N. Y. S. M.
13	Unknown........	....	14th Regiment, N. Y. S. M.
14	George A. Atkin..	D......	14th Regiment, N. Y. S. M.
15	Unknown.............................	....	147th Regiment, N. Y. V.
16	Unknown.............................	....	147th Regiment, N. Y. V.
17	Unknown.............................	....	147th Regiment, N. Y. V.
18	Unknown.............................	....	147th Regiment, N. Y. V.
19	Unknown.............................	....	147th Regiment, N. Y. V

New York.—Section A—*Continued.*

No. of grave.	Names.	Comp'y.	Regiment.
20	John Wood........................	B......	76th Regiment, N. Y. V.
21	Unknown.........................	....	147th Regiment, N. Y. V.
22	Sergt. Lawrence Hennessy ...	F......	94th Regiment, N. Y. V.
23	Unknown.........................	....	157th Regiment, N. Y. V.
24	Unknown.........................	....	157th Regiment, N. Y. V.
25	Henry Kellog....................	G......	157th Regiment, N. Y. V.
26	Joseph Pharett	E......	157th Regiment, N. Y. V.
27	Unknown.........................	....	157th Regiment, N. Y. V.
28	Unknown.........................	....	157th Regiment, N. Y. V.
29	Unknown.........................	....	157th Regiment, N. Y. V.
30	Unknown.........................	....	157th Regiment, N. Y. V.
31	J. A. Casad.......................	I......	137th Regiment, N. Y. V.
32	Unknown.........................	....	N. Y. V.
33	Venerabie Wesley	B......	137th Regiment, N. Y. V.
34	Ira Martin, Jr.....................	K......	137th Regiment, N. Y. V.
35	John Nickels.....................	B......	149th Regiment, N. Y. V.
36	William Besimer.................	D......	137th Regiment, N. Y. M.
37	Corp. William Miller...........	....	137th Regiment, N. Y. M.
38	Unknown		
39	John Barrey......................	B......	1st N. Y. Artillery.
40	Sergt. Benjamin F. Elliott.....	F......	2d Regiment, N. Y. S. M.
41	L. W. M'Clelland................	D......	20th Regiment, N. Y. S. M.
42	Thomas James..................	A......	42d Regiment, N. Y. V.
43	I. Heimbacker....................	B......	39th Regiment, N. Y. V.
44	R. Snyder.........................	E......	125th Regiment, N. Y. V.
45	John K. Philips..................	F......	126th Regiment, N. Y. V.
46	Marx Englert.....................	I......	108th Regiment, N. Y. V.

New York.—Section A—*Continued.*

No. of grave.	Names.	Comp'y.	Regiment.
47	Unknown		111th Regiment, N. Y. V.
48	H. Burch	K	111th Regiment, N. Y. V.
49	Unknown		111th Regiment, N. Y. V.
50	Edmund Stone, Jr., color bearer	D	64th Regiment, N. Y. V.
51	Francis W. Howard	D	64th Regiment, N. Y. V.
52	Lieut. Julius Ferretzy	D	119th Regiment, N. Y. V.
53	Chester Smith	A	44th Regiment, N. Y. V.
54	Rowland L. Ormsby	G	64th Regiment, N. Y. V.
55	James F. Joloph	G	66th Regiment, N. Y. V.
56	Richard Corcoran	G	2d Regiment, N. Y. V.
57	Frederick Rempmir	B	52d Regiment, N. Y. V.
58	Patrick Martin	D	61st Regiment, N. Y. V.
59	John O'Brian	C	63d Regiment, N. Y. V.
60	Corp. George Dalgleish	K	2d Regiment, N. Y. V.
61	Corp. Peter Junk	E	119th Regiment, N. Y. V.
62	L. A. Godfrey		9th Regiment, N. Y. Cav.
63	W. A. G	A	125th Regiment, N. Y. V.
64	Z. C. Wiggins	D	136th Regiment, N. Y. V.
65	Elias Gage	B	136th Regiment, N. Y. V.
66	Arzy West	H	136th Regiment, N. Y. V.
67	John Salsbury	E	64th Regiment, N. Y. V.
68	Sergt. Platt		86th Regiment, N. Y. S. M.
69	Mike Caddy, Color Sergeant	I	42d Regiment, N. Y. V.
70	Lieut. Col. Max. A. Thoman,		59th Regiment, N. Y. V.
71	Corp. George S. Smith	G	64th Regiment, N. Y. V.
72	Myron H. Van Winkle	E	111th Regiment, N. Y. V.
73	H. Williams	F	2d Regiment, N. Y. V.

New York.—Section A—*Continued.*

No. of grave.	Names.	Comp'y.	Regiment.
74	Sergt. J. B. Wilson	C	2d Regiment, N. Y. S. M.
75	Sergt. James M. Martin	H	59th Regiment, N. Y. S. M.
76	George Shaffer	A	39th Regiment, N. Y. S. M.
77	J. D. Slattery	K	40th Regiment, N. Y. V.
78	E. A. Potter	I	40th Regiment, N. Y. V.
79	A. Krappman	A	40th Regiment, N. Y. V.
80	Thomas Sebring	I	126th Regiment, N. Y. V.
81	1st Lieut. Theodore C. Pausch,		39th Regiment, N. Y. V.
82	Conrad Schuler	D	2d Excelsior.
83	Jacob Van Pelk	B	11th Regiment, N. Y. V.
84	2d Lieut. C. A. Foss	C	12th Regiment, N. Y. V.
85	John C. Curren	E	4th Excelsior.
86	Edwin A. Hess	F	5th Excelsior.
87	Corp. Henry Burk	B	5th Excelsior.
88	Eldridge G. Thompson	G	86th Regiment, N. Y. V.
89	Daniel O'Hara	G	40th Regiment, N. Y. V.
90	C. J. Crandell	K	125th Regiment, N. Y. V.
91	A. B. Usher	D	125th Regiment, N. Y. V.
92	Stephen Baldwin	B	122d Regiment, N. Y. V.
93	Sergt. I. L. Decker	F	70th Regiment, N. Y. V.
94	Philip Bansell	E	10th Regiment, N. Y. C.
95	David Knapp	I	111th Regiment, N. Y. V.
96	Unknown.		
97	John G. Bigg		5th N. Y. Ind. Battery.
98	Unknown.		
99	Frederick Feight	F	140th Regiment, N. Y. V.
100	E. Bryant	K	137th Regiment, N. Y. V.

New York.—Section A—*Continued.*

No. of grave.	Names.	Comp'y.	Regiment.
101	Unknown		
102	J. Dore	B	137th Regiment, N. Y. V.
103	H. Moore	H	149th Regiment, N. Y. V.
104	Thomas Gannon		6th N. Y. Cavalry.
105	Samuel Stills	F	40th Regiment, N. Y. V.
106	Frederick Wentz	I	41st Regiment, N. Y. V.
107	Color Corp. Albert Miracle	H	154th Regiment, N. Y. V.
108	Henry Rhoades	B	108th Regiment, N. Y. V.
109	Sergt. Lewis Bishop	C	154th Regiment, N. Y. V.
110	Jeremiah Barry	E	134th Regiment, N. Y. V.
111	William Weight	K	84th Regiment, N. Y. V.
112	Horace Anguish	I	157th Regiment, N. Y. V.
113	Corp. J. B. Thomas	E	134th Regiment, N. Y. V.
114	Thurston Thomas	D	134th Regiment, N. Y. V.
115	Samuel Hague	B	119th Regiment, N. Y. V.
116	Philip Daney	E	134th Regiment, N. Y. V.
117	P. C. Wilber	E	134th Regiment, N. Y. V.
118	Thaddeus Reynolds	I	154th Regiment, N. Y. V.
119	Lewis Frento	G	76th Regiment, N. Y. V.
120	Charles F. Webber	A	14th Regiment, N. Y. S. M.
121	Henry Miller	B	147th Regiment, N. Y. V.
122	George A. Douglass	F	14th Regiment, N. Y. S. M.
123	Sergt. F. Leaffled	D	104th Regiment, N. Y. V.
124	Albert D. Wilson	E	157th Regiment, N. Y. V.
125	Sergt. W. Shea	I	104th Regiment, N. Y. V.
126	J. Lohruss		104th Regiment, N. Y. V.
127	Mortimer Garrison	B	126th Regiment, N. Y. V.

New York.—Section A—*Continued.*

No. of grave.	Names.	Comp'y.	Regiment.
128	Corp. George W. Forrester...	C......	14th Regiment, N. Y. V.
129	Unknown.		
130	Unknown.		
131	Unknown..........................	....	134th Regiment, N. Y. V.
132	Unknown, with Testament......	....	134th Regiment, N. Y. V.
133	P. Lappen........................	H.....	2d Regiment, N. Y. V.
134	Marshall E. Hiscox, 2d Sergt.,	D......	125th Regiment, N. Y. V.
135	John Bell..........................	E......	123d Regiment, N. Y. V.
136	W. W. Scott	C.....	145th Regiment, N. Y. V.
137	D. Welch	E......	147th Regiment, N. Y. V.
138	W. Pooke	G......	76th Regiment, N. Y. V.
139	1st Sergt. Thomas J. Curtis...	A......	104th Regiment, N. Y. V.
140	Sergt. H. Roberts...............	C......	104th Regiment, N. Y. V.
141	Chauncey Snell..................	F......	147th Regiment, N. Y. V.
142	Elias Hannis.......................	C......	147th Regiment, N. Y. V.
143	Unknown............................	C......	
144	Lieut. Theodore Blume.........	....	2d N. Y. Battery.

Section B.

No. of grave.	Names.	Comp'y.	Regiment.
1	William Cranston................	....	76th Regiment, N. Y. V.
2	Unknown............................	....	76th Regiment, N. Y. V.
3	Unknown............................	....	76th Regiment, N. Y. V.
4	Unknown	....	76th Regiment, N. Y. V.
5	Unknown	....	76th Regiment, N. Y. V.
6	Sergt. Carey	F......	9th Regiment, N. Y. V.
7	Unknown	....	157th Regiment, N. Y. V.

New York.—SECTION B—*Continued.*

No. of grave.	Names.	Comp'y.	Regiment.
8	Amasa Topping.	D	157th Regiment, N. Y. V.
9	Unknown		157th Regiment, N. Y. V.
10	Unknown		157th Regiment, N. Y. V.
11	Unknown		157th Regiment, N. Y. V.
12	Corp. Philander Stone	K	157th Regiment, N. Y. V.
13	Unknown		157th Regiment, N. Y. V.
14	Sergt. Amos Hummiston	C	154th Regiment, N. Y. V.
15	——— Chamburg		134th Regiment, N. Y. V.
16	Unknown		134th Regiment, N. Y. V.
17	Edward Van Dyke	C	134th Regiment, N. Y. V.
18	Levi Carpenter	D	164th Regiment, N. Y. V.
19	Harris Henschell	E	140th Regiment, N. Y. V.
20	John P. Van Altype	A	150th Regiment, N. Y. V.
21	John P. Wing	A	150th Regiment, N. Y. V.
22	G. Ulmer	B	149th Regiment, N. Y. V.
23	Corp W. Foster	C	137th Regiment, N. Y. V.
24	Sergt. C. Gray	I	60th Regiment, N. Y. V.
25	P. Ayres	K	60th Regiment, N. Y. V.
26	James H. Mullin	B	127th Regiment, N. Y. V.
27	John Carnine	E	137th Regiment, N. Y. V.
28	Benjamin Clark	K	137th Regiment, N. Y. V.
29	Sergt. Henry Johnson	E	137th Regiment, N. Y. V.
30	Hannibal Dorset	F	60th Regiment, N. Y. V.
31	Hugh Murphy	G	42d Regiment, N. Y. V.
32	Peter Brentzel	I	42d Regiment, N. Y. V.
33	Unknown.		
34	Lieut. R. P. Holmes	G	126th Regiment, N. Y. V.

New York.—Section B—*Continued.*

No. of grave.	Names.	Comp'y.	Regiment.
35	Unknown.		
36	A. M'Gillora	G	111th Regiment, N. Y. V.
37	G. Bemis	K	111th Regiment, N. Y. V.
38	Albert Bruner		2d N. Y. Battery.
39	Franklin Cole	G	61st Regiment, N. Y. V.
40	John F. Fanssen	K	2d Regiment, N. Y. V.
41	Unknown		N. Y. Artillerist.
42	Daniel Mahoney	B	69th Regiment, N. Y. V.
43	John Burns	I	59th Regiment, N. Y. V.
44	William M. Stewart	C	2d Regiment, N. Y. S. M.
45	Daniel L. Confer	H	136th Regiment, N. Y. V.
46	John Stowell	K	136th Regiment, N. Y. V.
47	C. C. Elwell	H	136th Regiment, N. Y. V.
48	James Doran	E	136th Regiment, N. Y. V.
49	Sergt. William Hoover	G	136th Regiment, N. Y. V.
50	David Reed	A	59th Regiment, N. Y. V.
51	William Bryan	K	42d Regiment, N. Y. V.
52	O. Sergt. Sigm. Webb		52d Regiment, N. Y. V.
53	Thomas J. Boyd	H	2d Regiment, N. Y. S. M.
54	John King	K	2d Regiment, N. Y. S. M.
55	J. B. Morse	E	124th Regiment, N. Y. V.
56	T. Harrigan	A	40th Regiment, N. Y. V.
57	Timothy Kelly	D	40th Regiment, N. Y. V.
58	Benjamin F. Atkins	F	40th Regiment, N. Y. V.
59	William Peisdale	C	68th Regiment, N. Y. V.
60	Simon Freer	F	40th Regiment, N. Y. V.
61	Frank Staley	A	40th Regiment, N. Y. V

New York.—SECTION B—*Continued.*

No. of grave.	Names.	Comp'y.	Regiment.
62	W. M. M'Aboy	G	4th Regiment, N. Y. Ex.
63	J. Galliger	I	4th Regiment, N. Y. Ex.
64	J. J. Conniff	K	4th Regiment, N. Y. Ex.
65	David Maywood	E	5th Regiment, N. Y. Ex.
66	Sergt. Thomas King	E	2d Regiment, N. Y. Ex.
67	Sergt. Ira Penoyar	D	111th Regiment, N. Y. Ex.
68	John J. Dunning	D	111th Regiment, N. Y. Ex.
69	J. K. Saulspaugh	E	126th Regiment, N. Y. Ex.
70	P. D'Vos	E	111th Regiment, N. Y. Ex.
71	B. Conrad		125th Regiment, N. Y. Ex.
72	Ambrose Paine		42d Regiment, N. Y. Ex.
73	George Nicholson	K	126th Regiment, N. Y. Ex.
74	Dennis M'Carthy	K	122d Regiment, N. Y. Ex.
75	John Norton	C	60th Regiment, N. Y. V.
76	William Marks	E	140th Regiment, N. Y V.
77	Unknown.		
78	Unknown.		
79	Unknown.		
80	Unknown.		
81	1st Lieut. M. Stanley	E	60th Regiment, N. Y. V.
82	T. Wood	C	150th Regiment, N. Y. V.
83	W. H. Keyes	G	78th Regiment, N. Y. V.
84	J. Kough	G	102d Regiment, N. Y. V.
85	Sergt. S. A. Smith	B	137th Regiment, N. Y. V.
86	W. Johnson	B	60th Regiment, N. Y. V.
87	G. W. Strong	G	137th Regiment, N. Y. V.
88	J. Bowie	I	102d Regiment, N. Y. V.

New York.—SECTION B—*Continued.*

No. of grave.	Names.	Comp'y.	Regiment.
89	James E. Homan	H	124th Regiment, N. Y. V.
90	Bernard Germann	D	119th Regiment, N. Y. V.
91	Daniel V. Hull	G	136th Regiment, N. Y. V.
92	Albert Hatch	E	157th Regiment, N. Y. V.
93	William Schumne	D	54th Regiment, N. Y. V.
94	J. E. Jayner	E	157th Regiment, N. Y. V.
95	Sergt. J. C. Weisensal	E	45th Regiment, N. Y. V.
96	G. M. Reagles	H	134th Regiment, N. Y. V.
97	Lieut. L. Dietrick		58th Regiment, N. Y. V.
98	John Cassidy	D	108th Regiment, N. Y. V.
99	Morgan L. Allen	C	147th Regiment, N. Y. V.
100	H. F. Morton	F	147th Regiment, N. Y. V.
101	George W. Lampheart	E	76th Regiment, N. Y. V.
102	Corp. Elias A. Norris	B	126th Regiment, N. Y. V.
103	Francis A. Chapman	K	76th Regiment, N. Y. V.
104	Corp. William M'Kendry	G	94th Regiment, N. Y. V.
105	D. Lynes	I	76th Regiment, N. Y. S. M.
106	Sergt. John Stratton	A	94th Regiment, N. Y. V.
107	John Kurk	H	97th Regiment, N. Y. V.
108	Charles A. Hyde	B	76th Regiment, N. Y. V.
109	P. Sheets	G	147th Regiment, N. Y. V.
110	W. S. Besey	C	104th Regiment, N. Y. V.
111	Unknown		134th Regiment, N. Y. V.
112	Unknown		134th Regiment, N. Y. V.
113	Unknown.		
114	Unknown.		
115	Unknown.		

New York.—SECTION B—*Continued.*

No. of grave.	Names.	Comp'y.	Regiment.
116	——— Chamberlain.		
117	———d ———ngton..........	....	N. Y. V.
118	Frank Deieenroth..............	A......	108th Regiment, N. Y. V.
119	John Hofer.		
120	George Clark....................	B......	65th Regiment, N. Y. V.
121	Patrick Burns	H......	9th Regiment, N. Y. S. M.
122	N. A. Thayer.........	K......	123d Regiment, N. Y. S. M.
123	Sergt. M. Buckingham.........	C......	104th Regiment, N.Y.S. M.
124	Samuel G. Spencer.............	D......	76th Regiment, N. Y. S. M.
125	John M. Dawson................	H......	76th Regiment, N. Y. S. M.
126	Unknown.		
127	Unknown.		
128	James Montgomery	E......	1st N. Y. Excelsior.
129	Dennis Brady.....	....	15th I. B.
130	Supposed Excelsior.		
131	Robert Shields....................	C......	140th Regiment, N. Y. V.
132	John Allen.........................	C......	140th Regiment, N. Y. V.
133	Unknown.		
134	John Zubber	B......	140th Regiment, N. Y. V.
135	Sanford Webb.....................	G......	140th Regiment, N. Y. V.
136	Unknown.		
137	Unknown.		
138	Lieut. Charles Clark	B......	9th Regiment, N. Y. S. M.

New York.—Section C.

No. of grave.	Names.	Comp'y.	Regiment.
1	Unknown	....	N. Y. V.
2	Unknown	....	N. Y. V.
3	Unknown	....	N. Y. V.
4	Unknown	....	157th Regiment, N. Y. V.
5	Unknown	....	157th Regiment, N. Y. V.
6	Unknown	....	157th Regiment, N. Y. V.
7	Sergeant, unknown	....	N. Y. V.
8	Orderly Sergeant, unknown	....	N. Y. V.
9	Levi Rush	A	150th Regiment, N. Y. V.
10	B. C. Blunt	G	150th Regiment, N. Y. V.
11	Chase Wingate	....	N. Y. V.
12	George Mabee	D	137th Regiment, N. Y. V.
13	Unknown.		
14	A. Wallace	A	111th Regiment, N. Y. V.
15	W. Brown	H	111th Regiment, N. Y. V.
16	J. Morgan	H	111th Regiment, N. Y. V.
17	James Cullen	F	42d Regiment, N. Y. V.
18	John Smith	D	42d Regiment, N. Y. V.
19	Thomas Barren	D	42d Regiment, N. Y. V.
20	John Enosense	K	59th Regiment, N. Y. V.
21	Sergt. M. Dicker	C	20th Regiment, N. Y. S. M.
22	Sergt. L. H. Dicker	K	20th Regiment, N. Y. S. M.
23	James Gallagher	F	2d Regiment, N. Y. S. M.
24	J. L. Halleck	G	20th Regiment, N. Y. S. M.
25	T. D. Hawkin	E	111th Regiment, N Y. V.
26	H. W. Roberts	E	111th Regiment, N. Y. V.
27	Corp. George Blackall	G	136th Regiment, N. Y. V.

New York.—Section C—*Continued.*

No. of grave.	Names.	Comp'y.	Regiment.
28	William Whitmore..............	E......	111th Regiment, N. Y. V.
29	John Cripps........	A......	111th Regiment, N. Y. V.
30	Unknown.		
31	Corp. A. G. M'Afee............	....	111th Regiment, N. Y. V.
32	D. M'Gill..........................	A......	10th Battalion N. Y.
33	William H. Cross...............	G......	61st Regiment, N. Y. V.
34	——— Conrad..................	C......	2d Regiment, N. Y. V.
35	2d Lieut. Frank K. Garland...	A......	71st Regiment, N. Y. V.
36	Corp. Amos Cogswell..........	F......	71st Regiment, N. Y. V.
37	John H. Philips	B......	95th Regiment, N. Y. V.
38	Unknown..........................	....	N. Y. V.
39	Unknown.		
40	Sergt. P. Rinboldt..............	B......	39th Regiment, N. Y. V.
41	August Ellenberger.	H......	59th Regiment, N. Y. V.
42	Sergt. John Larkins............	E......	2d Regiment, N. Y. V.
43	Peter West.........................	K......	42d Regiment, N. Y. V.
44	William L. Stuart...............	K......	80th Regiment, N. Y. V.
45	John Bloekman.................	I.......	86th Regiment, N. Y. V.
46	James Partington...............	H......	124th Regiment, N. Y. V.
47	John Carrigan..............	I.......	186th Regiment, N. Y. V.
48	Ira W. Ross.........................	B......	86th Regiment, N. Y. V.
49	Walter Gloobson................	K......	40th Regiment, N. Y. V.
50	William Morgan..................	K......	126th Regiment, N. Y. V.
51	G. Huskey..........................	....	3d N. Y. Excelsior.
52	Wilson M. Molloy	C......	4th N. Y. Excelsior.
53	Lieut. George Dennen..........	C......	4th N. Y. Excelsior.
54	George Andrews.................	B......	4th N. Y. Excelsior.

New York.—SECTION C—*Continued.*

No. of grave.	Names.	Comp'y.	Regiment.
55	Alfred G. Armes	H	2d N. Y. Excelsior.
56	1st Sergt. George E. Smith	G	120th Regiment, N. Y. V.
57	Daniel Cauty	C	2d N. Y. Excelsior.
58	Corp. J. A. Thompson		4th N. Y. Battery.
59	James Higgins	I	1st N. Y. Excelsior.
60	Jacob Raish	I	125th Regiment, N. Y. V.
61	J. F. M'Cormick	D	10th Regiment, N. Y. V.
62	William N. Norris	C	44th Regiment, N. Y. V.
63	Unknown		64th Regiment, N. Y. V.
64	Joseph Laroost	H	140th Regiment, N. Y. V.
65	Ezra Hyde	B	146th Regiment, N. Y. V.
66	Unknown.		
67	P. Tillbury	B	137th Regiment, N. Y. V.
68	Capt. J. N. Warner, removed,	K	86th Regiment, N. Y. V.
69	Charles Rosebill	H	119th Regiment, N. Y. V.
70	John Paugh	I	154th Regiment, N. Y. V.
71	Henry Miller	B	141st Regiment, N. Y. V.
72	M. A. Culver	C	157th Regiment, N. Y. V.
73	Peter Linck	K	134th Regiment, N. Y. V.
74	George Rodeloff	E	119th Regiment, N. Y. V.
75	J. F. Chace	D	154th Regiment, N. Y. V.
76	Benjamin Bice	A	134th Regiment, N. Y. V.
77	Corp. Peter Berer	K	134th Regiment, N. Y. V.
78	Ord. Sergt. Augustus Willman,	F	54th Regiment, N. Y. V.
79	Thomas Haley	E	157th Regiment, N. Y. V.
80	George Conner	D	157th Regiment, N. Y. V.
81	Broughton Hough	K	157th Regiment, N. Y. V.

New York.—Section C—*Continued.*

No. of grave.	Names.	Comp'y.	Regiment.
82	George Halbring	G	119th Regiment, N. Y. V.
83	Henry Limerick	F	136th Regiment, N. Y. V.
84	Corp. Jerry Johnson	C	157th Regiment, N. Y. V.
85	J. B. Church	F	147th Regiment, N. Y. V.
86	C. E. Day	D	94th Regiment, N. Y. V.
87	Sergt. A. W. Swart	I	20th Regiment, N. Y. S. M.
88	J. Glair, Jr	D	94th Regiment, N. Y. V.
89	John Glair	B	104th Regiment, N. Y. V.
90	Horace Burgess	D	104th Regiment, N. Y. V.
91	Sergt. F. E. Munsun	D	97th Regiment, N. Y. V.
92	James Mahoney	B	147th Regiment, N. Y. V.
93	Sergt. Henry Sanders	C	94th Regiment, N. Y. V.
94	J. M. Bouren	C	154th Regiment, N. Y. V.
95	Unknown		154th Regiment, N. Y. V.
96	Unknown.		
97	Unknown		154th Regiment, N. Y. V.
98	Unknown		154th Regiment, N. Y. V.
99	Unknown		134th Regiment, N. Y. V.
100	C. W. Radeu	B	1st N. Y. Artillery.
101	Unknown.		
102	John Fitzner	F	108th Regiment, N. Y. V.
103	Henry J. Davis	B	125th Regiment, N. Y. V.
104	Edward Beren	I	125th Regiment, N. Y. V.
105	J. O'Brien	A	2d N. Y. Excelsior.
106	D. Hammond		N. Y. V.
107	Lafayette Burns	I	2d N. Y. Excelsior.
108	Unknown.		

New York.—SECTION C—*Continued.*

No. of grave.	Names.	Comp'y.	Regiment.
109	Corp. D. Casey...........	G.....	122d Regiment, N. Y. V.
110	William Raymond	B......	126th Regiment, N. Y. V.
111	Asa Pettingill......................	F......	147th Regiment, N. Y. V.
112	Jo. Stowtenger.........	G......	147th Regiment, N. Y. V.
113	James Pfeiffer......................	E......	145th Regiment, N. Y. V.
114	Unknown.		
115	Unknown.		
116	James Gray.........................	....	Cowan's Battery.
117	Edward Peto	....	1st N. Y. Battery.
118	R. Ellot.............................	K......	2d Regiment, N. Y. S. M.
119	Ord. Serg't Thomas Devine...	D......	2d Regiment, N. Y. S. M.
120	Unknown.		
121	Unknown.		
122	Unknown, supposed Excelsior.		
123	K. E. Claflin, Testament.......	....	N. Y. V.
124	Unknown, Letters................	....	N. Y. V.
125	Unknown.............................	....	N. Y. Excelsior.
126	Unknown.............................	....	N. Y. Excelsior.
127	Unknown........	....	N. Y. Excelsior.
128	Unknown...........	....	N. Y. Excelsior.
129	Ord. Serg't Edward F. Krause,	K......	19th Regiment, N. Y. V.
130	Unknown.		
131	Unknown.		
132	Unknown.		

New York.—Section D.

No. of grave.	Names.	Comp'y.	Regiment.
1	Frederick D. Clark	K	78th Regiment, N. Y. V.
2	Unknown		N. Y. V.
3	William C. Marsh	H	78th Regiment, N. Y. V.
4	Loren Eaton	D	149th Regiment, N. Y. V.
5	Frederick Phelps	C	137th Regiment, N. Y. V.
6	William Murphy	I	60th Regiment, N. Y. V.
7	Michael Moloy	C	149th Regiment, N. Y. V.
8	E. B. Roberts	B	14th Regiment, N. Y. V.
9	Unknown Cavalryman.		
10	Unknown Cavalryman.		
11	Ord. Serg't James P. Cush	B	59th Regiment, N. Y. V.
12	Unknown		N. Y. V.
13	N. Southerd	K	20th Regiment, N. Y. S. M.
14	John Capper	E	2d Regiment, N. Y. S. M.
15	Patrick M'Marra	E	43d Regiment, N. Y. S. M.
16	Frederick Tybal	K	42d Regiment, N. Y. S. M.
17	Serg't Darvoe	B	1st N. Y. Battery.
18	H. Wood		111th Regiment, N. Y. V.
19	Unknown		N. Y. V.
20	Unknown		N. Y. V.
21	James H. Griswald	E	111th Regiment, N. Y. V.
22	J. J. Beck	D	45th Regiment, N. Y. V.
23	Henry C. Dunnell	D	1st N. Y. Excelsior
24	Serg't Patrick Farrington	G	2d Regiment, N. Y. S. M.
25	Corp. Albert H. Edson	A	8th N. Y. Cavalry.
26	Unknown, Cavalryman.		
27	Patrick M'Donald		N. Y. V

New York,—SECTION D—*Continued.*

No. of grave.	Names.	Comp'y.	Regiment.
28	Wm. Kreis	I	52d Regiment, N Y. V.
29	Casper Bonnell	C	66th Regiment, N. Y. V.
30	Elisha Allen	A	59th Regiment, N. Y. V.
31	Wessel Whitbeck	E	111th Regiment, N. Y. V.
32	Serg't Edwin G. Aylesworth	G	147th Regiment, N. Y. V.
33	Unknown		20th Regiment, N. Y. V.
34	George M'Connell	I	14th Regiment, N. Y. S. M.
35	Francis Chapman	K	76th Regiment, N. Y. S. M.
36	Serg't James Harrigan	E	136th Regiment, N. Y. S. M.
37	Thomas Hurley	G	2d Regiment, N. Y. S. M.
38	David R. Johnson	I	2d Regiment, N. Y. S. M.
39	Philip Martyler		39th Regiment, N. Y. V.
40	George Shumdeher	B	39th Regiment, N. Y. V.
41	Serg't L. Stone	G	42d Regiment, N. Y. V.
42	J. W. Cresler	K	1st N. Y. Excelsior.
43	Unknown		1st N. Y. Excelsior.
44	Unknown		1st N. Y. Excelsior.
45	F. Platt	E	72d Regiment, N. Y. S. M.
46	Patrick Lynch	D	4th N. Y. Excelsior.
47	Serg't J. Murphy	B	4th N. Y. Excelsior.
48	W. M. Brown	G	4th N. Y. Excelsior.
49	Corp. Samuel Lambert	F	1st N. Y. Excelsior.
50	H. Rose	F	111th Regiment, N. Y. V.
51	Joseph Battel	A	2d N. Y. Excelsior.
52	J. D. B.	I	129th Regiment, N. Y. V.
53	Corp. N. W. Winship	K	86th Regiment, N. Y. V.
54	Jabez Fisk	K	86th Regiment, N. Y. V.

New York.—SECTION D—*Continued.*

No. of grave.	Names.	Comp'y.	Regiment.
55	Matthew Bryan	C	2d Regiment, N. Y. V.
56	Serg't C. Farnsborth	G	126th Regiment, N. Y. V.
57	William M'Cort	C	39th Regiment, N. Y. V.
58	E. Whitmore	E	111th Regiment, N. Y. V.
59	William Danice		39th Regiment, N. Y. V.
60	John Furgeson	E	39th Regiment, N. Y. V.
61	Serg't Carlton Sanders	H	120th Regiment, N. Y. V.
62	John Cain	K	122d Regiment, N. Y. V.
63	C. H. Carpenter	I	44th Regiment, N. Y. V.
64	Unknown.		
65	Unknown.		
66	H. M'Dowell	C	60th Regiment, N. Y. V.
67	J. Walton	H	14th Regiment, N. Y. S. M.
68	James Ivers	A	14th Regiment, N. Y. S. M.
69	Jacob Eiser	A	134th Regiment, N. Y. V.
70	—— Heyden		147th Regiment, N. Y. V.
71	Unknown.		
72	Unknown.		
73	J. Finlin		15th Indep't N. Y. Battery.
74	Unknown Zouave		14th Regiment, Brooklyn.
75	Unknown Zouave Serg't		14th Regiment, Brooklyn.
76	Unknown		N. Y. Excelsior.
77	Unknown.		N. Y. Excelsior.
78	Unknown		N. Y. Excelsior.
79	Robert Blair	D	140th Regiment, N. Y. V.
80	Unknown, (with Prayer Book	of Fr.	Deisenroth.)
81	Daniel Casey	D	44th Regiment, N. Y. V.

New York.—Section D—*Continued.*

No. of grave.	Names.	Comp'y.	Regiment.
82	Josephus Simmons	E	44th Regiment, N. Y. V.
83	James Look	A	44th Regiment, N. Y. V.
84	Charles Speisberger	D	140th Regiment, N. Y. V.
85	Philip Beckner	D	140th Regiment, N. Y. V.
86	Justice Eisenberg	D	140th Regiment, N. Y. V.
87	David Nash	F	44th Regiment, N. Y. V.
88	George Lervy	F	44th Regiment, N. Y. V.
89	Serg't Sidney S. Skinner	D	44th Regiment, N. Y. V.
90	Jesse White	G	44th Regiment, N. Y. V.
91	Corp. William C. Crafts	A	44th Regiment, N. Y. V.
92	George Strobridge	E	140th Regiment, N. Y. V.
93	Ross Thomas	E	140th Regiment, N. Y. V.
94	Corp. Goodman	H	44th Regiment, N. Y. V.
95	George Nole	E	44th Regiment, N. Y. V.
96	Leander T. Burnham	E	44th Regiment, N. Y. V.
97	R. M'Elligot	C	44th Regiment, N. Y. V.
98	F. Griswald	C	44th Regiment, N. Y. V.
99	Peter Beers	B	44th Regiment, N. Y. V.
100	John M. Irons	E	44th Regiment, N. Y. V.
101	E. Strong	K	34th Regiment, N. Y. V.
102	Unknown.		
103	Unknown.		
104	Unknown.		
105	Joseph Sneebacker	F	146th Regiment, N. Y. V.
106	Unknown, (with ambrotype and papers.)		
107	Unknown Cavalryman.		
108	Unknown.		

New York.—SECTION D—*Continued.*

No. of grave.	Names.	Comp'y.	Regiment.
109	Martin Roe........	K......	111th Regiment, N. Y. V.
110	H. W. D..............................	....	111th Regiment, N. Y. V.
111	J. C. K..............................	....	N. Y. V.
112	Charles Johnrid..................	H......	5th N. Y. Excelsior.
113	Unknown Cavalry Sergeant.		
114	Unknown.		
115	Unknown.		
116	Unknown.		
117	Unknown.		
118	W. L. Bort........................	B......	157th Regiment, N. Y. V.
119	J. C. Kent........................	K......	136th Regiment, N. Y. V.
120	W. W. Clark......................	B......	60th Regiment, N. Y. V.
121	T. Manly............	A......	63d Regiment, N. Y. V.
122	D. Smith.......	I.......	57th Regiment, N. Y. V.
123	George S. Moss..................	C......	125th Regiment, N. Y. V.
124	William Wyer.....................	A......	119th Regiment, N. Y. V.
125	F. M. Stowell........	D......	N. Y. Excelsior.
126	H. Dale..............................	C......	135th N. Y. Excelsior.
127	Unknown Cavalryman.		

SECTION E.

No. of grave.	Names.	Comp'y.	Regiment.
1	James Gray........................	C......	2d Regiment, N. Y. S. M.
2	Unknown............................	....	2d Regiment, N. Y. S. M.
3	Unknown.		
4	Unknown, (with knife, inkstand, medal, purse and 75 cents.)		

New York.—Section E—*Continued.*

No. of grave.	Names.	Comp'y.	Regiment.
5	Nicholas Paquet	E	49th Regiment, N. Y. V.
6	Charles Root.		
7	John P. Conn		Battery L, 1st Artillery.
8	Frederick Blackstein	A	40th Regiment, N. Y. V.
9	A. R. Townsend	I	60th Regiment, N. Y. V.
10	Charles Manning	C	137th Regiment, N. Y. V.
11	H. W. Nichols	F	137th Regiment, N. Y. V.
12	E. Van Tassel	C	60th Regiment, N. Y. V.
13	P. Stevenson	A	60th Regiment, N. Y. V.
14	P. M'Donald	I	60th Regiment, N. Y. V.
15	Corp. W. W. Rand	E	102d Regiment, N. Y. V.
16	Corp. L. Vinning	A	137th Regiment, N. Y. V.
17	Serg't Charles F. Fox	A	137th Regiment, N. Y. V.
18	Mahlon J. Pardee	F	137th Regiment, N. Y. V.
19	Oliver English	A	137th Regiment, N. Y. V.
20	F. A. Archibald	C	137th Regiment, N. Y. V.
21	Serg't J. W. Brockham	C	137th Regiment, N. Y. V.
22	William W. Wheeler	F	137th Regiment, N. Y. V.
23	Richard W. Rush	A	137th Regiment, N. Y. V.
24	A. Stanton	C	137th Regiment, N. Y. V.
25	Peter Hill	A	137th Regiment, N. Y. V.
26	Dean Swift	A	137th Regiment, N. Y. V.
27	Serg't Daniel Corbett	B	60th Regiment, N. Y. V.
28	Serg't Hiram G. Hilts	C	122d Regiment, N. Y. V.
29	P. Fanning	C	122d Regiment, N. Y. V.
30	W. P. Huntington	C	123d Regiment, N. Y. V.
31	James W. Wickham	E	122d Regiment, N. Y. V.

New York.—Section E—*Continued.*

No. of grave.	Names.	Comp'y.	Regiment.
32	J. Vandyke	K	107th Regiment, N. Y. V.
33	R. Gandley	B	44th Regiment, N. Y. V.
34	G. Christanna	A	120th Regiment, N. Y. V.
35	Daniel Cook, U. S. Ambulance	driver.	
36	Serg't F. Jell	I	95th Regiment, N. Y. V.
37	R. T. Myres	K	111th Regiment, N. Y. V.
38	Felix M'Cram	K	42d Regiment, N. Y. V.
39	Josephus Gee	G	137th Regiment, N. Y. V.
40	A. J. Chafee	E	44th Regiment, N. Y. V.
41	William J. Sutliff	B	137th Regiment, N. Y. V.
42	John Jolloff	F	Excelsior Brigade.
43	Elisha Loomis	C	137th Regiment, N. Y. V.
44	Michael Burns	C	140th Regiment, N. Y. V.
45	James Giles	I	104th Regiment, N. Y. V.
46	Serg't S. Lasage	A	147th Regiment, N. Y. V.
47	John Sloven	I	61st Regiment, N. Y. V.
48	Heinrich Droeber	C	119th Regiment, N. Y. V.
49	John Riley	B	145th Regiment, N. Y. V.
50	H. Hawkins		94th Regiment, N. Y. V.
51	Jacob Dilber	G	119th Regiment, N. Y. V.
52	Joseph Cotrell	A	43d Regiment, N. Y. V.
53	Orin Shepherd	A	60th Regiment, N. Y. V.
54	Lieut. A. Wagner	F	39th Regiment, N. Y. V.
55	P. Newman	K	73d Regiment, N. Y. V.
56	John M. Wastrant	G	111th Regiment, N. Y. V.
57	A. S. Van Volkenburg	G	64th Regiment, N. Y. V.
58	Tyler J. Snyder	G	126th Regiment, N. Y. V.

New York.—Section E.

No. of grave.	Names.	Comp'y.	Regiment.
59	Unknown, (on cap).............	D......	157th Regiment, N. Y. V.
60	Hendrick [illegible]man...........	....	39th Regiment, N. Y. V.
61	J. Clegg...........................	I.......	Excelsior.
62	Corp. A. Ralph....................	C......	62d Regiment, N. Y. V.
63	J. E. Bailey........................	I.......	111th Regiment, N. Y. V.
64	F. Sweney.	D......	40th Regiment, N. Y. V.
65	Thomas Smith.........	K......	1st N. Y. Excelsior.
66	Serg't S. Vanderpool............	I.......	125th Regiment, N. Y. V.
67	Unknown Captain.................	....	N. Y. V.
68	Unknown............................	....	N. Y. Excelsior.
69	1st Lieut. J. Ross Horner....	K......	20th Regiment, N. Y. V.
70	H. Berman..........................	E......	41st Regiment, N. Y. V.
71	Unknown.		
72	—— Delmot, ($2 75, diary and ambrotype)......................	E......	41st Regiment, N. Y. V.
73	Unknown Corporal.............	E......	41st Regiment, N. Y. V.
74	Solomon Lesser, ($36, &c.,)....	E......	41st Regiment, N. Y. V.
75	Corp. Bollinger....................	E......	41st Regiment, N. Y. V.
76	——— Klebenspies.............	E......	41st Regiment, N. Y. V.
77	Corp. Conrad Waelde...........	K......	41st Regiment, N. Y. V.
78	Albert Spitz.......................	H......	41st Regiment, N. Y. V.
79	——— Eiershan....................	B......	41st Regiment, N. Y. V.
80	Corp. Woell.........................	B......	41st Regiment, N. Y. V.
81	J. Smith........	....	4th N. Y. Battery.
82	C. A. Caldwell....................	E......	64th Regiment, N. Y. V.
83	H. C. Rosegrant.................	B......	1st Regiment, N. Y. V.
84	Timothy Kearns..................	A......	1st N. Y. Excelsior.
85	P. Owens...........................	A......	61st Regiment, N. Y. V.

New York.—SECTION E—*Continued.*

No. of grave.	Names.	Comp'y	Regiment.
86	G. W. Secose ..	F......	4th N. Y. Cavalry.
87	Unknown	....	4th N. Y. Cavalry.
88	P. Trainer	D......	4th N. Y. Cavalry.
89	Jo n Kenton	C......	4th N. Y. Cavalry.
90	John Smith	D......	57th Regiment, N. Y. V.
91	Serg't William H. Ambler	D......	57th Regiment, N. Y. V.
92	John Lanegar	D......	5th N. Y. Cavalry.
93	1st Serg't Selden D. Wales	A......	5th N. Y. Cavalry.
94	Adjutant Gaulk	....	5th N. Y. Cavalry.
95	J. B. Cowill	E......	108th N. Y. Cavalry.
96	John P. Wells	E......	104th N. Y. Cavalry.
97	William Franklin	H......	136th N. Y. Cavalry.
98	A. N. Post	A......	43d N. Y. Cavalry.
99	hn I rry	I......	88th Regiment, N. Y. V.
100	1st Sergeant—unknown	....	116th Regiment, N. Y. V.
101	James M'Bride	A......	88th Regiment, N. Y. V.
102	Unknown.		
103	Patrick Kenney	B......	63d Regiment, N. Y. V.
104	Ch es Hogan	A......	63d Regiment, N. Y. V.
105	Henry Hitchcock	....	1st Ind't N Y. Battery.
106	George Clax	C......	111th Regiment, N. Y. V.
107	Amos Otis	K......	146th Regiment, N. Y. V.
108	Serg't Samuel Fuller	G......	105th Regiment, N. Y. V.
109	Unknown	....	Excelsior.
110	E. Develin	A......	4th Regiment, N. Y. V.
111	J. Raetchner	D......	Excelsior.
112	Unknown Zouave.		

New York.—Section E—*Continued.*

No. of grave.	Names.	Comp'y.	Regiment.
113	Corp. Richard Sheridan.........	E......	2d Regiment, N. Y. S. M.
114	D. C., (with bible)		
115	Unknown.		
116	Unknown.		
117	Unknown..........................	....	Excelsior.
118	Unknown..........................	....	Excelsior.
119	Unknown..........................	....	Excelsior.
120	Unknown..........................	....	Excelsior.

Section F.

No. of grave.	Names.	Comp'y.	Regiment.
1	Capt. J. S. Corbin............	F......	20th Regiment, N. Y. V.
2	Cicero Tolls.......................	A......	134th Regiment, N. Y. V.
3	A. D. Tice..........................	E......	20th Regiment, N. Y. V.
4	Unknown..........................	....	147th Regiment, N. Y. V.
5	Unknown..........................	....	147th Regiment, N. Y. V.
6	Unknown..........................	....	147th Regiment, N. Y. V.
7	Unknown..........................	....	76th Regiment, N. Y. V.
8	Unknown..........................	....	76th Regiment, N. Y. V.
9	Unknown..........................	....	76th Regiment, N. Y. V.
10	Serg't Frederick Derbin........	I.......	78th Regiment, N. Y. V.
11	Thomas Dawson..................	A......	78th Regiment, N. Y. V.
12	Alfred Trudell..................	A.....	78th Regiment, N. Y. V.
13	Fred. Hei———.....................	....	N. Y. V.
14	Elbert Traver.....................	E......	44th Regiment, N. Y. V.
15	Unknown..........................	....	N. Y. V.

New York.—Section F—*Continued.*

No. of grave.	Names.	Comp'y.	Regiment.
16	William Lacy......................	H......	4th N. Y. Excelsior.
17	J. Simond..........................	D......	4th N. Y. Excelsior.
18	Serg't T. Lally....................	K......	4th N. Y. Excelsior.
19	Unknown..............................	....	Excelsior.
20	Unknown..............................	....	Excelsior.
21	Unknown..............................	....	Excelsior.
22	Unknown..............................	....	Cavalry.
23	Unknown.		
24	Unknown..............................	....	Cavalry.
25	David Holland, (with medal,)	F......	2d Excelsior.
26	Unknown..............................	....	Excelsior.
27	Michael Flanegan..............	B......	1st N. Y. Excelsior.
28	Ord. Serg't Patrick Sullivan...	K......	4th N. Y. Excelsior.
29	K. H. P..............................	....	126th Regiment, N. Y. V.
30	Unknown..............................	....	N. Y. V.
31	Unknown, (with ring,).........	....	N. Y. V.
32	Charles W. Gaylord............	B......	126th Regiment, N. Y. V.
33	Unknown..............................	....	Excelsior.
34	Charles Welden, (with diary,)	D......	111th Regiment, N. Y. V.
35	Unknown Corporal..............	....	N. Y. V.
36	Unknown..............................	....	Cavalry.
37	Unknown.		
38	Unknown.		
39	Lieut. A. W. Estes.............	H......	2d N. Y. Excelsior.
40	Unknown..............................	....	Excelsior.
41	Unknown..............................	....	1st Division 5th Corps
42	Unknown..............................	....	1st Division 5th Corps.

New York.—SECTION F—*Continued.*

No. of grave.	Names.	Comp'y.	Regiment.
43	Unknown.		
44	Unknown.		
45	Unknown.		
46	Unknown.		
47	Unknown, (with knife)		N. Y. V.
48	Unknown	E	5th Corps.
49	Unknown.		
50	John Kapp	K	1st Excelsior.
51	Michael Ryan	C	1st Excelsior.
52	Unknown.		
53	Unknown.		
54	Charles M'Kenney	B	1st Excelsior.
55	Unknown.		
56	Unknown.		
57	Unknown		2d Brig. 2d Div. 5th Corps.
58	Unknown Corporal, (with pipe.)		
59	Unknown.		
60	James Brady		2d Excelsior
61	Unknown.		
62	Unknown.		
63	Unknown.		
64	Unknown		N. Y. V.
65	Unknown		N. Y. V.
66	Charles Gorman	E	2d Excelsior.
67	Unknown		2d Excelsior.
68	Patrick Olvany	A	2d Excelsior.
69	Alonzo Henstreat, (with pocket book and 50 cents.)		

New York.—Section F—*Continued.*

No. of grave.	Names.	Comp'y.	Regiment.
70	Supposed...........................	....	N. Y.
71	George W. Douglass	I......	1st Excelsior.
72	Supposed...........................	....	N. Y.
73	Supposed...........................	....	N. Y.
74	Supposed...........................	....	N. Y.
75	Supposed...........................	....	N. Y.
76	Supposed...........................	....	N. Y.
77	Supposed.........................	....	N. Y. V.
78	Supposed...........................	....	N. Y. V.
79	Supposed...........................	....	N. Y. V.
80	Supposed...........................	....	N. Y. V.
81	Unknown...........................	....	N. Y. V.
82	Unknown...........................	....	N. Y. V.
83	Unknown Orderly Sergeant...	....	Excelsior.
84	Unknown, (with ambrotype)..	E......	5th Corps.
85	Supposed...........................	....	N. Y. V.
86	Supposed...........................	....	Excelsior.
87	Supposed...........................	....	Excelsior.
88	Jacob Jones, (with letter.)		
89	Unknown.		
90	Unknown.		
91	Unknown...........................	....	11th Corps.
92	Unknown.........................	....	Artillerist.
93	William M'Clellan	G......	88th Regiment, N. Y. V.
94	Unknown.		
95	P. J. Hopkins......................	H......	126th Regiment, N. Y. V.
96	Unknown.		

New York.—SECTION F—*Continued.*

No. of grave.	Names.	Comp'y.	Regiment.
97	Unknown Corporal.............	....	126th Regiment, N. Y. V.
98	Lieut. R. D. Lower............	I.......	157th Regiment, N. Y. V.
99	Unknown Corporal.............	....	157th Regiment, N. Y. V.
100	Supposed..........................	....	Excelsior.
101	Unknown..........................	....	Excelsior.
102	Unknown..........................	....	Excelsior.
103	G. M'Cleary	F......	4th Excelsior.
104	Unknown..........................	....	Excelsior.
105	Unknown..........................	....	Excelsior.
106	Edmund Holmes.................	F......	4th Excelsior.
107	T. Tetworth........................	D......	4th Excelsior.
108	Adam Shaw.........................	....	4th Excelsior.
109	Supposed..........................	....	Excelsior.
110	Supposed..........................	....	Excelsior.
111	William H. Bell	F......	120th Regiment, N. Y. V.
112	Corp. James M. Delaney	I	120th Regiment, N. Y. V.
113	Corp. Andrew De Wit	H......	120th Regiment, N. Y. V.
114	Supposed..........................	....	N. Y. V.
115	Theodore Bogart, (with medal and breastpin)................	I.......	120th Regiment, N. Y. V.

SECTION G.

No. of grave.	Names.	Comp'y.	Regiment.
1	2d Lieut. F. F	....	N. Y. V.
2	Supposed, (with ambrotype)..	....	N. Y. V.
3	Supposed..........................	....	N. Y. V.
4	Supposed..........................	....	120th Regiment, N. Y. V.
5	Daniel Smith......................	E......	120th Regiment, N. Y. V.

New York.—Section G—*Continued.*

No. of grave.	Names.	Comp'y.	Regiment.
6	Supposed, (with watch chain)...	....	3d Excelsior.
7	Corp. Gilbert Myer..............	I.......	120th Regiment, N. Y. V.
8	Supposed..........................	....	Excelsior.
9	Theodore Van Deborgert.......	I.......	120th Regiment, N. Y. V.
10	R. M. W....	....	Supposed N. Y. V.
11	Supposed..........................	....	Excelsior.
12	Supposed..........................	....	Excelsior.
13	Supposed..........................	....	Excelsior.
14	Supposed..........................	....	Excelsior.
15	Supposed..........................	....	Excelsior.
16	Supposed..........................	....	Excelsior.
17	Supposed..........................	....	Excelsior.
18	Supposed..........................	....	Excelsior.
19	Supposed..........................	....	Excelsior.
20	Supposed..........	....	Excelsior.
21	Supposed..........................	....	Excelsior.
22	W. H. Ackerman	I.......	1st Excelsior.
23	Supposed..........................	....	Excelsior.
24	Supposed..........................	....	Excelsior.
25	Corporal, supposed.............	....	Excelsior.
26	Supposed......	....	Excelsior.
27	Supposed..........................	....	Excelsior.
28	Supposed...........	....	Excelsior.
29	Supposed..........................	....	Excelsior.
30	Supposed..........................	....	N. Y. V.
31	Supposed..........................	....	N. Y. V.
32	Corp. Lewis Solomon..........	B......	1st Regiment, N. Y. V.

New York.—SECTION G—*Continued.*

No. of grave.	Names.	Comp'y.	Regiment.
33	Supposed..........................	....	N. Y. V.
34	Supposed..........	....	N. Y. V.
35	Orderly Sergeant P. Farrel...	D	4th Excelsior.
36	Rufus Thomson..........	C......	120th Regiment, N. Y. V.
37	Seth Harpell........................	C......	5th Excelsior.
38	Henry Wilson......................	E......	126th Regiment, N. Y. V.
39	Alexander Gacon...............	B......	5th N. Y. Excelsior.
40	W. H. Piper..........................	H......	1st N. Y. Excelsior.
41	Sergeant Bie———...............	A......	1st N. Y. Excelsior.
42	Charles Gorman..................	E......	2d N. Y. Excelsior.
43	Sergeant Washington Knight,	C......	5th N. Y. Excelsior.
44	George Buggins	I.......	1st N. Y. Excelsior.
45	Michael Riley......................	G......	42d Regiment, N. Y. V.
46	Elbert Brown	G.....	111th Regiment, N. Y. V.
47	John Carey.........................	H......	5th Regiment, N. Y. V.
48	Unknown.		
49	Unknown.		
50	Unknown, (2 knives and comb,)	....	N. Y. V.
51	Unknown..................	....	N. Y. V.
52	Unknown................	....	N. Y. V.
53	Unknown..........................	....	N. Y. V.
54	Unknown..........................	....	N. Y. V.
55	Unknown..........................	... .	N. Y. V.
56	O. W. Hotchkiss, (breast pin,)	F......	120th Regiment, N. Y. V.
57	William Shuly, (ambrotype,)..	....	N. Y. V.
58	Supposed..........................	....	N. Y. V.
59	Supposed..........................	....	N. Y. V.

New York.—Section G—*Continued.*

No. of grave.	Names.	Comp'y.	Regiment.
60	Justus Warner, (with snuff box,)...........................	I......	120th Regiment, N. Y. V.
61	Supposed.....	....	N. Y. V.
62	Unknown Corporal..............	....	Excelsior.
63	Unknown.		
64	Unknown, supposed............	....	N. Y. V.
65	Serg't John Knox................	K......	5th N. Y. Excelsior.
66	John Nolan.....	K......	1st N. Y. Excelsior.
67	Serg't J. H. Mead..............	....	N. Y. V.
68	Supposed..................	....	Excelsior.
69	Supposed............................	....	Excelsior.
70	George Washington Sprague..	G......	2d Regiment, N. Y. V.
71	Serg't L. H. Lee................	B......	2d Regiment, N. Y. V.
72	Corp. Luke Kelly................	F......	2d Regiment, N. Y. S. M.
73	Thomas Murphy.......	F......	2d Regiment, N. Y. S. M.
74	Henry Irvin........................	F......	2d Regiment, N. Y. S. M.
75	Henry Diemer.....	F......	2d Regiment, N. Y. S. M.
76	Supposed............................	....	N. Y. S. M.
77	H. Thompson...........	I.......	111th Regiment, N. Y. V.
78	Adam C. Cadmus	I.......	126th Regiment, N. Y. V.
79	Jacob Frey...............	B......	149th Regiment, N. Y. V.
80	M. Stout...........................	F......	136th Regiment, N. Y. V.
81	Charles Jones......................	C	9th Regiment, N. Y. Cav.
82	Serg't James Melchen..........	H......	2d Regiment, N. Y. S. M.
83	Thomas Hunt	H......	2d Regiment, N. Y. S. M.
84	Supposed............................	....	N. Y. V.
85	Robert Laning....................	K.....	86th Regiment, N. Y. V.
86	John Sloat..........................	E......	126th Regiment, N. Y. V.

New York.—Section G—*Continued.*

No. of grave.	Names.	Comp'y.	Regiment.
87	Serg't George Baker............	A.....	40th Regiment, N. Y. V.
88	Supposed............................	....	N. Y. V.
89	Joshua Pursel......................	C......	126th Regiment, N. Y. V.
90	Daniel Day.........................	B... ..	126th Regiment, N. Y. V.

Total, 866.

NEW JERSEY.

Section A.

No. of grave.	Names.	Comp'y.	Regiment.
1	2d Lt. Richard H. Townsend,	....	12th Regiment, N. J. V.
2	1st Serg't T. Sutphin..	E......	5th Regiment, N. J. V.
3	I. L. T.		
4	L. Kreisel................................	....	Battery A, 1st N. J. V.
5	G. Cutter.....	....	Battery A, 1st N. J. V.
6	Isaac H. Copeland...............	E......	12th Regiment, N. J. V.
7	John Albright.		
8	Joseph Spacious....................	....	12th Regiment, N. J. V.
9	George Martin	A......	12th Regiment, N. J. V.
10	O. S. Platt....................	B......	12th Regiment, N. J. V.
11	Unknown.		
12	Daniel Hierman................ .	H......	12th Regiment, N. J. V.
13	Unknown.		
14	George W. Adams...............	F......	12th Regiment, N. J. V.
15	William Redrow.......	....	12th Regiment, N. J. V.

New Jersey.—SECTION A—*Continued.*

No. of grave.	Names.	Comp'y.	Regiment.
16	William Spencer.		
17	Unknown.		
18	Unknown.		
19	Jacob Sheik	I	4th Regiment, N. J. V.
20	——— Creamer		12th Regiment, N. J. V.
21	J. W. Button	K	5th Regiment, N. J. V.
22	R. S. Price		Battery B, 1st N. J. Artil.
23	Swart Perew	G	11th Regiment, N. J. V.

SECTION B.

No. of grave.	Names.	Comp'y.	Regiment.
1	Patrick Ryan	A	5th Regiment, N. J. V.
2	Sergeant John M'Iver	B	5th Regiment, N. J. V.
3	Thomas Van Cleaf	F	8th Regiment, N. J. V.
4	B. C. Jackson	B	11th Regiment, N. J. V.
5	John Rue	B	11th Regiment, N. J. V.
6	James Fletcher	G	7th Regiment, N. J. V.
7	Michael Goff	G	11th Regiment, N. J. V.
8	Joseph Burroughs	B	8th Regiment, N. J. V.
9	Henry Elberson	G	N. J. V.
10	Serg't Samuel Stockton	K	5th Regiment, N. J. V.
11	William Preser		Egg Harbor City Cavalry.
12	Henry Dammig	G	13th Regiment, N. J. V.
13	Charles B. Yearkes	B	6th Regiment, N. J. V.
14	Daniel Shuk		3d Regiment, N. J. V.
15	J. Parliament	C	13th Regiment, N. J. V.

New Jersey.—SECTION B—*Continued.*

No. of grave.	Names.	Comp'y.	Regiment.
16	John Smith, (with pocket book, 15 cents, &c.)		
17	W. T. Hawkins....................	H......	12th Regiment, N. J. V
18	—— Riley....................	E......	2d Regiment, N. J. V.
19	J. B..............................	F......	7th Regiment, N. J. V.
20	J. H., (with comb).............	F......	7th Regiment, N. J. V.
21	H. R..............................	F......	7th Regiment, N. J. V.
22	Unknown, (with Testament)...		

SECTION C.

No. of grave.	Names.	Comp'y.	Regiment.
1	W. A. E..........................	I.......	7th Regiment, N. J. V.
2	Unknown, (with knife).........	....	7th Regiment, N. J. V.
3	Unknown............................	....	N. J. V.
4	Unknown	....	7th Regiment, N. J. V.
5	John Ryan........................	C......	5th Regiment, N. J. V.
6	J. F...............................	A......	7th Regiment, N. J. V.
7	Unknown, (with blanket shawl.)		
8	Unknown.		
9	Unknown.		
10	Unknown.		
11	Unknown.		
12	Unknown.		
13	Unknown.		
14	Unknown.		
15	Unknown.		
16	Unknown.		
17	Unknown.		

New Jersey.—SECTION C—*Continued.*

No. of grave.	Names.	Comp'y.	Regiment.
18	Thomas Flanagen	G......	7th Regiment, N. J. V.
19	M. V	A......	7th Regiment, N. J. V.
20	George W. Berry	B......	7th Regiment, N. J. V.

SECTION D.

No. of grave.	Names.	Comp'y.	Regiment.
1	Unknown	....	7th Regiment, N. J. V.
2	Unknown, (with needle case.)		
3	Unknown	....	N. J. V.
4	Supposed	....	N. J. V.
5	Supposed	....	N. J. V.
6	Corp. William H. Ray..........	F	12th Regiment, N. J. V.
7	Serg't James B. Rister.........	C......	11th Regiment, N. J. V.
8	E. Baner............................	H	11th Regiment, N. J. V.
9	Supposed	....	N. J. V.
10	Supposed	....	N. J. V.
11	J. M'N..............................	F......	7th Regiment, N. J. V.
12	Unknown.		
13	P. Weene.............	H.....	6th Regiment, N. J. V.

TOTAL, 78.

DELAWARE.

Section A.

No. of grave.	Names.	Comp'y.	Regiment.
1	Corp. William Strong	D	2d Regiment, D. V.
2	Serg't Thomas Seymore	B	1st Regiment, D. V.
3	William Dorsey	D	1st Regiment, D. V.
4	John B. Sheets	D	1st Regiment, D. V.
5	T. P. Carey	E	1st Regiment, D. V.
6	John S. Black	K	1st Regiment, D. V.
7	Serg't Michael Cavanagh	G	2d Regiment, D. V.

Section B.

No. of grave.	Names.	Comp'y.	Regiment.
1	Peter Boster	A	2d Regiment, D. V.
2	Jacob Stiles	A	2d Regiment, D. V.
3	——— Downey	B	1st Regiment, D. V.
4	Serg't Jacob Boyd	E	2d Regiment, D. V.
5	A. Huhn	A	1st Regiment, D. V.
6	Lieut. George G. Plank	E	2d Regiment, D. V.

Section C.

No. of grave.	Names.	Comp'y.	Regiment.
1	James Dougherty	I	1st Regiment, D. V.
2	Stephen Carey	A	2d Regiment, D. V.

Total, 15.

MARYLAND.

Section A.

No. of grave.	Names.	Comp'y.	Regiment.
1	Southey Stirling	K	1st Regiment, Md. V.
2	Unknown.		
3	Wm. P. Jones	B	1st E. Shore Md. V.
4	Edward Pritchard	B	1st Regiment, Md. V.
5	Unknown.		
6	Unknown.		
7	Unknown.		
8	H. Miller	C	1st Regiment, P. H. B.

Section B.

No. of grave.	Names.	Comp'y.	Regiment.
1	Wm. H. Eaton	E	1st E. Shore Md. V.
2	G. H. Barger	H	1st Regiment, Md. V.
3	A. Saterfield	I	1st E. Shore Md. V.
4	Joseph Bailey	B	1st Regiment, Md. V.
5	Teter French	E	1st Regiment, P. H. B.
6	Unknown.		
7	Stephen Ford	D	1st Regiment, Md. V.

Section C.

No. of grave.	Names.	Comp'y.	Regiment.
1	G. W. Lowry	K	1st Regiment, P. H. B.
2	John Conner	F	1st Regiment, P. H. B.
3	David Krebs	G	1st Regiment, P. H. B.

Maryland.—SECTION C—*Continued.*

No of grave.	Names.	Comp'y.	Regiment.
4	M. F. Knott......................	F......	1st Regiment, Md. V.
5	Frank Baxter......................	D......	1st Regiment, Md. V.
6	John W. Stockman..............	....	1st Brigade.

SECTION D.

No. of grave.	Names.	Comp'y.	Regiment.
1	Unknown, (killed at Hanover,	Pa.)	

TOTAL, 22.

WEST VIRGINIA.

SECTION A.

No. of grave.	Names.	Comp'y.	Regiment.
1	Simon Maine......................	F......	7th Regiment, Va. V.
2	John Brown......................	....	7th Regiment, Va. V.
3	Aaron Austin......................	E......	7th Regiment, Va. V.
4	Theodore Stewart..............	C.....	7th Regiment, Va. V.
5	George Berger..................	C......	7th Regiment, Va. V.
6	Martin L. Scott..................	B......	7th Regiment, Va. V.
7	Capt. William N. Harris.......	E......	1st Cavalry.

SECTION B.

No. of grave.	Names.	Comp'y.	Regiment.
1	Serg't Garret Selby............	F......	1st Regiment, Va. Cavalry.
2	Serg't George Collins..........	L......	1st Regiment, Va. Cavalry.
3	Charles Lacey....................	C.....	1st Artillery.
4	William Bailey....................	E......	1st Cavalry.

TOTAL, 11.

OHIO.

SECTION A.

No. of grave.	Names.	Comp'y.	Regiment.
1	Enoch M. Detty	G	73d Regiment, O. V.
2	2d Lieut. George W. M'Gary,		82d Regiment, O. V.
3	William Folk	D	82d Regiment, O. V.
4	Martin Jacob	D	82d Regiment, O. V.
5	John Wiser	D	82d Regiment, O. V.
6	Richard Bradler	D	82d Regiment, O. V
7	E. A. Hain	H	82d Regiment, O. V.
8	——— Busk	H	82d Regiment, O. V.
9	J. Warner	H	82d Regiment, O. V.
10	Elmer L. Ross	C	82d Regiment, O. V.
11	Francis H. Blough	C	82d Regiment, O. V.
12	Unknown.		
13	Unknown.		
14	Unknown.		
15	John M'Cleary	D	66th Regiment, O. V.
16	George K. Wilson	B	8th Regiment, O. V.
17	Orville A. Warren	K	8th Regiment, O. V.
18	Ozro Moore	I	8th Regiment, O. V.
19	William Brown	B	8th Regiment, O. V.
20	Serg't John K. Barclay	C	8th Regiment, O. V.
21	Frank Shaffer	D	8th Regiment, O. V.
22	Danford Parker	K	8th Regiment, O. V.
23	Jeremiah N. Crabaugh	C	75th Regiment, O. V.
24	John Edmunds	H	1st Regiment, O. V.

Ohio.—SECTION A—*Continued.*

No. of grave.	Names.	Comp'y.	Regiment.
25	Frederick Meyer		Battery 1st, O. V.
26	A. Houck	F	82d Regiment, O. V.
27	Joseph Klinefelter	F	55th Regiment, O. V.

SECTION B.

No. of grave.	Names.	Comp'y.	Regiment.
1	Edward T. Lovett	I	25th Regiment, O. V.
2	William Williams	I	73d Regiment, O. V.
3	Henry Ophir	E	55th Regiment, [illegible]
4	William Ackerman	D	72d Regiment, O. V.
5	John R. Meyer	C	55th Regiment, O. V.
6	Serg't Caleb Dewees	F	73d Regiment, O. V.
7	Ai Maddox	G	73d Regiment, O. V.
8	Ozias C. Ford	A	55th Regiment, O. V.
9	William Whitby	H	73d Regiment, O. V.
10	Joseph R. Blake	I	73d Regiment, O. V.
11	Andrew Miller	I	73d Regiment, O. V.
12	William M'Clue	B	13th Regiment, O. V.
13	Corp. James H. Lee	H	73d Regiment, O. V.
14	William E. Haynes	B	73d Regiment, O. V.
15	Allen Yaple	A	73d Regiment, O. V.
16	A. M. Campbell	E	185th Regiment, O. V.
17	Henry Stark	I	4th Regiment, O. V.
18	James W. Harl	A	4th Regiment, O. V.
19	Bernard M'Guire	B	8th Regiment, O. V.
20	John M'Kellips	C	8th Regiment, O. V.
21	George H. Martin	G	4th Regiment, O. V.

Ohio.—SECTION B—*Continued.*

No. of grave.	Names.	Comp'y.	Regiment.
22	Serg't Philip Tracey...........	G......	8th Regiment, O. V.
23	Color Corp'l William Welch...	I.......	30th Regiment, O. V.
24	Samuel Mowery..................	....	107th Regiment, O. V.
25	Corp. Edward G. Ranney......	D......	61st Regiment, O. V.
26	Unknown........................	....	1st Ohio Battery.

SECTION C.

No. of grave.	Names.	Comp'y.	Regiment.
1	Anthony Mervale...............	G......	5th Regiment, O. V.
2	J. Senard.........................	D......	5th Regiment, O. V.
3	Charles Rhinehart..............	....	Battery I, 1st Artillery.
4	George Nixon.....................	B......	73d Regiment, O. V.
5	August Raber.....................	F......	107th Regiment, O. V.
6	Elisha L. Leake..................	G......	73d Regiment, O. V.
7	Lucas Struble....................	A......	107th Regiment, O. V.
8	John Davis........................	K......	75th Regiment, O. V.
9	Thomas Gilleran................	F......	61st Regiment, O. V.
10	Corp. George B. Greiner......	G......	73d Regiment, O. V.
11	Jacob Swackhamer.............	G......	73d Regiment, O. V.
12	Isaac J. Sperry...................	G......	73d Regiment, O. V.
13	Jacob Mitchell....................	C......	55th Regiment, O. V.
14	Chauncey Haskell...............	F......	82d Regiment, O. V.
15	William E. Pollock	C......	55th Regiment, O. V.
16	Benjamin F. Hartley...........	E......	75th Regiment, O. V.
17	Serg't Thomas H. Rice........	B......	73d Regiment, O. V.
18	Joseph Barrett...................	G......	73d Regiment, O. V.
19	Andrew Samiller................	A......	107th Regiment, O. V.

Ohio.—SECTION C—*Continued.*

No. of grave.	Names.	Comp'y.	Regiment.
20	William R. Call	B	73d Regiment, O. V.
21	Isaac Richards	A	82d Regiment, O. V.
22	Adam Snyder	H	107th Regiment, O. V.
23	Corp. James H. Goodspeed	D	75th Regiment, O. V.
24	William Miller	G	25th Regiment, O. V.
25	Nathan Heald	H	73d Regiment, O. V.

SECTION D.

No. of grave.	Names.	Comp'y.	Regiment.
1	Serg't Charles Ladd	E	25th Regiment, O. V.
2	Caspar Bohrer	G	107th Regiment, O. V.
3	Jacob Hoff	E	107th Regiment, O. V.
4	Joseph W. Cunningham	I	25th Regiment, O. V.
5	John Aigle	K	107th Regiment, O. V.
6	Balts Beverly	C	107th Regiment, O. V.
7	George Richards	D	75th Regiment, O. V.
8	Serg't Philip Shiplin	F	75th Regiment, O. V.
9	Samuel L. Conner	E	82d Regiment, O. V.
10	Joseph Gasler	K	107th Regiment, O. V.
11	William M'Vey	H	73d Regiment, O. V.
12	Asa Hines		11th Corps.
13	Serg. William Norton Williams	C	108th Regiment, O. V.
14	David W. Callins	G	4th Regiment, O. V.
15	William Bain	G	4th Regiment, O. V.
16	Lieut. Addison Edgar	G	4th Regiment, O. V.
17	Andrew Myers	G	4th Regiment, O. V.
18	1st Lieut. George Hayward	E	29th Regiment, O. V.

Ohio.—Section D—*Continued.*

No. of grave.	Names.	Comp'y.	Regiment.
19	Jeremiah Myers	G	74th Regiment, O. V.
20	John Owens	G	75th Regiment, O. V.
21	Ira L. Brigham	H	8th Regiment, O. V.
22	G. Walker	F	82d Regiment, O. V.
23	John Glouchlen	H	25th Regiment, O. V.

Section E.

No. of grave.	Names.	Comp'y.	Regiment.
1	Thomas Durm	K	25th Regiment, O. V.
2	B. F. Pontious	D	29th Regiment, O. V.
3	George H. Thompson	G	5th Regiment, O. V.
4	B. F. Sherman	G	61st Regiment, O. V.
5	Corp. John Debolt	B	4th Regiment, O. V.
6	Haskell Farr	G	55th Regiment, O. V.
7	Corp. William Myers	A	8th Regiment, O. V.
8	J. Laveden	E	75th Regiment, O. V.
9	Perry Taylor	G	75th Regiment, O. V.
10	T. M'Cain	E	29th Regiment, O. V.
11	George Case	C	5th Regiment, O. V.
12	Corp. Isaac Johnson	K	1st Artillery.
13	Asa O. Davis	G	4th Regiment, O. V.
14	William Overholt	I	73d Regiment, O. V.
15	Lewis Davis	D	75th Regiment, O. V.
16	1st Serg't John W. Pierce	C	25th Regiment, O. V.
17	Hiram Hughes	H	25th Regiment, O. V.
18	Wesley Rakes	G	75th Regiment, O. V.
19	Samuel P. Baughman	C	75th Regiment, O. V

Ohio.—SECTION E—*Continued.*

No. of grave.	Names.	Comp'y.	Regiment.
20	Joseph Juchem	G......	107th Regiment, O. V.
21	Jacob Bise.	K......	107th Regiment, O. V.
22	H. Schram...........................	H......	1st Regiment, O. V.

SECTION F.

No. of grave.	Names.	Comp'y.	Regiment.
1	Serg't Jasper C. Briggs........	G......	73d Regiment, O. V.
2	Serg't John C. Kisska.........	A......	8th Regiment, O. V.
3	Andrew J. Dildine..............	A......	8th Regiment, O. V.
4	Jacob I. Ranch..................	A......	8th Regiment, O. V.
5	Josiah D. Johnson...............	F......	29th Regiment, O. V.
6	Serg't Isaac Willis........	G......	73d Regiment, O. V.
7	Daniel Palmer....................	D......	73d Regiment, O. V.
8	James Ray..........................	G......	73d Regiment, O. V.

TOTAL, 131.

INDIANA.

SECTION A.

No. of grave.	Names.	Comp'y.	Regiment.
1	Lieut. R. Jones	B......	19th Regiment, I. V.
2	Serg't Dougherty...............	....	19th Regiment, I. V.
3	James Sticklep...................	C......	19th Regiment, I. V.
4	W. Hoover, (or Houer).........	C......	19th Regiment, I. V.
5	Alexander Burk	C......	19th Regiment, I. V.
6	R. Clark............................	C......	19th Regiment, I. V.

Indiana.—Section A—*Continued.*

No. of grave.	Names.	Comp'y.	Regiment.
7	A. Sulgroof	F	19th Regiment, I. V.
8	Unknown.		
9	Peter L. Faust	C	19th Regiment, I. V.
10	Wm. Simmons	E	19th Regiment, I. V.
11	Serg't Ferguson		19th Regiment, I. V.
12	Wesley Smith	A	20th Regiment, I. V.
13	Amos D. Ashe	A	20th Regiment, I. V.
14	John Sager	A	20th Regiment, I. V.

Section B.

No. of grave.	Names.	Comp'y.	Regiment.
1	F. H. K.	H	6th Regiment, I. V.
2	Joshua Richmond	B	20th Regiment, I. V.
3	George Sylvester		20th Regiment, I. V.
4	Unknown		20th Regiment, I. V.
5	Unknown		20th Regiment, I. V.
6	Unknown		20th Regiment, I. V.
7	Unknown		20th Regiment, I. V.
8	Unknown		20th Regiment, I. V.
9	Unknown	A	20th Regiment, I. V.
10	Unknown		20th Regiment, I. V.
11	Unknown		20th Regiment, I. V.
12	Unknown		20th Regiment, I. V.
13	Unknown		20th Regiment, I. V.

Indiana.—Section C.

No. of grave.	Names.	Comp'y.	Regiment.
1	P. Umphill	D	27th Regiment, I. V.
2	J. Gilmore	I	27th Regiment, I. V.
3	E. Stallup	H	27th Regiment, I. V.
4	J. Gardner	K	27th Regiment, I. V.
5	Silas Upham	G	19th Regiment, I. V.
6	John E. Weaver	A	3d Regiment, Ind. Cav.
7	Serg't A. C. Lamb	E	120th Regiment, I. V.
8	Serg't G. H. Redrick	F	20th Regiment, I. V.
9	P. A. Bussard	K	20th Regiment, I. V.
10	J. Williams	B	20th Regiment, I. V.
11	C. Showalter	A	27th Regiment, I. V.
12	E. Holt	G	27th Regiment, I. V.

Section D.

No. of grave.	Names.	Comp'y.	Regiment.
1	John Shehan, (Orderly for Gen. Gibbons.)		
2	A. G. Wright	A	20th Regiment, I. V.
3	C. E. Wishmyer	A	27th Regiment, I. V.
4	L. C. Antrim	C	27th Regiment, I. V.
5	D. C. Calvin	C	27th Regiment, I. V.
6	John Tice	A	20th Regiment, I. V.
7	Ord. Serg't E. Tumey	D	27th Regiment, I. V.
8	Levi Bulla	C	20th Regiment, I. V.
9	James W. Whitlow	B	19th Regiment, I. V.
10	Jesse Smith	D	3d Regiment Cavalry.
11	George Bales	A	27th Regiment, I. V.
12	T Hunt	A	27th Regiment, I. V.

Indiana.—Section E.

No. of grave.	Names.	Comp'y.	Regiment.
1	J. K. Fletcher	F	27th Regiment, I. V.
2	Jesse Wills.	C	27th Regiment, I. V.
3	Samuel R. Lewis	D	27th Regiment, I. V.
4	John D. Noble	K	27th Regiment, I. V.
5	James Chapman	E	27th Regiment, I. V.
6	J. D. Lynn	D	27th Regiment, I. V.
7	Thomas J. Lett	H	27th Regiment, I. V.
8	W. H. Wilson	E	27th Regiment, I. V.
9	Unknown	K	27th Regiment, I. V.
10	E. M'Knight	F	27th Regiment, I. V.
11	D. T. David	G	27th Regiment, I. V.

Section F.

No. of grave.	Names.	Comp'y.	Regiment.
1	Serg't Jeremiah Davis	H	20th Regiment, I. V.
2	Unknown.		
3	F. W		14th Regiment, I. V.
4	R. Pavy	B	3d Regiment, I. V.
5	J. Robinson	K	7th Regiment, I. V.
6	F. W. Smith	K	27th Regiment, I. V.
7	H. Ambrose	H	20th Regiment, I. V.
8	A. J. Crabb	D	20th Regiment, I. V.
9	Serg't George W. Batchelor	H	27th Regiment, I. V.
10	Wm. Tillottson	I	14th Regiment, I. V

Indiana.—SECTION G.

No. of grave.	Names.	Comp'y.	Regiment.
1	Corp. H. S. B.....................	I.......	14th Regiment, I. V.
2	Unknown, (with letter.)		
3	A. Lister...........................	F......	27th Regiment, I. V.
4	Supposed.		
5	Supposed.		
6	Supposed.		
7	Supposed.		
8	Thomas J. Wasson..............	B......	19th Regiment, I. V.

TOTAL, 80.

ILLINOIS.

SECTION A.

No. of grave.	Names.	Comp'y.	Regiment.
1	J. Wallikeck......................	H.....	82d Regiment, Ill. V
2	John Ellis..........................	G......	12th Regiment, Ill. V.
3	Charles Wm. Miner.		
4	David Dieffenbaugh............	....	8th Regiment, Ill. Cav.
5	Corp. John Ackerman..........	K......	82d Regiment, Ill. V.
6	Supposed, (comb and very light	hair)..	8th Regiment, Ill. V.

TOTAL, 6.

MICHIGAN.

SECTION A.

No. of grave.	Names.	Comp'y.	Regiment.
1	George Colburn	G	24th Regiment, M. V.
2	Edward B. Harrison	K	24th Regiment, M. V.
3	Erson H. Smith	A	3d Regiment, M. V.
4	Silas E. Thurston	G	3d Regiment, M. V.
5	Serg't George Pettinger	G	24th Regiment, M. V.
6	Charles B. Burgess	A	3d Regiment, M. V.
7	Lieut. G. A. Dickey	G	24th Regiment, M. V.
8	James O'Neil	H	3d Regiment, M. V.
9	R. K. Horman	H	24th Regiment, M. V.
10	Corp. Otis Southworth	C	24th Regiment, M. V.
11	Charles Phelps	B	4th Regiment, M. V.
12	Corp. F. P. Worden	C	4th Regiment, M. V.
13	Corp. Wm. A. Pryor	D	4th Regiment, M. V.
14	Charles A. Rouse	D	4th Regiment, M. V.
15	Charles A. Thurlach	A	4th Regiment, M. V.
16	Charles W. Gregory	H	4th Regiment, M. V.
17	James H. Pendleton	H	4th Regiment, M. V.
18	George Purdy	H	4th Regiment, M. V.
19	Joseph Brink	H	4th Regiment, M. V.
20	Serg't Nicholas Gosha	F	7th Regiment, M. V.
21	Edwin Beebe	E	7th Regiment, M. V.
22	A. R. Evans	A	5th Cavalry.
23	James T. Bedell	F	7th Michigan Cavalry.
24	George W. Lundy		7th Michigan Cavalry.

Michigan.—Section B.

No. of grave.	Names.	Comp'y.	Regiment.
1	John Durre	D	24th Regiment, M. V.
2	A. Jenks	A	24th Regiment, M. V.
3	Corp. W. H. Luce	G	24th Regiment, M. V.
4	William H. Cole	G	5th Regiment, M. V.
5	Herson Blood	I	3d Regiment, M. V.
6	E. B. Browning	G	24th Regiment, M. V.
7	Corp. J. T. Fails	G	24th Regiment, M. V.
8	Serg't George Kline	B	24th Regiment, M. V.
9	Serg't John Powell	H	24th Regiment, M. V.
10	Corp. Norman King	D	4th Regiment, M. V.
11	Ellis Comstock	D	4th Regiment, M. V.
12	A. Hoisington	F	24th Regiment, M. V.
13	Corp. Charles H. Ladd	A	24th Regiment, M. V.
14	H. B. Fountain	F	4th Regiment, M. V.
15	Corp. Jerome Shook	B	5th Regiment, M. V.
16	Corp. A. Benson	A	4th Regiment, M. V.
17	Robert Sligh	K	3d Regiment, M. V.
18	Oliver N. Culver	K	3d Regiment, M. V.
19	Serg't Reuben Power	K	3d Regiment, M. V.
20	1st Serg't Daniel A. Vodria	A	5th Regiment, M. V.
21	Thomas Shanahan	H	1st Cavalry.
22	D. C. Laird	A	4th Regiment, M. V.
23	C. Pease	C	4th Regiment, M. V.

Michigan.—Section C.

No. of grave.	Names.	Comp'y.	Regiment.
1	S. Bisonette	A	4th Regiment, M. V.
2	Corp. Charles A. Turner	B	5th Regiment, M. V.
3	Charles Jelioke	K	5th Regiment, M. V.
4	1st Serg't James Hazzard	C	5th Regiment, M. V.
5	Serg't John Sholes	G	7th Regiment, M. V.
6	Wm. Underwood	F	7th Regiment, M. V.
7	——— Almas.		
8	1st Serg't Thomas J. Divit	D	5th Michigan Cavalry.
	John Lavaby	A	5th Michigan Cava..
10	John Roberts	C	5th Regiment, M. V.
11	Frank Barbour	A	5th Michigan Cavalry.
12	Samuel Christopher	D	5th Regiment, M. V.
13	Andrew R. Evans	A	5th Michigan Cavalry.
14	Nelson A. Allen	A	5th Michigan Cavalry.
15	Charles Masters	A	5th Michigan Cavalry.
16	Corp. Horace Barse	E	5th Michigan Cavalry.
17	Frank Anderson	D	5th Regiment, M. V.
18	Unknown—Supposed		3d or 5th Michigan Cav.
19	Serg't Charles E. Miner		7th Michigan Cavalry.
20	L. Gibbs	C	5th Michigan Cavalry.
21	J. Falketts	H	5th Michigan Cavalry.
22	W. B. Hunt	I	16th Regiment, M. V.

Section D.

No. of grave.	Names.	Comp'y.	Regiment.
1	Henry Butler	I	5th Regiment, M. V.
2	Serg't Charles Ballard	E	5th Michigan Cavalry.

Michigan.—Section D—*Continued.*

No. of grave.	Names.	Comp'y.	Regiment.
3	Christopher Miller...............	E......	5th Michigan Cavalry.
4	Edward A. Warner..............	I.......	5th Michigan Cavalry.
5	Serg't Henry Bicker	F......	5th Michigan Cavalry.
6	Richard Alwayra	E	5th Regiment, M. V.
7	Henry Riolo......................	F......	5th Michigan Cavalry.
8	D. M. Merefield	F......	5th Michigan Cavalry.
9	Francis R. Kent..................	G......	5th Michigan Cavalry.
10	J. M. Skinner......................	G......	5th Michigan Cavalry.
.	Artemus Clark.....................	G......	5th Michigan Cavalry
12	Corp. Delos Harris..............	C......	7th Michigan Cavalry.
13	John M. Brown...................	K......	3d Michigan Cavalry.
14	Corp. Wm. A. Cole.......	G......	5th Michigan Cavalry.
15	James M. Pierce.......	A	3d Regiment, M. V.
16	George Lawrence.........	C......	5th Regiment, M. V.
17	John Roberts...........	C......	5th Regiment, M. V.
18	2d Serg't R. B. Godfrey.......	B......	7th Regiment, M. V.
19	J. K. Beagle...............	I.......	16th Regiment, M. V.
20	Isaac H. Scott	K......	16th Regiment, M. V.
21	Serg't Henry Raw.............	I.......	16th Regiment, M V.

Section E.

No. of grave.	Names.	Comp'y.	Regiment.
1	Mason Palmer....................	B......	24th Regiment, M. V.
2	Luther Franklin.....	C......	5th Regiment, M. V.
3	Richard Aylward................	E......	5th Regiment, M. V.
4	Peter E. Roy	C	5th Regiment, M. V.
5	1st Lieut. John P. Thelan....	A......	5th Regiment, M. V.

Michigan.—SECTION E—*Continued.*

No. of grave.	Names.	Comp'y.	Regiment.
6	1st Serg't James Hazzard.....	C......	5th Regiment, M. V.
7	D. Zimmerman....................	D......	4th Regiment, M. V.
8	G. W. Stevens......	D......	16th Regiment, M. V.
9	Serg't E. Trip......................	H	4th Regiment, M. V.
10	J. Geiner............................	G......	16th Regiment, M. V.
11	G. W. Ervey........................	H......	16th Regiment, M. V.
12	Serg't Hiram Hopkins..........	I.......	7th Regiment, M. V.
13	Serg't D. C. Kimbal.............	B......	4th Regiment, M. V.
14	Serg't Joseph Mallenbre.......	B......	4th Regiment, M. V.
15	C. H. Wilson.......................	H......	4th Regiment, M. V.
16	R. Moody...........................	K.....	4th Regiment, M. V.
17	Serg't Fred. Sheets..............	D......	4th Regiment, M. V.
18	J. Bags.........	I.......	16th Regiment, M. V.
19	J. Hart...............................	G......	16th Regiment, M. V.
20	Edward Burton....................	K.....	16th Regiment, M. V.

SECTION F.

No. of grave.	Names.	Comp'y.	Regiment.
1	C. W. Martin	C......	16th Regiment, M. V.
2	C. H. Hulmer..	G......	7th Regiment, M. V.
3	Peter La Valley	A......	5th Cavalry.
4	Thomas Motley...................	G......	7th Cavalry.
5	Nelson Walters...................	A......	7th Cavalry.
6	Philip Wilcox	L......	1st Cavalry.
7	Robert Hasty	I.......	7th Cavalry.
8	George Ketchler..................	E......	5th Cavalry.
9	Philip Hill...........................	E......	5th Cavalry.

Michigan.—SECTION F—*Continued.*

No. of grave.	Names.	Comp'y.	Regiment.
10	W. A. Crowell	G	5th Cavalry.
11	Miles A. Webster	G	5th Cavalry.
12	A. S. Norris	G	5th Cavalry.
13	John Nothing	I	5th Cavalry.
14	Moses Cole	I	5th Cavalry.
15	John G. Folkerts	K	5th Regiment, M. V.
16	J. Mason	D	16th Regiment, M. V.
17	Corp. J. M. Weston	A	16th Regiment, M. V.
18	Emery Tuttle	B	16th Regiment, M. V.

SECTION G.

No. of grave.	Names.	Comp'y.	Regiment.
1	Carlisle Bennett	I	1st Cavalry.
2	Corp. Reuben Hone	C	5th Regiment, M. V.
3	S. G. Harris	B	7th Regiment, M. V.
4	J. S. Rider	B	24th Regiment, M. V
5	W. Williams	B	24th Regiment, M. V.
6	J. M'Nish	F	24th Regiment, M. V.
7	Col. Serg't E. Moore	E	7th Cavalry.
8	Corp. Albert Smith	D	5th Regiment, M. V.
9	Capt. Peter Generous	B	5th Regiment, M. V.
10	Chester W. Alex	D	5th Regiment, M. V.
11	Joseph Sutter	E	5th Regiment, M. V.
12	Serg't Alexander Moore		7th Regiment, M. V.
13	2d Lieut. Albert Slafter	E	7th Regiment, M. V.
14	John W. Barber		1st Artillery.
15	Serg't J. M. Stevens	E	16th Regiment, M. V.

Michigan.—Section G—*Continued.*

No. of grave.	Names.	Comp'y.	Regiment.
16	J. R. Hall	D	16th Regiment, M. V.
17	Corp. Beck	I	16th Regiment, M. V.

Section H.

No. of grave.	Names.	Comp'y.	Regiment.
1	Lieut. B. Brown	E	16th Regiment, M. V.
2	Lieut. W. Jewett	K	16th Regiment, M. V.
3	Corp. Charles M'Brahmie	D	16th Regiment, M. V.
4	Orin D. Wade	D	3d Regiment, M. V.
5	J. Hyde	D	4th Regiment, M. V.
6	Asher D. Ashley	F	5th Regiment, M. V.
7	Corp. Charles Thayer	I	5th Regiment, M. V.
8	George H. Miller		5th Regiment, M. V.
9	John Dover	K	5th Regiment, M. V.
10	Charles Sits	L	1st Cavalry.
11	William Brennan	B	5th Cavalry.
12	Joseph Tucker	I	5th Regiment, M. V.
13	Lieut. M'Ilhenny		1st Cavalry.
14	Corp. Josiah G. Bond	F	16th Regiment, M. V.
15	Serg't H. H. Barret	B	15th Regiment, M. V.
16	Corp. H. Hart	C	6th Cavalry.

Section I.

No. of grave.	Names.	Comp'y.	Regiment.
1	C. J. Pattin	E	24th Regiment, M. V.
2	L. W. Lampman	K	4th Regiment, M. V.

Michigan.—Section I—*Continued.*

No. of grave.	Names.	Comp'y.	Regiment.
3	Unknown.		
4	Corp. Thomas Sugget..........	G	20th Regiment, M. V.
5	Charles Ruff......................	D......	24th Regiment, M. V.
6	Corp. David Rounds............	D......	24th Regiment, M. V.
7	Serg't W. H. Jackson, Detroit.		
8	Corp. R. Howe..................	C	5th Regiment, M. V.
9	Charles Crouse....................	A......	6th Cavalry.
10	Corp. Wm. C. Harlan..........	F	5th Regiment, M. V.
11	Maj. Noah H. Ferry, (removed)	....	5th Cavalry.

Total, 172.

WISCONSIN.

Section A.

No. of grave.	Names.	Comp'y.	Regiment.
1	Unknown.		
2	Unknown.		
3	Unknown.		
4	Corp. Edward H. Heath......	H......	2d Regiment, W. V.
5	Unknown.		
6	Unknown.		
7	Unknown.		
8	Lieut. William S. Winnegan..	H......	2d Regiment, W. V.
9	Unknown.		
10	Unknown.		
11	Unknown.		
12	Unknown.		

Wisconsin.—SECTION A—*Continued.*

No. of grave.	Names.	Comp'y.	Regiment.
13	Unknown.		
14	Unknown.		
15	Unknown.		
16	Lieut. Charles Broket...........	I.......	26th Regiment, W. V.
17	Christian Stier....................	F......	26th Regiment, W. V.
18	Corp. James Kelly...............	B......	6th Regiment, W. V.
19	Corp. William E. Evans.......	B......	6th Regiment, W. V.
20	Serg't George W. Sain	C......	7th Regiment, W. V.
21	Unknown.		
22	Unknown.		
23	Unknown.		

SECTION B.

No. of grave.	Names.	Comp'y.	Regiment.
1	Unknown.		
2	Unknown.		
3	Marcellus Chase.................	A......	7th Regiment, W. V.
4	Unknown.		
5	Unknown.		
6	Corp. John T. Christie.........	F......	2d Regiment, W. V.
7	Corp. Frank M. Bull............	D.....	7th Regiment, W. V.
8	Edward Leaman.........	E......	6th Regiment, W. V.
9	1st Serg't Fred'k A. Nichols..	A.....	2d Regiment, W. V.
10	Corp. John M'Donald...... ...	A	2d Regiment, W. V.
11	Charles Branstetter	A.....	2d Regiment, W. V.
12	1st Serg't James Gow..........	C......	2d Regiment, W. V.

Wisconsin.—SECTION B—*Continued.*

No. of grave.	Names.	Comp'y.	Regiment.
13	Henry R. M'Collum	H	2d Regiment, W. V.
14	Hanford C. Tupper	G	2d Regiment, W. V.
15	Serg't William Gallup	D	6th Regiment, W. V.
16	Henry Anderson	B	6th Regiment, W. V.
17	Peter Kraescher	C	26th Regiment, W. V.
18	Peter Kuhn	G	26th Regiment, W. V.
19	Joseph Balmes	C	26th Regiment, W. V.
20	Mathias Scheivester	E	26th Regiment, W. V.
21	Leion Stedoman	C	6th Regiment, W. V.

SECTION C.

No. of grave.	Names.	Comp'y.	Regiment.
1	Corp. Abraham Fletcher	K	6th Regiment, W. V.
2	Corp. William H. Barnum	K	7th Regiment, W. V.
3	George H. Hawes	B	7th Regiment, W. V.
4	John B. Straight	E	7th Regiment, W. V.
5	William Rampthen	K	2d Regiment, W. V.
6	Silas Castor	B	7th Regiment, W. V.
7	Philip Bennetts	F	7th Regiment, W. V.
8	John W. Scott	D	7th Regiment, W. V.
9	William D. M'Kinney	K	7th Regiment, W. V.
10	A. Fowler	A	7th Regiment, W. V.
11	Corp. Ernst Shuhart	K	2d Regiment, W. V.
12	William Wagner	F	3d Regiment, W. V.
13	Thomas Barton	F	3d Regiment, W. V.
14	Philonas Kinsman	K	7th Regiment, W. V.
15	Lewis H. Eggleson	H	6th Regiment, W. V.

Wisconsin.—SECTION C—*Continued.*

No. of grave.	Names.	Comp'y.	Regiment.
16	Corp. John Krauss.............	A.....	26th Regiment, W. V.
17	Frank King......................	E......	6th Regiment, W. V.
18	James C. Perrine.......	I.......	2d Regiment, W. V.
19	Frantz Benda	F......	26th Regiment, W. V.

SECTION D.

No. of grave.	Names.	Comp'y.	Regiment.
1	1st Lieut. Martin Young.......	A	26th Regiment, W. V.
2	Serg't Spencer M. Train.......	C......	2d Regiment, W. V.
3	Uriah Palmer......................	A.....	6th Regiment, W. V.
4	Ord. Serg't W. S. Rouse.......	E	2d Regiment, W. V.
5	1st Serg't Andrew Miller......	I.......	6th Regiment, W. V.
6	1st. Serg't Albert E. Tarbor,	K......	6th Regiment, W. V.
7	2d Lieut. Orin D. Chapman...	C.....	6th Regiment, W. V.
8	Fritz Zilsdorf......................	G......	26th Regiment, W. V.
9	Charles Hasse....................	F	6th Regiment, W. V.
10	Lt. Col. George H. Stevens...	....	2d Regiment, W. V.

TOTAL, 73.

MINNESOTA.

SECTION A.

No. of grave.	Names.	Comp'y.	Regiment.
1	Joseph V. Sisler	G	1st Regiment, Minn. V.
2	Alonzo C. Hayden	D	1st Regiment, Minn. V.
3	George W. Grands	D	1st Regiment, Minn. V.
4	Capt. Nathan S. Messick	G	1st Regiment, Minn. V.
5	Corp. William N. Peck	I	1st Regiment, Minn. V.
6	Charles H. Gove	B	1st Regiment, Minn. V.
7	Freder Glave	A	1st Regiment, Minn. V.
8	Corp. Wilber F. Wellman	I	1st Regiment, Minn. V.
9	Israel Durr	K	1st Regiment, Minn. V.
10	Serg't Philip Hamlin	F	1st Regiment, Minn. V.
11	Unknown	F	1st Regiment, Minn. V.
12	Unknown	F	1st Regiment, Minn. V.
13	Unknown		1st Regiment, Minn. V.
14	Unknown		1st Regiment, Minn. V.
15	Unknown		1st Regiment, Minn. V.
16	Unknown		1st Regiment, Minn. V.
17	J. H. Prime	D	1st Regiment, Minn. V.
18	Unknown		1st Regiment, Minn. V.

SECTION B.

No. of grave.	Names.	Comp'y.	Regiment.
1	Supposed		1st Regiment, Minn. V.
2	Supposed		1st Regiment, Minn. V.
3	Supposed		1st Regiment, Minn. V.
4	Serg't Frederick Diehr	H	1st Regiment, Minn. V.

Minnesota.—SECTION B—*Continued.*

No. of grave.	Names.	Comp'y.	Regiment.
5	John Ellsworth	C	1st Regiment, Minn. V.
6	Clark Brandt	A	1st Regiment, Minn. V.
7	Corp. Timothy Crowley	A	1st Regiment, Minn. V.
8	Corp. Peter Marks	A	1st Regiment, Minn. V.
9	Capt. Joseph Periam	K	1st Regiment, Minn. V.
10	Charles Baker	D	1st Regiment, Minn. V.
11	Byron Welch	I	1st Regiment, Minn. V.
12	Unknown		1st Regiment, Minn. V.
13	Unknown		1st Regiment, Minn. V.
14	Lieut. Waldo Farrer	I	1st Regiment, Minn. V.
15	W. Moore		1st Regiment, Minn. V.
16	Henry Nickels	A	1st Regiment, Minn. V.
17	John M'Kenzie	E	1st Regiment, Minn. V.

SECTION C.

No. of grave.	Names.	Comp'y.	Regiment.
1	Edward P. Hale	I	1st Regiment, Minn. V.
2	Unknown		Minn. V.
3	Unknown		Minn. V.
4	Unknown		Minn. V.
5	Unknown		Minn. V.
6	Unknown		Minn. V.
7	Serg't Wade Lufkin	C	1st Regiment, Minn. V.
8	Serg't Oscar Woodward	I	1st Regiment, Minn. V.
9	Unknown		Minn. V.
10	Unknown		Minn. V.
11	Unknown Orderly Sergeant		Minn. V.

Minnesota.—Section D.

No. of grave.	Names.	Comp'y.	Regiment.
1	Edwin Parl	I	1st Regiment, Minn. V.
2	Corp. Phineas L. Dunham	G	1st Regiment, Minn. V.
3	Ervine Lawrence	D	1st Regiment, Minn. V.
4	Corp. L. J. Squires	F	1st Regiment, Minn. V.
5	Corp. Peter Welm	E	1st Regiment, Minn. V.
6	Hans Simonson	A	1st Regiment, Minn. V.

Total, 52.

UNITED STATES INFANTRY.

Section A.

No. of grave.	Names.	Comp'y.	Regiment.
1	T. E. Sheets	G	14th Regiment, U. S. I.
2	Unknown	B	2d Battalion, U. S. I.
3	Unknown	B	2d Battalion, U. S. I.
4	Unknown	B	2d Battalion, U. S. I.
5	Unknown	B	2d Battalion, U. S. I.
6	Unknown	B	2d Battalion, U. S. I.
7	Unknown	B	2d Battalion, U. S. I.
8	Unknown	B	2d Battalion, U. S. I.
9	Unknown Sergeant	B	2d Battalion, U. S. I.
10	Serg't D. W. Clock		11th U. S. I.
11	Unknown	B	2d Battalion, U. S. I.
12	Christian Engers	H	4th Battalion, U. S. I.
13	Peter M'Manimus	H	4th Battalion, U. S. I.
14	Corp. Barrington	B	4th Battalion, U. S. I.
15	Peter Robinson	F	4th Battalion, U. S. I.

U. S. Infantry.—SECTION A—*Continued.*

No. of grave.	Names.	Comp'y.	Regiment.
16	Roger M'Denald	H	4th Battalion, U. S. I.
17	Christian Albett	H	4th Battalion, U. S. I.
18	Serg't John Reily	K	4th Battalion, U. S. I.
19	Unknown		2d Battalion, U. S. I.
20	W. Mare		4th Battalion, U. S. I.
21	Unknown	A	Battalion, U. S. I.
22	T. H. Mulligan	A	14th Battalion, U. S. I.
23	John Creridon	B	11th Regiment, U. S. I.
24	Ransom B. Russell	F	6th Regiment, U. S. I.
25	Corp. John Small	D	17th Regiment, U. S. I.
26	William Curtis	A	7th Regiment, U. S. I.
27	John Keenan	A	7th Regiment, U. S. I.
28	Corp. John Fallbright	B	2d Regiment, U. S. I.
29	William D. Hammond	F	14th Regiment, U. S. I.
30	Serg't S. P. Blanchard	B	17th Regiment, U. S. I.
31	C. H. Whitney	C	17th Regiment, U. S. I.
32	William Duffy	D	17th Regiment, U. S. I.
33	John O. Keefer	F	11th Regiment, U. S. I.
34	Thomas Murry	F	14th Regiment, U. S. I.
35	Charles Horton	G	11th Regiment, U. S. I.
36	J. Lutz	E	14th Regiment, U. S. I.
37	Lieut. Rockford		11th Regiment, U. S. I.
38	Capt. Thomas O'Barre		11th Regiment, U. S. I.

U. S. Infantry.—SECTION B.

No. of grave.	Names.	Comp'y.	Regiment.
1	Thomas Whitford	Bat. F.	U. S. Artillery.
2	Amest Fassette	A	4th U. S. Artillery.
3	Unknown	A	U. S. Infantry.
4	John Porter	Bat. C.	5th U. S. Artillery.
5	Martin Slograt.	Bat. A.	U. S. Artillery.
6	Thomas Padgett	Bat. I.	1st U. S. Artillery.
7	Joseph W. Erwin		4th U. S. Artillery.
8	William Patton	Bat. A.	4th U. S. Artillery.
9	James Murphy	Bat. A.	4th U. S. Artillery.
10	John Marklein	Bat. H.	1st U. S. Artillery.
11	William Becker	K	4th Regiment, U. S. I.
12	Serg't Charles Giles	B	11th Regiment, U. S. I.
13	Serg't Judas Thetart	I	6th Regiment, U. S. I.
14	Playford Woods	B	14th Regiment, U. S. I.
15	Wm. Byrne	D	17th Regiment, U. S. I.
16	Benjamin Way.	A	14th Regiment, U. S. I.
17	John Willis	K	2d Regiment, U. S. I
18	Corp. Mills Jamson	G	2d Battalion, 14th U. S. I.
19	Corp. Frank Berchard	G	14th Regiment, U. S. I.
20	J. Reeman	G	6th Regiment, U. S. I.
21	John Pine.	I	3d Regiment, U. S. I.
22	John Hare	I	2d Regiment, U. S. I.
23	M. Carroll	H	14th Regiment, U. S. I.
24	G. Moran	D	12th Regiment, U. S. I.
25	——— Sullivan		5th Corps, U. S. I.
26	Unknown.		
27	Lieut. Williaam Chamberlain,		1st. Bat. 7th Reg't U. S. I.

U. S. Infantry.—Section B—*Continued.*

No. of grave.	Names.	Comp'y.	Regiment.
28	Patrick Tighe	I.......	3d U. S. Artillery.
29	L. Griswold........................	Bat. D.	5th U. S. Artillery.
30	E. Brower..........................	Bat. D.	5th U. S. Artillery.
31	O. F. Drake, detailed from 16th Reg't Michigan Vol.........	Bat. D.	5th U. S. Artillery.
32	G. H. White	G......	2d U. S. S. S.
33	Serg't J. Gray......................	D......	2d U. S. S. S.
24	Serg't Henry Lye................	G......	1st U. S. S. S.
35	Benjamin Hamlet.................	A......	1st U. S. S. S.
36	Eli S. B. Vincent................	G......	1st U. S. S. S.
37	Charles Thatcher	E......	1st U. S. S. S.

Section C.

No. of grave.	Names.	Comp'y.	Regiment.
1	Levi G. Strickland	C......	11th Regiment, U. S. I.
2	James Agin........................	D......	14th Regiment, U. S. I.
3	Unknown.		
4	Unknown.		
5	Unknown.		
6	Unknown.		
7	Charles Wilson....................	G......	11th Regiment, U. S. I.
8	Charles Schmidt..................	E......	14th Regiment, U. S. I.
9	D. A. M'Kean......................	....	11th Regiment, U. S. I.
10	Unknown.		
11	Unknown.		
12	Unknown.		
13	Unknown.		
14	M. Kennedy......................	D......	10th Regiment, U. S. I.

U. S. Infantry.—SECTION C—*Continued.*

No. of grave.	Names.	Comp'y.	Regiment.
15	W. R. Davis	H	10th Regiment, U. S. I.
16	S. Coriell	A	2d Battery, 17th U. S. I.
17	Julius Fergeson	A	7th Regiment, U. S. I.
18	B. M. M.		
19	Unknown.		
20	E. M. Williams	I	3d Regiment, U. S. I.
21	Casper Kupferly	G	3d Regiment, U. S. I.
22	Robert Furlong	C	3d Regiment, U. S. I.
23	Unknown.		
24	W. F. M.		7th Regiment, U. S. I.
25	Daniel Kinney	C	1st Battery, 12th U. S. I.
26	Serg't H. Rogers	D	12th Regiment, U. S. I.
27	Robert Morrison	Bat. C,	3d Regiment, U. S. I.
28	Unknown, (on cap)	Bat. I,	U. S. Infantry.
29	Unknown		6th Regiment, U. S. Cav.
30	Unknown		6th Regiment, U. S. Cav.
31	Unknown		6th Regiment, U. S. Cav.
32	1st. Lieut. Christian Balder		6th Regiment, U. S. Cav.
33	Unknown		6th Regiment, U. S. Cav.
34	J. Moles	C	12th Regiment, U. S. I.
35	C. T. Ridder	Bat. D,	4th U. S. Artillery.
36	E. Dennis	Bat. D,	4th U. S. Artillery.

U. S. Infantry.—SECTION D.

No. of grave.	Names.	Comp'y.	Regiment.
1	Silas A. Miller		12th Regiment, U. S. I.
2	H. Gaertner.		

U. S. Infantry.—SECTION D—*Continued.*

No. of grave.	Names.	Comp'y.	Regiment.
3	Unknown		6th Regiment, U. S. Cav.
4	William Reynolds	C	6th Regiment, U. S. Cav.
5	Augustus Nelson	E	6th Regiment, U. S. Cav.
6	William S. Mottern	H	6th Regiment, U. S. Cav.
7	John Pattinson		6th Regiment, U. S. Cav.
8	Unknown, (with diary & handkerchief)		6th Regiment, U. S. Cav.
9	Unknown		6th Regiment, U. S. Cav.
10	Unknown		6th Regiment, U. S. Cav.
11	Unknown		6th Regiment, U. S. Cav.
12	Charles Bodman	G	11th Regiment, U. S. I.
13	C. F. Smetzer	G	6th Regiment, U. S. I.
14	J. Conway	F	11th Regiment, U. S. I.
15	James Stanton	H	11th Regiment, U. S. I.
16	D. Wallace	Bat. I,	5th U. S. Artillery.
17	George Smith	I	7th Regiment, U. S. I.
18	C. Miller	E	7th Regiment, U. S. I.
19	P. M'Grinity	I	1st U. S. Artillery.
20	F. Rovey	G	14th Regiment, U. S. I.
21	Serg't Alfred E. Cook	C	11th Regiment, U. S. I.
22	Unknown		U. S. I.
23	2d Lieut. G. W. Sheldon	I	U. S. S. S.
24	William H. Woodruff	G	1st U. S. S. S.
25	George Van Buskirk		11th Regiment, U. S. I.
26	Edmund W. Howard	C	14th Regiment, U. S. I.
27	Unknown		13th Reg., 2d Div., U. S. I.
28	1st Lieut. Wesley F. Miller,*		7th Regiment, U. S. I.

*Son of Gov. Miller, of Minnesota, removed to Harrisburg.

TOTAL, 138.

LIST OF DEAD WHOSE RESIDENCES ARE UNKNOWN, AND WHO ARE BURIED IN THE UNKNOWN LOTS.

No. of grave.	Names.	Section.	
30	J. H., (on bone ring)…………	C……	South.
18	Jeremiah Chadwick………….	F……	
41	Orderly Serg't Michael ……..	F……	
18	Hooker, (on cap.)…………….	G……	South.
37	——— Hutchkins …………….	G ……	South.
43	Unknown, (with gold watch,)	G……	South.
2	Serg't C. M. Hall, (paper on coat, child's likeness, &c.)..	H…..	South.
24	M. Riggs …….. ……………….	H…..	South.
12	William Martin……………….	H…..	South.
22	G. W. Miley ………………….	A……	North.
4	Corp. I. Hilton……………….	B……	North.
44	Unknown, ("4 F," on belt,)…	C……	North.
22	E. Gilbert…………………….	F……	North.
35	H. Irvin……………… ………	F……	North.
38	I. D. H………………………….	F……	North.
29	John Morrison………………..	G……	North.
34	S. J. Braddock ……………….	G……	North.
35	Isaac Cavalry…………………	G……	North.
23	Cyrus A. Drot………………..	L……	
27	W. M'———……… …………	L……	
2	Oley P. Thompson……………	K……	
	H. R. Clark…….. …………….	K……	

LIST OF NAMES OF SOLDIERS BURIED IN EVERGREEN CEMETERY, GETTYSBURG, PA.

Names.	Company.	Regiment.
Edward Stinson	I	5th New Hampshire Vol.
Aaron A. Clark	G	14th Connecticut Vol.
Lieut. Herman Donarth	C	19th Massachusetts Vol.
George Kelley	C	126th New York Vol.
Samuel Blew	C	126th New York Vol.
Charles F. Harris	C	126th New York Vol.
Cornelius S. Baley	C	126th New York Vol.
John E. Dougall	H	134th New York Vol.
C. P. Le Clear		New York Vol.
Robert C. Burns	A	144th New York Vol.
Henry Comstock	F	108th New York Vol.
Albert E. Dixon	B	94th New York Vol.
John B. Owen	D	157th New York Vol.
L. Willie Hobart	B	126th New York Vol.
James H. Bump	A	111th New York Vol.
S. Potter		147th New York Vol.
Serg't A. E Banta		140th New York Vol.
Corp. Wentworth E. Dudley	E	64th New York Vol.
Arthur M'Alpine	G	111th New York Vol.
Jeremiah Bigelow	K	111th New York Vol.
Benjamin Van Wirt	K	111th New York Vol.
Capt. J. K. Backus	E	157th New York Vol.
Edward Grinnell	K	111th New York Vol.
Capt. A. J. Sofield	A	149th Regiment, P. V.
James M'Cleary	Battery B,	1st Pennsylvania Artillery.
A. P. Alcorn	Battery B,	1st Pennsylvania Artillery.

EVERGREEN CEMETERY—*Continued.*

Names.	Company.	Regiment.
Evan Edwards, Philadelphia.		
Sidney R. Breidninger	E	15th Regiment, P. V.
S. B. Stewart	F	2d Regiment, R. C. P. V.
Charles Gibbs	K	62d Regiment, P. V.
Corp. L. S. Greenlee	A	140th Regiment, P. V.
Jacob F. Strouse	C	143d Regiment, P. V.
W. D. Millard	F	Pennsylvania Vol.
George W. Wood	K	26th Regiment, P. V.
[illegible]bert Otterson	F	62d Regiment, P. V
George Stuart	C	72d Regiment, P. V.
A. Graw	F	68th Regiment, P. V.
Serg't William Shaffer		62d Regiment, P. V.
Corp. J. M. Young	I	83d Regiment, P. V.
Lieut. W. S. Briggs		27th Regiment, P. V.
Hiram H. Hartman	F	1st Regiment, Maryland V.
Serg't Alpheas M'Vickers	E	7th Regiment, Virginia V.
George W. Stuart	H	55th Regiment, Ohio V.
Lewis A. Sanford	C	73d Regiment, Ohio V.
Corp. William Gridley	D	8th Regiment, Ohio V.
Lieut. S. H. Shoub	I	4th Regiment, Ohio V.
Corp. J. S. Allison	K	75th Regiment, Ohio V.
Mathias Frey		Cleveland, Ohio.
E. Welsh	I	14th Regiment, Indiana V.
Serg't William Park	E	3d Regiment, Indiana Cav.
Marcus A. Past	D	1st Regiment, Minnesota V.
W. K. Allen		1st Regiment, Minnesota V.
Lieut. A. J. Barber		11th U. S. Infantry.

EVERGREEN CEMETERY.—*Continued.*

Names.	Company.	Regiment.
Serg't Frank Littinger..........	K...........	3d Regiment, U. S. I.
Joseph A. Campbell.............	Battery C,	4th U. S. Artillery.
Charles Long.....................	F...........	3d Regiment, U. S. I.
Unknown	....	134th.
Unknown.		
Unknown.		
J. S. Hopping.		
Unknown.		
Matthew M'Grow................	E...........	1st N. Y. Excelsior.
Serg't Jeremiah Gallagher.....	D...........	69th Regiment, P. V.
Thomas C. Diver................	I...........	69th Regiment, P. V.
Charles August..........	G...........	2d Regiment, Del. V.
Unknown.		
Unknown.		
Unknown.		
Unknown.		
Unknown.		

LIST OF NAMES OF SOLDIERS BURIED IN THE UNITED PRESBYTERIAN BURYING GROUND, GETTYSBURG, PA.

Names.	Company.	Regiment.
William W. Story................	F...........	3d Regiment, Ind. Cav.
Ebenezer H. James.............	A...........	122d Regiment, P. V.

LIST OF MEN BURIED AT YORK, PA., WHO DIED AT THE U. S. A. GENERAL HOSPITAL, YORK, PA., FROM WOUNDS RECEIVED AT THE BATTLE OF GETTYSBURG.

No. of grave.	Names.	Comp'y.	Regiment.
1	Serg't Vincent A. Keiflin,* ...	K......	105th Regiment, P. V.
2	D. L. Wade,*	K......	2d Regiment, Mass. V.
3	Serg't James M. Coroden......	I.......	149th Regiment, P. V.
4	D. Zimmerman	B......	9th Regiment, N. Y. S. M.
5	Serg't Samuel Lamb	C......	3d Ind. Cavalry.
6	Charles C. Holmes........	K......	149th Regiment, N. Y. V.
7	Henry Brehl.......	A.......	44th Regiment, N. Y. V.
8	Michael Donovan.................	D......	12th Regiment, U. S. I.
9	Franklin A. Rollins.............	D......	1st Regiment, Minn. V.
10	August Stein......................	H.....	1st U. S. Artillery.
11	Michael Hagden..................	B......	6th Regiment, Wis. V.
12	Thomas A. Reedy,*.............	A.....	73d Regiment, Ohio V.
13	Serg't Winslow A. Morril.....	A.....	16th Regiment, Maine V.
14	Thomas Moriartz................	B......	22d Regiment, Mass. V.
15	Ira Hunt	I.......	27th Regiment, Indep't V.
16	William H. Dinsmore..	F......	140th Regiment, P. V.
17	Charles Groesot	B......	83d Regiment, P V.
18	Corp Henry J. Smith,*........	G......	12th Regiment, N. H. V.
19	William H. Heise................	B......	107th Regiment, Ohio V.
20	George Werner....................	A.....	12th Regiment, U. S. I.
21	William Patent.......	A.....	107th Regiment, P. V.
22	Sylvester L. Brown.............	....	5th Maine Battery.
23	William H. Batcheldor	I.	16th Regiment, Maine V.
24	Corp. Emet Kneirin............	E......	143d Regiment, P. V.
25	Michael Vogelbach.............	F......	5th Regiment, Ohio V.

* Removed.

YORK HOSPITAL—*Continued.*

No. of grave.	Names.	Comp'y.	Regiment.
26	John Cooley..........................	B......	2d Regiment, U. S. I.
27	Serg't Charles Herbstritt	D......	74th Regiment, Va. V.
28	Job B. Flagg......................	B......	19th Regiment, Maine V.
29	Corp. Simeon Cooper............	G......	111th Regiment, N. Y. V.
30	Adam Eckler......................	A.....	74th Regiment, P. V.
31	Nicholas Conner,*................	E......	136th Regiment, N. Y. V.
32	Ephraim Guyer....................	D......	151st Regiment, P. V.

* Removed.

NOTE.—Two removals have been made to the Pennsylvania lot, since the foregoing list was printed, which makes the total number buried in that lot, eighty, viz:

SECTION F.

No. of grave.	Names.	Comp'y.	Regiment.
79	W. D. Millard......................	F......	149th Regiment, P. V.
80	Andrew R. M'Kinney..........	B......	21st Cavalry.

SYNOPSIS.

Maine	104
New Hampshire	49
Vermont	61
Massachusetts	159
Rhode Island	12
Connecticut	22
New York	866
New Jersey	78
Pennsylvania	526
Delaware	15
Maryland	22
West Virginia	11
Ohio	131
Indiana	80
Illinois	6
Michigan	171
Wisconsin	73
Minnesota	52
U. S. Regulars	138
Unknown—Lot North	411
Do.........Lot South	425
Do.........Lot Inner circle	143
Total buried in the Soldiers' National Cemetery	3,555

LIST OF ARTICLES

TAKEN FROM THE BODIES OF THE SOLDIERS REMOVED TO THE SOLDIERS' NATIONAL CEMETERY, BY WHICH MANY UNKNOWN WERE RECOGNIZED, AND WHICH ARE IN POSSESSION OF THE CEMETERY ASSOCIATION AT GETTYSBURG, PENN'A.

MAINE.

William S. Hodgdon, Company F, 20th Regiment, letter and fish book.
Unknown, 20th Regiment, Testament, and letter signed Anna Grove.
Richard Shuley, Company K, 7th Regiment, bugle off cap.
M. Davis, Company C, 20th Regiment, Thanksgiving book.
E. Cunningham, Co. L, 1st Regiment, $3 95, comb and postage stamps.
S. R. White, Company C, 20th Regiment, stencil plate and two cents.
Capt. G. D. Smith, Co. I, 19th Regiment, gold plate, with artificial tooth.
J. D. Sampson, Company C, 20th Regiment, gold ring.
Gordin Ireland, Co. F, 20th Regiment, Testament, purse, glass, and letters.
Hugh C. W. Hall, Company B, 17th Regiment, pencil.

NEW HAMPSHIRE.

Joseph Bond, 5th Regiment, comb.

VERMONT.

M. M'Kartney, Company A, 13th Regiment, gun wiper.
M. P. Baldwin, Company C, 16th Regiment.
C. Whiting, Company E, 13th Regiment, to rings.
L. L. Baird, Company H, 14th Regiment, $3 35 and two combs.
R. Archer, Company B, 14th Regiment, ring.

CONNECTICUT.

James Monterth, Testament.
William Cannell, letters, $8 rebel money, diary, &c.

NEW YORK.

R. Burman, Company E, 41st Regiment, comb.
Sergeant Hiram Hilts, Company C, 122d Regiment, diary, likeness, &c.
A. Stanton, Company C, 137th Regiment, ring and Testament.
Charles Manning, Co. C, 137th Regiment, knife, comb and gun wiper.
Theodore Bogart, Company I, 120th Regiment, medal, breastpin, comb and pencil.

P. Fanning, Company C, 122d Regiment, match and tobacco box.

H. W. Nichols, Company F, 137th Regiment, letters off cap, knife.

Theophilus Bascarick, Testament.

Unknown, supposed New York, ambrotype of mother and two daughters.

Albert D. Traver, Company E, 44th Regiment, S. M. diary, Testament and pencil.

E. Van Tassel, Company A, 60th Regiment, ring and glass.

Unknown, Company D, 137th Regiment, letters cut off cap.

G. W. Sprague, the grape shot that killed him, two knives, two rings and comb.

Frank Deisenroth, Company A, 108th Regiment, book, "Path to Pardon."

Amos Otis, Company K, 146th Regiment, diary.

Alonzo Henstreat, pocket book, small Bible, and fifty cents.

Charles Weden, Company D, 111th Regiment, diary, letter, &c.

P. M'Donald, Company F, 137th Regiment, twenty-seven cents, piece of silver, "quarter."

Unknown, Excelsior, knife and spoon.

Lieut. Charles Clark; Company B, 9th Regiment, S. M., two cents.

Tyler J. Snyder, order for $20 on U. S. Treasury, $7 15 in greenbacks.

George W. Lecase, Company F, 4th Excelsior, knife.

Corp. Andrew DeWitt, Company H, 120th Regiment, bullet moulds and screw driver.

2d Lieut. John F. Cox, Company I, 57th Regiment, letter and Testament.

George W. Douglass, Company I, 1st Excelsior, pipe.

Solomom Lisser, $30 in gold, $6 in greenbacks, and certificates of deposit for $300 in German Savings Bank, New York.

J. Smith, 4th New York Battery, comb.

James Gray, Company C, 2d Regiment, S. M., ring.

James W. Wickham, Company E, 122d Regiment, diary and Testament.

O. W. Hotchkiss, Company F, 120th Regiment, breast pin.

Corp. ——— Delmont, supposed New York, $2 75, diary, likeness and inkstand.

Justus Warner, snuff box.

F. Sweeney, Company D, 40th Regiment, gun pivot.

Charles Hagan, Company A, 63d Regiment, forty cents.

David Holland, Company F, 22d Excelsior, M'Clellan pin, medal and diary.

Serg. Bel——, (balance obliterated,) Company A, 1st Regimemt, pipe, comb, &c.

W. H. Piper, Company H, 1st Excelsior, comb and gun wiper.

Albert Brown, Company G, 111th Regiment, spoon and "11" off cap.

Jacob Jones, letter.

Corp. Walde, Company K, 4th Regiment, $12 85, comb and knife.

J. E. Bail, or Bailey, Company I, 111th Regiment, ring.

John M'Kenney, Excelsior, water purifier.

PENNSYLVANIA.

Sergeant E. N. Somercamp, Company I, 29th Regiment, likeness, letter, and diary.

Sanford Boyden, Company A, 149th Regiment, letter.

Charles Webster, letter.

Matthew Johnson, diary, express receipt and comb.

Samuel Finnifrock, letter.

J. J. Finnifrock, letter.

Corporal W. H. Burrill, Company F, 149th Regiment, Bible.

Lieut. William H. Beaver, Company D, 15th or 150th Regiment, shoulder straps and paper.

B. E. True, glass, &c.

G. H. Allen, Company C, 57th Regiment, Testament and letter.

James Morrow, Company I, 29th Regiment, pipe.

Unknown, diary, with name Agnes Jones, Pittsburg, Pa.

John Harvey, Company A, 69th Regiment, medal and comb.

James Kelley, Company K, 69th Regiment, ambrotype, sixty cents, comb, medal.

T. Miller, Company G, 1st Cavalry, diary.

William Crowl, Company K, 1st Regiment, needle case, pencil, &c.

J. Kleppinger, Company D, 153d Regiment, comb and bullet.

Peter M'Mahon, Company E, 26th Regiment, name on envelope.

Thomas Shields, Company H, 99th Regiment, medal.

Patrick O'Conner, Company D, 91st Regiment, $1 50, gun wrench, cross, medal, gimblet, &c.

Isaac Eaton, Company D, 10th P. R. C., ring with two red sets.

John O'Conner, Company G, 69th Regiment, medal.

Milton Campbell, Company C, 11th P. R. C., ring.

Tobias Jones, (removed,) letter, diary, &c.

John C. Coyle, $6, diary, &c., (sent to wife.)

John Aker, pipe.

Charles M'Connell, Company K, 11th Regiment, handkerchief, diary and letter.

Henry Adams, 83d Regiment, book and glass.

William Orr, Company I, 62d Regiment, watch case.

George M'Intosh, Company L, 62d Regiment, book cut out of wood, and letter A.

W. N. Williams, Co. K, 143d Regiment, diary, needle case, comb and handkerchief.

John Long, Company D, 62d Regiment, comb, &c.

William Kelley, Company A, 121st Regiment, Testament, fifty-five cents, comb, pencil, medal.

John M'Nutt, Company G, 140th Regiment, key, two watch keys.

M. Townsend, Company C, 1st Regiment, case knife, tooth brush.

NEW JERSEY.

J. M., Company F, 7th Regiment, comb.

J. Parliament, Company C, 13th Regiment, comb.

W. F. Harkins, Company H, 12th, Regiment, Testament.

Thomas Flanagan, Company G, 7th Regiment, medal and comb.

J. F., 7th Regiment, knife, fork and spoon.

John Smith, purse, fifteen cents, knife and comb.

——— Riley, Company E, 7th Regiment, letter and needle case.

W. A. E., Company I, 7th Regiment, table spoon.

MARYLAND.

David Krebs, Co. G, 1st P. H. B., twenty-five cents, tassel, smoker, &c.

WEST VIRGINIA.

Capt. W. N. Harris, 1st Cavalry, shoulder straps.

William Bailey, 1st Cavalry, letters, comb, &c.

George Berger, Company G, 7th Infantry, comb and glass.

L. Lacey, Battery C, 1st Va., glass and comb.

Martin L. Scott, Company B, 7th Infantry, silver watch.

P. Stewart, Company C, 7th Cavalry, pencil.

OHIO.

Lewis Davis, Company D, 75th Regiment, Testament and letters.

John C. Owens, Company C, 75th Regiment, book.

B. F. Pontious, Company D, 25th Regiment, letter, ring, diary, book and glass.

Louis A. Sandford, Company H, 73d Regiment, Testament and letters.

Samuel Baughman, Company C, 75th Regiment, pencil.

J. D. Johnson, Company F, 29th Regiment, knife.

Asa O. Davis, Company G, 4th Regiment, gun wrench, comb and ring.

Thomas Doman, Company K, 25th Regiment, $4 and gold locket.

Jacob Biese, Company K, 107th Regiment, handkerchief.

A. Myers, Company G, 4th Regiment, Testament.

Daniel Palmer, Company D, 107th Regiment, ambrotype and Testament.

B. F. Sherman, Company G, 61st Regiment, match box.

Serg. John Pierce, Company C, 25th Regiment, pipe.

INDIANA.

Levi Bulla, Company G, 20th Regiment, medal.

Wm. Tillottson, letter.

ILLINOIS.

Unknown cavalryman, very light hair.

MICHIGAN.

Peter LeValley, letter and ambrotype. (Sent to wife.)

Wm. Brennan, Company B, 3d Cavalry, hair.

James F. Bedel, Company F, 7th Regiment, muster roll list, and certificate for back pay from April to July, diary, &c.

——— Scott, Company K, 16th Regiment, needle case, comb and letters.

WISCONSIN.

Philip Bennetts, Company F, 7th Regiment, glass, photograph, pencil, diary, letters and knife.

F. C. Seibentral, Company D, 6th Regiment, medal.

MINNESOTA.

Solomon Moore, Company I, 1st Regiment, diary and letters.

U. S. REGULARS.

C. Schmidt, Company E, 4th U. S. A., pipe.

M. Kennedy, Company, D, 10th Infantry, knife.

S. Cornell, Company A, 2d Bat. 7th Infantry, two pictures, two knives, two gun wrenches.

Peter G. Febery, Company G, 6th U. S. Cavalry, diary, letter and handkerchief, &c.

UNKNOWN.

Unknown, two rings and small book cut of wood.

Unknown, jet heart.

Unknown, ring.

Unknown, knife with three white sets on handle.

Unknown, gun wrench.

Henry Dieman, gun wiper.

Unknown, knife, fork and spoon.

Unknown, knife, fork and spoon.

Unknown, gun wrench.

Unknown, knife.

Luke Kelly, medal and small bag.

Unknown, large diary and papers.

G. Turner, Bible, Testament and needle case.

Unknown, knife, postage stamps, pocket book and water purifier.
Unknown, pocket book, fifty-one cents, knife, two bones and comb.
John Boyer, ambrotype and letter.
Unknown, knife and comb.
Unknown, glass inkstand and spoon.
Unknown, twenty cents.
William Vasberg, small vice, comb and pencil.
Unknown, two ambrotypes.
Unknown, gun wrench.
William Sheley, two handkerchiefs, letters and comb.
Unknown, two purses, gun wrench, gun pivot.
T. D. Allen, diary, glass and letters.
Unknown, piece plaid blanket—colors, white, blue and green.
Sullivan Syes, purse, ring and comb.
Unknown, twenty cents.
Unknown, knit woollen cap for head, with tassel.
Unknown, two knives and comb.
Unknown, two knives and comb.
Corporal W. K., glass, comb and knife.
Unknown, handkerchief and gun wrench.
Unknown, Testament.
Unknown, letter, Testament and pocket book.
Unknown, knife.
Orderly Sergeant, knife and gun wrench.
G. M. S., knife, comb and four slides.
Unknown, needle case and pencil.
Unknown, black thread, ring, pin cushion and pipe.
Unknown, knife, gun wrench, comb and glass.
J. K. Beagle, knife and comb.
Unknown, knife.
G. W. Penn, marked on knife.
Unknown, handkerchief.
Unknown, tooth brush, &c.
Unknown, pipe, tooth brush and pencil.
Unknown, three pipes.
Unknown, glass, comb and sundries.
Unknown, two cents, and parts of five and ten cent notes.
Unknown, pipe.
Unknown, table knife.
Unknown, pocket knife.
R. E. Claffen, N. Y., Testament.
Unknown, shawl pin.

Unknown, pocket book, $1, pin cushin, gun wrench, knife, &c.

Unknown, needle case.

Samuel Ault, inkstand, keys and cross.

Unknown, inkstand and tooth brush.

Unknown, hand-vice.

Unknown, match box.

Charles Sets, pocket book, and hair of father, mother, sister and brother.

Unknown, knife, handkerchief and pencil.

Unknown, pipe.

Corporal Samuel Fitzinger, Pa., corps badge off cap.

Unknown, two combs and ambrotype.

Unknown, snuff box.

Unknown, handkerchief and comb.

Henry Irvin, pipe.

Unknown, ring and small candlestick.

George M'Cleary, N. Y., flag breast pin.

Unknown, with inkstand.

Unknown, diary.

Timothy Kears, book, "Key of Heaven."

Unknown, gun wrench.

Unknown, plate with V. M. M.

Unknown, ambrotype of woman.

Unknown, German Testament from Catharine Detaupafer.

Unknown, ambrotype, knife, two pipes, keys, inkstand, &c.

Unknown, hymn book, medal and gun wiper.

Unknown, letter from Carrisa Smith.

Corp. J. J. Bond, needle case, comb and letter.

Unknown, book, "Morning Exercises."

Unknown, with likeness on which is marked Charles Keller, July 4, 1859.

Unknown, ring, three buttons, with hooks, and water purifier.

Unknown, ornamental affair, consisting of a cross, figure of the Saviour, Virgin Mary, Apostles, &c.

Unknown, snuff box.

Unknown, handkerchief.

Unknown, ambrotype.

Unknown, knife.

Unknown, gun wrench.

Serg't. S. Vandertool, N. Y., letters.

Unknown, two rings.

Unknown, gold ring and steel watch keys.

B. W. Laigh, $10, "Reb" money.

Unknown, $25.

Thomas Shanahik, rosary.
Unknown, gold ear rings.
Unknown, ambrotype of young lady and letter.
Unknown, match box, spoon and Minnie ball.
Unknown, ring.
Unknown, bone ring, marked I. H.
Unknown, silver watch.
Unknown, gold watch.
Unknown, purse, $5 30, knife and tobacco box.
Unknown, pocket book and seven cents.
Unknown, razor and brush.
Unknown, pipe,
Unknown, book, ambrotype and pipe.
Unknown, handkerchief, which was spread over his face.
Unknown, pipe.
Unknown, pipe stem.
Unknown, (supposed Minnesota,) Bible.
Unknown, sick list.
Unknown, two gun wrenches.
Unknown, pipe.
Unknown, three ambrotypes.
Charles Kelley, Pa , letter, Testament, knife, keys, fifteen cents.
Unknown, snuff box.
Unknown, Testament.
Melville C. Day, diary, letters, &c.
Edmond F. Crouse.
Unknown, watch chain, gun wiper, salve box and keys.
Unknown, comb.
John ———, pipe.
Corporal W. W. W., from old Cemetery, pipe.
Unknown, pipe.
Joseph Wentworth, letter.
Byron Welch, paper, diary and pencil.
Unknown, knife.
Unknown, knife.
James Wallace, Pa., purse and twenty-five cents.
Unknown, inkstand, knife, letter and seventy-five cents.
A. Calhoun, diary.
Unknown Corporal, ambrotype of female.
Unknown, "Soldier's Pocket Book."
Unknown, pipe.
Sergeant L. H. Lee, two combs, diary, and bullet that killed him.

LIST OF REGIMENTS,

IN THE DIFFERENT CORPS OF THE ARMY OF THE POTOMAC, IN THE BATTLE OF GETTYSBURG.

MAINE.

Regiment.	Corps.	Regiment.	Corps.	Regiment.	Corps.
3d..........	3d..........	6th..........	6th..........	17th..........	3d..........
4th..........	3d..........	7th..........	6th..........	19th..........	2d..........
5th..........	6th..........	16th..........	1st..........	20th..........	5th..........

NEW HAMPSHIRE.

Regiment.	Corps.	Regiment.	Corps.	Regiment.	Corps.
2d..........	3d..........	5th..........	2d..........	12th..........	3d..........

VERMONT.

Regiment.	Corps.	Regiment.	Corps.	Regiment.	Corps.
2d..........	6th..........	6th..........	6th..........	14th..........	1st..........
3d..........	6th..........	1st..........	2d..........	15th..........	1st..........
4th..........	6th..........	12th..........	1st..........	16th..........	1st..........
5th..........	6th..........	13th..........	1st..........	19th..........	2d..........

MASSACHUSETTS.

Regiment.	Corps.	Regiment.	Corps.	Regiment.	Corps.
1st..........	1st..........	12th..........	1st..........	20th..........	2d..........
2d..........	12th..........	13th..........	1st..........	22d..........	5th..........
7th..........	6th..........	15th..........	2d..........	28th..........	2d..........
9th..........	5th..........	16th..........	3d..........	32d..........	5th..........
10th..........	6th..........	18th..........	5th..........	33d..........	11th..........
11th..........	3d..........	19th..........	2d..........	37th..........	6th..........

CONNECTICUT.

Regiment.	Corps.	Regiment.	Corps.	Regiment.	Corps.
5th..........	12th..........	17th..........	11th..........	20th..........	12th..........
14th..........	2d..........	27th..........	2d..........	....	....

NEW YORK.

Regiment.	Corps.	Regiment.	Corps.	Regiment.	Corps.
9th	1st	64th	2d	108th	2d
14th	1st	65th	6th	111th	2d
20th	1st	66th	2d	119th	11th
30th	1st	67th	6th	120th	3d
33d	6th	68th	11th	121st	6th
39th	2d	69th	2d	122d	6th
40th	3d	70th	3d	123d	12th
41st	11th	71st	3d	124th	3d
42d	2d	72d	3d	125th	2d
43d	6th	73d	3d	126th	2d
44th	5th	74th	3d	137th	12th
45th	11th	76th	1st	140th	2d
49th	6th	77th	6th	145th	12th
52d	2d	78th	12th	146th	5th
54th	11th	82d	2d	147th	1st
57th	2d	86th	3d	149th	12th
58th	11th	88th	2d	150th	12th
59th	2d	94th	1st	153d	11th
60th	12th	95th	1st	154th	11th
61st	2d	97th	1st	157th	11th
62d	6th	104th	1st		
63d	2d	107th	12th		

PENNSYLVANIA.

Regiment.	Corps.	Regiment.	Corps.	Regiment.	Corps.
P. R. V. C.	5th	75th	11th	114th	3d
11th	1st	81st	2d	115th	3d
23d	6th	82d	6th	116th	2d
26th	3d	83d	5th	118th	5th
27th	11th	84th	3d	119th	6th
28th	12th	88th	1st	121st	1st
29th	12th	90th	1st	134th	11th
46th	12th	91st	5th	139th	6th
49th	6th	93d	6th	140th	2d
53d	2d	95th	6th	141st	3d
57th	3d	96th	6th	142d	1st
61st	6th	98th	6th	143d	1st
62d	5th	99th	3d	146th	5th
63d	3d	102d	6th	147th	12th
68th	3d	105th	3d	148th	2d
69th	2d	106th	2d	149th	1st
71st	2d	107th	1st	150th	1st
72d	2d	109th	12th	151st	1st
73d	11th	110th	3d	154th	11th
74th	11th	111th	12th	155th	5th

NEW JERSEY.

Regiment.	Corps.	Regiment.	Corps.	Regiment.	Corps.
1st..........	....	7th..........	....	12th..........	....
2d..........	....	8th..........	....	13th..........	....
3d..........	....	5th..........	....	15th..........	....
6th..........	....	11th..........	....	....	....

DELAWARE.

Regiment.	Corps.	Regiment.	Corps.	Regiment.	Corps.
1st..........	2d..........	2d..........	2d..........	....	....

MARYLAND.

Regiment.	Corps.	Regiment.	Corps.	Regiment.	Corps.
1st..........	12th..........	3d..........	12th..........	....	....

VIRGINIA.

7th Regiment, 2d Corps.

OHIO.

Regiment.	Corps.	Regiment.	Corps.	Regiment.	Corps.
5th..........	12th..........	23d..........	11th..........	75th..........	11th..........
7th..........	12th..........	29th..........	12th..........	82d..........	11th..........
4th..........	2d..........	61st..........	11th..........	107th..........	11th..........
8th..........	2d..........	66th..........	12th..........		

ILLINOIS.

82d Regiment, 11th Corps.

INDIANA.

Regiment.	Corps.	Regiment.	Corps.	Regiment.	Corps.
7th..........	1st..........	19th..........	1st..........	27th..........	12th..........
14th..........	2d..........	20th..........	1st..........		

MICHIGAN.

Regiment.	Corps.	Regiment.	Corps.	Regiment.	Corps.
1st..........	5th....... ..	4th..........	5th..........	16th........	5th..........
5th..........	3d..........	7th..........	12th........	24th........	1st..........

WISCONSIN.

Regiment.	Corps.	Regiment.	Corps.	Regiment.	Corps.
2d..........	1st..........	5th..........	6th..........	7th..........	11th..........
3d..........	12th........	6th..........	1st..........	26th........	....

MINNESOTA.

1st Regiment, 2d Corps.

UNITED STATES.

Regiment.	Corps.	Regiment.	Corps.	Regiment.	Corps.
2d sharp s..	3d..........	4th Inft'ry.	5th..........	11th Inft'y.	5th..........
1st....do...	3d..........	6th....do...	5th..........	12th...do...	5th..........
2d Infant'y	5th..........	7th....do...	5th..........	14th...do...	5th..........
3d.....do...	5th..........	10th...do...	5th..........	17th...do...	5th..........

CAVALRY CORPS.

MAINE.—1st Regiment.

VERMONT.—1st Regiment.

MASSACHUSETTS.—1st Regiment.

RHODE ISLAND.—1st Regiment.

NEW YORK.—2d, 4th, 5th, 6th, 8th, 9th and 10th Regiments.

NEW JERSEY.—1st Regiment.

PENNSYLVANIA.—1st, 2d, 3d, 4th, 6th, 8th, 16th, 17th and 18th Regiments.

VIRGINIA.—1st and 3d Regiments.

OHIO.—6th Regiment.

INDIANA.—3d Regiment.

ILLINOIS.—8th and 12th Regiments.

MICHIGAN.—1st, 5th, 6th and 7th Regiments.

WISCONSIN.—1st Regiment.

UNITED STATES.—1st, 2d, 5th and 6th Regiments.

ARTILLERY RESERVE CORPS.

MASSACHUSETTS.—5th and 9th Regiments.

NEW YORK.—1st Regiment, B and G, 7th Independent, 15th Independent, 30th Independent, 32d Independent and 1st Independent.

NEW JERSEY.—1st Regiment, (A.)

PENNSYLVANIA.—1st Regiment, (C,) 4th Regiment, Independent.

MARYLAND.—1st and 6th Regiments.

VIRGINIA.—1st Regiment.

OHIO.—1st Regiment, (H.)

UNITED STATES.—1st Regiment, (H,) 3d Regiment, (K,) 4th Regiment, (C,) 4th Regiment, (K.)

REMARKS

ON THE DESIGN FOR THE SOLDIERS' NATIONAL CEMETERY, GETTYSBURG, PENNSYLVANIA.

In constructing a design for the Cemetery, the following considerations and details suggested themselves, as objects of paramount importance:

First.—The great disparity that exists, with reference to the space required for the interments of each State, necessitates a discrimination as to position and extent, while the peculiar solemnity of the interest attached by each State to each interment, allows of no distinction. Therefore, the arrangement must be of a kind that will obviate criticism as to position, and at the same time possess other equally important requirements and relations to the general design. (*a*)

Second.—The principal expression of the improvement should be that produced by simple grandeur and propriety. (*b*)

Third.—To arrange the roads, walks, trees and shrubs, so as to answer every purpose required by utility, and realize a pleasing landscape and pleasure ground effect, at the same time paying due regard to economy of construction, as well as to the future cost of maintenance and keeping the grounds. (*c*)

Fourth.—To select an appropriate site for the monument. (*d*)

(*a*) In order to secure the conditions embraced in the first of the above propositions, a semi-circular arrangement was adopted for the interments. By referring to the plan, the propriety of this mode will, I think, be conceded without further explanation. The ground appropriated to each State, is part, as it were, of a common centre; the position of each lot, and indeed of each interment, is relatively of equal importance, the only difference being that of extent, as determined by the number of interments belonging to each State. The coffins are deposited side by side, in parallel trenches. A space of twelve feet is allowed to each parallel, about five feet of which forms a grass path between each row of interments. The configuration of the ground surface is singularly appropriate at the point selected, falling away in a gradual and regular slope in every direction, from the centre to the circumference, a feature alike pleasing and desirable. In order to secure regularity, the head-stones are precisely alike throughout the entire area of lots, and are constructed so as not to detract from the effect and prominence of the monument. The head-stones form a continuous line of granite blocks, rising nine inches above the ground, and showing a face or width of ten inches on their upper surface. The name, company and regiment being carved in the granite, opposite each interment, thus securing a simple and expressive arrangement, combined with great permanence and durability.

(b) The prevailing expression of the Cemetery should be that of *simple grandeur*. Simplicity is that element of beauty in a scene that leads gradually from one object to another, in easy harmony, avoiding abrupt contrasts and unexpected features. Grandeur, in this application, is closely allied to solemnity. Solemnity is an attribute of the sublime. The sublime in scenery may be defined as continuity of extent, the repetition of objects in themselves simple and common place. We do not apply this epithet to the scanty tricklings of the brook, but rather to the collected waters of the ocean. To produce an expression of grandeur, we must avoid intricacy and great variety of parts, more particularly must we refrain from introducing any intermixture or meretricious display of ornament.

(c) The disposition of trees and shrubs is such as will ultimately produce a considerable degree of landscape effect. Ample spaces of lawn are provided; these will form vistas, as seen from the drive, showing the monument and other prominent points. Any abridgment of these lawns by planting further than is shown in the design, will tend to destroy the massive effect of the groupings, and in time would render the whole confused and intricate. As the trees spread and extend, the quiet beauty produced by these open spaces of lawn will yearly become more striking; designs of this character require time for their development, and their ultimate harmony should not be impaired or sacrificed to immediate and temporary interest. Further, to secure proper *breadth* of scene, few walks or roads are introduced. A main roadway or drive of sufficient width courses round the grounds; a few paths or walks are also provided for facilitating the inspection of the interment lots. Roads and walks are exclusively objects of utility; their introduction can only be justified by direct necessity.

(d) The centre of the semi-circle is reserved for the monument. An irregularly shaped belting of dwarf shrubbery borders partially isolate it from the lots. It may be suggested that the style of the monument should be in keeping with the surrounding improvements, showing no effort to an exhibition of cost or ostentatious display on the one hand, and no apparent desire to avoid reasonable expense on the other.

The gateway and gatehouse should also be designed in the same spirit, massive, solid, substantial and tasteful.

With regard to the future keeping of the ground, the walks should be smooth, hard and clean, the grass kept short, and maintained as clean and neat as the best pleasure ground in the country. No effort should be wanting to attain excellence in this respect.

WILLIAM SAUNDERS.

DEP'T OF AGRICULTURE, *Washington, D. C.*

REPORT OF SAMUEL WEAVER.

GETTYSBURG, *March* 19, 1864.

TO DAVID WILLS, ESQ.,

Agent for A. G. CURTIN, *Gov. of Penn'a:*

SIR:—I herewith submit the following brief report of the results of my labors as the Superintendent of the exhuming of the bodies of the Union soldiers that fell on the battle field of Gettysburg:

The contractor commenced the work of exhuming on Tuesday, the 27th of October last, and finished yesterday. The work has been protracted much beyond our original anticipations, by reason of the ground being frozen for a long time during the winter, thus entirely suspending the work, and also by the number of bodies exceeding our first calculations.

The number taken up and removed to the SOLDIERS' NATIONAL CEMETERY is thirty-three hundred and fifty-four, (3,354,) and to these add the number of the Massachusetts soldiers taken up by the authorities of the city of Boston, by special contract, amounting to one hundred and fifty-eight, (158,) makes the total number of removals thirty-five hundred and twelve (3,512) bodies. Of these, nine hundred and seventy-nine were bodies nameless, and without any marks or surroundings to designate the State from which they volunteered. The rest were, in most instances, marked with boards, on which the name, company, and regiment, were written in pencil, or cut, by their comrades who buried them. In some instances, the regiment to which the soldier belonged was discovered, and sometimes only the State from which he volunteered; and in these cases they were buried in their appropriate State lot.

There was not a grave permitted to be opened or a body searched unless I was present. I was inflexible in enforcing this rule, and here can say, with the greatest satisfaction to myself and to the friends of the soldiers, that I saw every body taken out of its temporary resting place, and all the pockets carefully searched; and where the grave was not marked, I examined all the clothing and everything about the body to find the name. I then saw the body, with all the hair and all the particles of bone, carefully placed in the coffin, and if there was a head-board, I required it to be at once nailed to the coffin. At the same time I wrote the name, company, and regiment, of the soldier on the coffin, and numbered the coffin, and entered in my book the same endorsement. This book was returned to your office every evening, to copy and compare with the daily return made by the Superintendent of the interments in the Cemetery. In these scrutinizing searches, the names of a number of lost soldiers were found. They were discovered in various ways. Sometimes by the pocket diaries, by letters, by names in Bible, or Testament, by photographs, names in pocketbooks, descriptive list, express receipts, medals, names on some part of the clothing, or on belt, or cartridge-box, &c., &c.

There were some articles of value found on the bodies; some money, watches, jewelry, &c. I took all relics, as well as articles of value, from the bodies, packed them up and labelled them, so that the friends can get them. There are many things, valueless to others, which would be of great interest to the friends. I herewith submit a list of names of persons and articles found upon them, and you will, no doubt, take means to get information to the friends, by advertisement or otherwise, so that they may give notice where, and to whom, these things shall be forwarded. I have two hundred and eighty-seven such packages.

Before we commenced our work, the battle field had been overrun by thousands of sorrowing friends in search of lost ones, and many of the graves opened and but partially or carelessly closed. Many of the undertakers who were removing bodies, also performed their work in the most careless manner, invariably leaving the graves open, and often leaving particles of the bones and hair lying scattered around. These things are frequently to be seen on every part of the battle field; and persons going over it might attribute such work to the contractors, but there cannot be one instance pointed out of such kind of work done by them. Every particle of the body was gathered up by them, and the grave neatly closed over and levelled.

The bodies were found in various stages of decomposition. On the battle field of the first day, the rebels obtained possession before our men were buried, and left most of them unburied from Wednesday until Monday following, when our men buried them. After this length of time, they could not be identified. The consequence was, that but few on the battle field of July 1st, were marked. They were generally covered with a small portion of earth dug up from along side of the body. This left them much exposed to the heat, air, and rains, and they decomposed rapidly, so that when these bodies were taken up, there was nothing remaining but the dry skeleton.

Where bodies were in heavy clay soil, or in marshy places, they were in a good state of preservation. Where they were in sandy, porous soil, they were entirely decomposed. Frequently our men were buried in trenches—a shallow ditch—in which they were laid side by side. In several instances the numbers in a trench amounted to sixty or seventy bodies.

In searching for the remains of our fallen heroes, we examined more than three thousand rebel graves. They were frequently buried in trenches, and there are instances of more than one hundred and fifty in a trench. In one place it is asserted by a reliable farmer who saw them buried, that there are over two hundred in one trench. I have been making a careful estimate, from time to time, as I went over the field, of the rebel bodies buried on this battle field and at the hospitals, and I place the number at not less than seven thousand bodies.

It may be asked how we could distinguish the bodies of our own men from those of the rebels. This was generally very easily done. In the first place, as a general rule, the rebels never went into battle with the United States coat on. They sometimes stole the pantaloons from our dead and wore them, but not the coat. The rebel clothing is made of cotton, and is of a grey or brown color. Occasionally I found one with a blue cotton jean roundabout on. The clothing of our men is of wool, and blue; so that the body having the coat of our uniform on was a pretty sure indication that he was a Union soldier. But if the body were without a coat, then there were other infallible marks. The shoes of the rebels were differently made from those of our soldiers. If these failed, then the underclothing was the next part examined. The rebel cotton undershirt gave proof of the army to which he belonged. In no instance was a body allowed to be removed which had any portion of the rebel clothing on it. Taking all these things together, we never had much trouble in deciding, with infallible accuracy, whether the body was that of a Union soldier or a rebel. And I here most conscientiously assert, that I firmly believe that there has not been a single mistake made in the removal of the soldiers to the Cemetery by taking the body of a rebel for a Union soldier.

All which is respectfully submitted.

SAMUEL WEAVER.

REPORT OF JAMES S. TOWNSEND.

To DAVID WILLS, Esq.,

Agent for A. G. CURTIN, *Governor of Pennsylvania:*

SIR:—The interments of all the Union soldiers on the battle field of Gettysburg, in the SOLDIERS' NATIONAL CEMETERY, have been completed in a very satisfactory manner, and according to the terms and specifications of the contract. There has been much delay, for weeks at a time, during the winter, in prosecuting the work, on account of the ground being frozen too hard to dig. Then, occasionally, the wet weather and the snows would stop the work, so that it has been protracted much beyond the time we at first anticipated having it completed.

I surveyed and laid out the grounds as designed by Mr. WM. SAUNDERS, and have since superintended the burials, personally, measuring the depth of every grave and the proper distance for each coffin. I, also, took the name, company and regiment of each body, as soon as placed in the ground, personally superintending the proper marking of the grave, with the appropriate head-board.

The graves are all numbered, and the list of interments of each day was returned to your office for comparison with the list of those taken up in the field, and to be registered daily in a permanent register. The total number of burials in the Cemetery is thirty-five hundred and twelve.

I herewith refer you to the registers you have made in your office, for the number buried in each State lot, and in the lots set apart for the United States Regulars, and the Unknown.

All which is respectfully submitted.

JAS. S. TOWNSEND,

Surveyor and Sup't of Burials.

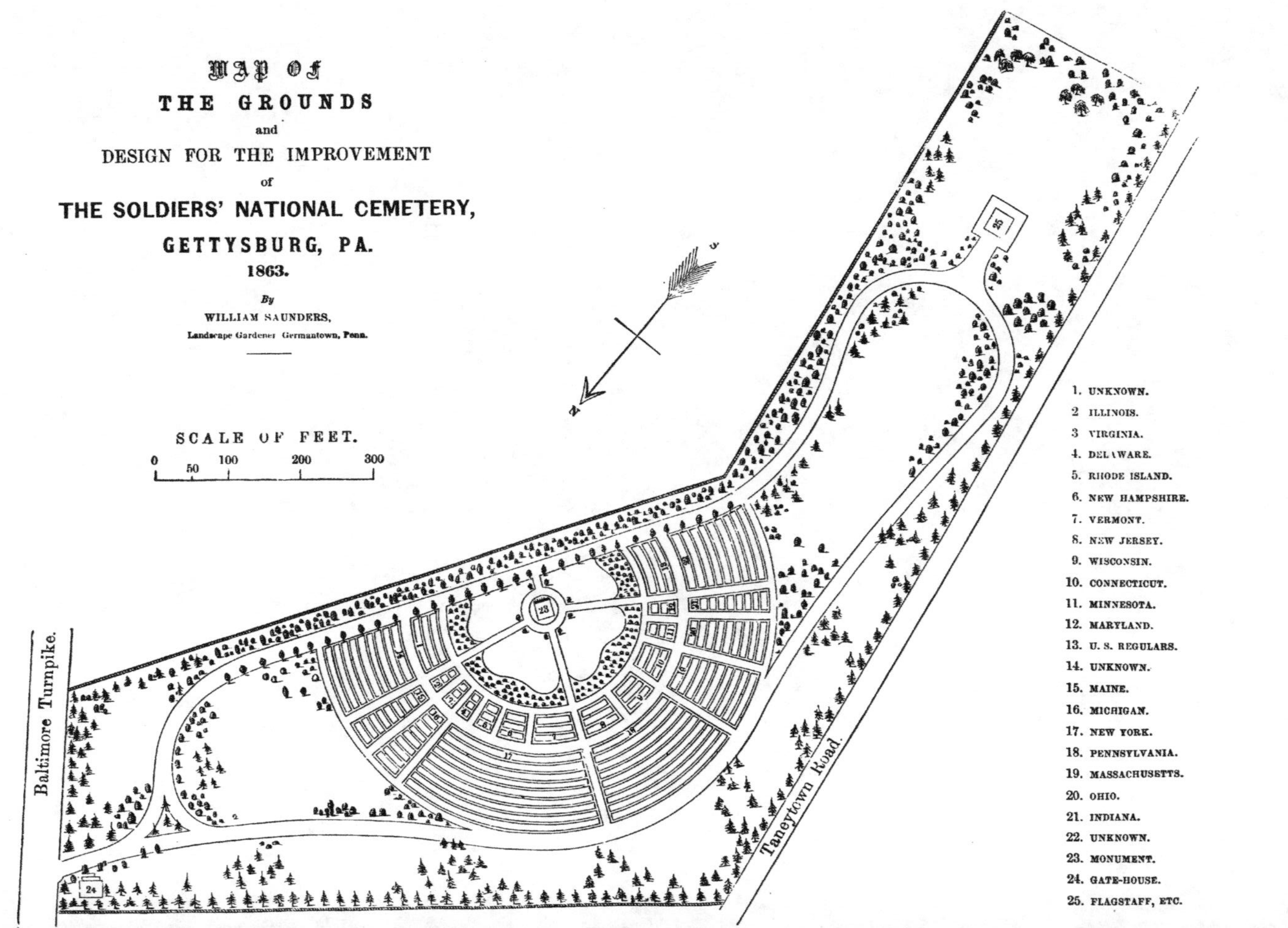
MAP OF
THE GROUNDS
and
DESIGN FOR THE IMPROVEMENT
of
THE SOLDIERS' NATIONAL CEMETERY,
GETTYSBURG, PA.
1863.
By
WILLIAM SAUNDERS,
Landscape Gardener Germantown, Penn.
SCALE OF FEET.
0 50 100 200 300
N
S
Baltimore Turnpike.
Taneytown Road.
1. UNKNOWN.
2 ILLINOIS.
3 VIRGINIA.
4. DELAWARE.
5. RHODE ISLAND.
6. NEW HAMPSHIRE.
7. VERMONT.
8. NEW JERSEY.
9. WISCONSIN.
10. CONNECTICUT.
11. MINNESOTA.
12. MARYLAND.
13. U. S. REGULARS.
14. UNKNOWN.
15. MAINE.
16. MICHIGAN.
17. NEW YORK.
18. PENNSYLVANIA.
19. MASSACHUSETTS.
20. OHIO.
21. INDIANA.
22. UNKNOWN.
23. MONUMENT.
24. GATE-HOUSE.
25. FLAGSTAFF, ETC.

DESCRIPTION OF THE GETTYSBURG MONUMENT.

The design of the Gettysburg monument is adapted for execution either in marble, or in granite and bronze, as may be deemed expedient, the material being of course controlled entirely by the amount appropriated. The whole rendering of the design is intended to be purely historical, telling its own story, with such simplicity that any discerning mind will readily comprehend its meaning and purpose.

The superstructure is sixty feet high, and consists of a massive pedestal, twenty-five feet square at the base, and is crowned with a colossal statue, representing the GENIUS OF LIBERTY. Standing upon a three-quarter globe, she raises with her right hand the victor's wreath of laurel, while with her left she gathers up the folds of our national flag under which the victory has been won.

Projecting from the angles of the pedestal are four buttresses, supporting an equal number of allegorical statues representing, respectively, WAR, HISTORY, PEACE and PLENTY.

WAR is personified by a statue of the American soldier, who, resting from the conflict, relates to History the story of the battle which this monument is intended to commemorate.

HISTORY, in listening attitude, records with stylus and tablet, the achievements of the field, and the names of the honored dead.

PEACE is symbolized by a statue of the American mechanic, characterized by appropriate accessories.

PLENTY is represented by a female figure, with a sheaf of wheat and fruits of the earth, typifying peace and abundance as the soldiers' crowning triumph.

The panels of the main die between the statues are to have inscribed upon them such inscriptions as may hereafter be determined.

The main die of the pedestal is octagonal in form, panelled upon each face. The cornice and plinth above are also octagonal, and are heavily moulded. Upon this plinth rests an octagonal moulded base bearing upon its face, in high relief, the National arms.

The upper die and cap are circular in form, the die being encircled by stars equal in number with the States whose sons contributed their lives as the price of the victory won at Gettysburg.

AN ACT

TO INCORPORATE THE SOLDIERS' NATIONAL CEMETERY.

WHEREAS, The Commonwealth of Pennsylvania has purchased seventeen acres of land on Cemetery Hill, on the Gettysburg battle field, in the county of Adams, for a Cemetery for the burial of the remains of the soldiers who fell in the battle of Gettysburg, and the skirmishes incident thereto, in defence of the Union, or died thereafter from wounds received in that battle and the skirmishes; therefore,

SECTION 1. *Be it enacted by the Senate and House of Representatives of the Commonwealth of Pennsylvania in General Assembly met, and it is hereby enacted by the authority of the same,* That the titles to the said lands purchased, as set forth in the foregoing preamble, are hereby ratified and confirmed, and shall vest and remain in said Commonwealth, in fee simple, in trust for all the States having soldiers buried in said grounds; and the said grounds shall be devoted in perpetuity to the purpose for which they were purchased, namely: for the burial and place of final rest of the remains of the soldiers who fell in defence of the Union, in the battle of Gettysburg; and, also, the remains of the soldiers who fell at other points north of the Potomac river, in the several encounters with the enemy during the invasion of LEE, in the summer of one thousand eight hundred and sixty-three, or died thereafter in consequence of wounds received in said battle and during said invasion.

SECTION 2. That B. W. NORRIS, of the State of Maine, ——— ———, of the State of New Hampshire, PAUL DILLINGHAM, of the State of Vermont, HENRY EDWARDS, of the State of Massachusetts, JOHN R. BARTLETT, of the State of Rhode Island, ALFRED COIT, of the State of Connecticut, EDWARD COOPER, of the State o New York, ——— ———, of the State of New Jersey, DAVID WILLS, of the State of Pennsylvania, BENJAMIN DEFORD, of the State of Maryland, JOHN R. LATIMER, of the State of Delaware, ——— ———, of the State of West Virginia, GORDON LOFLAND, of the State of Ohio, JOHN G. STEPHENSON, of the State of Indiana, CLARK E. CARR, of the State of Illinois, W. Y. SELLECK, of the State of Wisconsin, THOMAS WHITE FERRY, of the State of Michigan, ——— ———, of the State of Minnesota, being one Commissioner from each State, having soldiers buried in said Cemetery, be and they and their successors are hereby created a body politic in law, under the name, style and title of the SOLDIERS' NATIONAL CEMETERY, and by that name, style and title shall have perpetual succession, and be able and capable in law to have and use a common seal, to sue and be sued, plead and be impleaded, in all courts of law and equity, and to do all such other things as are incident to a corporation.

SECTION 3. The care and management of the grounds referred to in the preamble and first section of this act, are hereby entrusted solely to the commissioners named in the second section of the same, and those hereafter appointed to represent the States therein named, and their successors in office; the said commissioners shall constitute a board of managers, whose duty it shall be, out of funds that may be in the hands of the treasurer of the corporation, by State appropriations, or otherwise, to remove the remains of all the soldiers referred to in the first section of this act, that have not already been removed to the Cemetery, and have them properly interred therein; and, also, to lay out, fence and ornament, to divide and arrange into suitable plots and burial lots, establish carriage-ways, avenues and foot-ways, erect buildings, and a monument, or monuments, and suitable marks to designate the graves, and generally to do all other things in their judgment necessary and proper to be done to adapt the ground and premises to the uses for which it has been purchased and set apart.

SECTION 4. The business of the corporation shall be conducted by the commissioners aforesaid, and their successors in office; the said commissioners shall meet within sixty days after the passage of this act, and organize by electing one of their number president; they shall also appoint a secretary and treasurer, and shall have power to employ such other officers and agents as may be needful; they shall require of the treasurer to enter into bonds, to the corporation, in double the probable amount of money that may be in his hands at any one time during his term of office, with two or more sufficient sureties, conditioned for the faithful discharge of his duties, and the correct accounting for and paying over of the money; which said bond or bonds, shall be approved by the court of common pleas of Adams county, and recorded in the office of the recorder of deeds, in and for said county; the term of office of the officers of the board of commissioners aforesaid shall expire on the first day of January, of each and every year, or as soon thereafter as their successors may be duly chosen and qualified to act.

SECTION 5. At the first meeting of the commissioners heretofore named, they shall be divided, by lot, into three classes, and the term of office of the first class shall expire on the first day of January, Anno Domini one thousand eight hundred and sixty-five; the second class, on the first day of January, Anno Domini one thousand eight hundred and sixty-six, and the third class on the first day of January, Anno Domini one thousand eight hundred and sixty-seven; the vacancies thus occurring shall be filled by the Governors of the States which the said commissioners represented; and the persons thus appointed to fill such vacancies, shall hold their office, as commissioners aforesaid, for the term of three years. In case of the neglect, or failure, of the Governor of any State, having burial lots in the Cemetery, to fill such vacancy, the board of commissioners may supply the place by appointing a citizen of the particular State which is not represented in the board by reason of such vacancy; any vacancies not yet filled, or hereafter occurring, in the board of commissioners, by death, resignation, or otherwise, shall be filled, by appointment, for the unexpired term, by the Governor of the State which the person represented, or in case of failure by such Governor to make said appointment, then the place shall be supplied as last above indicated; such other States of the Union, not having burial lots in said Cemetery, but that may at any time hereafter desire to be represented in this corporation, shall have the privilege of nominating a Commissioner to represent them severally in the board of commissioners, and thereafter pay their proportionate share of the expense of maintaining said Cemetery.

SECTION 6. The board of commissioners shall annually, at the end of each fiscal year, make a report of the condition and management of the Cemetery; which report shall contain a detailed statement of the receipts and expenditures of the corporation, and a copy thereof shall be forwarded to the Governor of each State represented in the corporation. The expenses incident to the removal of the dead, the enclosing and ornamenting the Cemetery, and all the work connected therewith, and its future maintenance, shall be apportioned among the States connecting themselves with the corporation, according to their population, as indicated by their representation in the House of Representatives of the United States.

SECTION 7. The board of commissioners shall adopt such by-laws, rules, and regulations, as they may deem necessary for their meetings and government, and for the government of their officers, agents and employees, and for the care and protection of the cemetery grounds, and the property of the corporation: *Provided,* Said by-laws, rules, and regulations, be not inconsistent with the Constitution and laws of the United States, the Constitution and laws of the Commonwealth of Pennsylvania, and this act of incorporation.

SECTION 8. The board of commissioners shall have no power to appropriate any of the funds of the corporation as a compensation for their services as commissioners.

SECTION 9. The grounds and property of said Cemetery shall be forever free from the levy of any State, county, or municipal taxes; and the Commonwealth of Pennsylvania hereby releases, and exempts, the corporation created by this act of Assembly, from the payment of any enrolment tax, or any tax, or taxes, whatever, that might be imposed by existing laws; all the laws of this Commonwealth now in force, or which may hereafter be enacted, for the protection of cemeteries, burial grounds, and places of sepulture, shall apply with full force and effect to the SOLDIERS' NATIONAL CEMETERY, hereby incorporated, immediately from and after the passage of this act.

SECTION 10. The corporation of the SOLDIERS' NATIONAL CEMETERY shall have power to receive appropriations from the United States, and from the State Legislatures, and also devises, and bequests, gifts, annuities, and all other kinds of property, real and personal, for the purposes of the burial of the dead, enclosing and ornamenting the grounds, and maintaining the same, and erecting a monument, or monuments, therein.

HENRY C. JOHNSON,
Speaker of the House of Representatives.

JOHN P. PENNEY,
Speaker of the Senate.

APPROVED—The twenty-fifth day of March, Anno Domini one thousand eight hundred and sixty-four.

A. G. CURTIN.

CORRESPONDENCE,

ADDRESSES AND CEREMONIES,

AT THE

CONSECRATION

OF THE

Soldiers' National Cemetery,

AT

GETTYSBUBG, NOVEMBER 19, 1863.

THE NATIONAL CEMETERY.

A few days after the terrific battle of Gettysburg, His Excellency, A. G. CURTIN, Governor of the State of Pennsylvania, hastened to the relief of the sick and wounded soldiers, visited the battle field, and the numerous hospitals in and around Gettysburg, for the purpose of perfecting the arrangements for alleviating the sufferings and ministering to the wants of the wounded and dying. His official duties soon requiring his return to Harrisburg, he authorized and appointed DAVID WILLS, Esq., of Gettysburg, to act as his special agent in this matter.

In traversing the battle field, the feelings were shocked and the heart sickened at the sights that presented themselves at every step. The remains of our brave soldiers, from the necessary haste with which they were interred, in many instances were but partially covered with earth, and, indeed, in some instances were left wholly unburied. Other sights, too shocking to be described, were occasionally seen. These appearances presented themselves promiscuously over the fields of arable land for miles around, which would, of necessity, be farmed over in a short time. The graves, where marked at all, were only temporarily so, and the marks were liable to be obliterated by the action of the weather. Such was the spectacle witnessed on going over the battle field—a field made glorious by victory achieved through the sacrifice of the lives of the thousands of brave men, whose bodies and graves were in such exposed condition. And this, too, on Pennsylvania soil! Humanity shuddered at the sight, and called aloud for a remedy. The idea, accordingly, suggested itself of taking measures to gather these remains together, and bury them decently and in order in a cemetery. Mr. WILLS submitted the proposition and plan for this purpose, by letter July 24th, 1863, to His Excellency, Governor CURTIN; and the Governor, with that profound sympathy, and that care and anxiety for the soldier which have always characterized him, approved of the design, and directed a correspondence to be entered into at once by Mr. WILLS with the Governors of the other States having soldiers dead on the battle field of Gettysburg. The Governors of the different States, with great promptness, seconded the project, and the details of the arrangement were subsequently agreed upon. Grounds favorably situated were selected by the Agent, and Governor CURTIN directed him to purchase them for the State of Pennsylvania, for the specific purpose of the burial of the soldiers who fell in defence of the Union in the battle of Gettysburg, and that lots in this Cemetery should be gratuitously tendered to each State having such dead on the field. The expenses of the removal of the dead, of the laying out, ornamenting, and enclosing the grounds, and erecting a lodge for the keeper, and of constructing a suitable monument to the memory of the dead, to be borne by the several States, and assessed in proportion to their population, as indicated by their representation in Congress. The Governor of Pennsylvania stipulated that the State of Pennsylvania would subsequently keep the grounds in order, and the buildings and fences in repair.

Seventeen acres of land on Cemetery Hill, at the apex of the triangular line of battle of the Union army, were purchased by Pennsylvania for this purpose. There were stone fences upon these grounds, which had been advantageously used by the infantry. On the elevated portions of the ground many batteries of artillery had been planted, which not only commanded the view of the whole line of battle of the Union army, but were brought to bear almost incessantly, with great effect, upon every position of the Rebel lines. We refer the reader to the excellent map of this battle field and its hospitals, in the front of this pamphlet. It was prepared by the Rev. ANDREW B. CROSS, who is one of the most active and zealous members of the Christian Commission, and who labored faithfully for months in the hospitals at Gettysburg, ministering to the temporal and spiritual wants of the wounded and dying soldiers. This map gives the locality of the National Cemetery, as well as many other points of interest connected with the battle field.

The Cemetery grounds were plotted and laid out in the original and appropiate style indicated by the plate accompanying this description, by the celebrated rural architect, Mr. WILLIAM SAUNDERS.

Such was the origin of this final resting place for the remains of our departed heroes, who nobly laid down their lives a sacrifice on their country's altar, for the sake of Universal Freedom and the preservation of the Union. Who can estimate the importance to us and all posterity of their valor and heroism? Their remains, above all others, deserve the highest honor that a grateful people can bestow on them. Their deeds will live in history long after their bodies have mouldered into dust; and the place where they now lie will be honored, protected, and preserved as a sad, but sacred memento of their brave conduct.

The design contemplates the erection of a monument to the memory of the dead; and the situation which seems to meet with the greatest favor is in the centre of the semi-circle of graves. It has been suggested, that each State having dead here should contribute a slab or stone tablet, to be placed the monument, with the names engraved upon it of those whose graves are not identified, and who consequently are interred in the lots set apart for the unknown.

The grounds are laid off in lots for each state, proportioned in size to the number of marked graves on the Gettysburg battle field. There is also a lot set apart for the burial of the remains of those who belonged to the regular service. The graves of about one-third of the dead were unmarked; but these bodies are deposited in prominent and honorable positions at each end of the semi-circular arrangement of the lots. The grounds naturally have a gradual slope in every direction from the centre of the semi-circle to the circumference. Each lot is laid off in sections, with a space of four feet for a walk between each section. The outer section is lettered A, and so on in alphabetical order. As the observer stands in the centre of the semi-circle, facing the circumference, the burials are commenced at the right hand of the section in each lot, and the graves are numbered from one up numerically. A register is made of the number, name, regiment and company of the occupant of each grave. Two feet space is allotted to each, and they are laid with the heads toward the centre of the semi-circle. At the head of the graves there is a stone wall, built up from the bottom as a foundation for the headstones, which are to be placed along the whole length of each section, and on which, opposite each grave, will be engraved the name, regiment and company of the deceased. These headstones will be all alike in size, the design being wholly adapted to a symmetrical order, and one which combines simplicity and durability. No other marks will be permitted to be erected. There will be about twenty-nine hundred burials in the Cemetery.

An application was made by Mr. WILLS to Hon E. M. STANTON, Secretary of War, for coffins for the interment of the dead, and the Quartermaster General was promptly ordered to furnish them. The Secretary of War, also, with a liberal considerateness, afforded many facilities for the proper and honorable solemnization of the exercises of the 19th of November. The removals and burials are made with the greatest care, and under the strictest supervision. Every precaution is taken to identify the unmarked graves, and also to prevent the marked graves from losing their identity, by the defacement of the original temporary boards, on which the names were written or cut by comrades in arms. The graves being all numbered, the numbers are registered every evening in a record book, with the name, company and regiment. This register will designate the graves, should the temporary marks become defaced by the action of the weather, or be otherwise lost, before the permanent headstones are put in place. After the burials are all made, the graves all permanently marked, and the style of monument determined upon, a map will be prepared and lithographed, showing the number of each grave in each section, and a key be published with the map, giving the full inscription on the headstone, corresponding with the number.

A few of the States sent agents to Gettysburg to superintend the removal and burial of their dead, while most of them entrusted the arrangements for that purpose to the Agent of the State of Pennsylvania. The Boston city authorities, in concert with the Governor of Massachusetts, sent an efficient committee to Gettysburg, who made the removals of the Massachusetts dead by their own special arrangement.

The consecration of these Cemetery grounds was, in due time, suggested by Governor CURTIN. The name of Hon. EDWARD EVERETT was submitted to the Governors of all the States interested, as the orator to deliver the address on that occasion, and they unanimously concurred in him as the person eminently suitable for the purpose. A letter of invitation was accordingly addressed to him, inviting him to deliver the oration. He accepted the duty, and the 19th of November was fixed upon as the day. Hon. W. H. LAMON, the United States Marshal for the District of Columbia, was selected as the Chief Marshal of the civic procession, and to Major General D. N. COUCH, commanding the Department of the Susquehanna, were committed the arrangements for the military. To all of these gentlemen great credit is due, for the admirable manner in which they discharged the duties of the positions assigned them. Birgfield's Brigade Band, of Philadelphia, was invited to furnish the music for the ceremonial of consecration, which was done gratuitously, and in a very acceptable manner. The Presidential party was accompanied by the Marine Band, from the Navy Yard at Washington, and the military detachment was attended by the Brass Band from Fort M'Henry, Baltimore.

The public generally were invited to be present and participate in these solemn exercises, and special invitations were sent to the PRESIDENT and VICE PRESIDENT of the United States, and the members of the Cabinet—to Major General GEORGE G. MEADE, commanding the army of the Potomac, and, through him, to the officers and privates of that army which had fought so valiantly, and gained such a memorable victory on the Gettysburg battle field—and to Lieutenant General WINFIELD SCOTT and Admiral CHARLES STEWART, the distinguished and time honored representatives of the Army and Navy. The PRESIDENT of the United States was present, and participated in these solemnities, delivering a brief dedicatory address. The occasion was further made memorable by the presence of large representations from the army and navy, of the Secretary of State of the United States, the Ministers of France and Italy, the French Admiral, and other distinguished foreigners, and several members of Congress, also, of the Governors of a large number of the States interested, with their staffs, and, in some instances, large delegations, besides a vast concourse of citizens from all the States.

Letters were received, in reply to the invitations addressed to them, from Major General MEADE, Lieutenant General SCOTT, Admiral CHARLES STEWART, and the Secretary of the Treasury, Hon. S. P. CHASE, regretting their inability to be present, and expressive of their approval of the project.

One of the most sad and impressive features of the solemnities of the 19th of November was the presence, in the procession and on the grounds, of a delegation of about fifty wounded soldiers of the army of the Potomac, from the York hospital. These men had been wounded in the battle of Gettysburg, and were present in a delegation to pay this just tribute to the remains of their fallen comrades. During the exercises, their bronzed cheeks were frequently suffused with tears, indicative of their heartfelt sympathy in the solemn scene before them. From none others could tears of unfeigned grief fall upon these graves with so much sad appreciation.—These scarred vaterans came and dropped the tear of sorrow on the last resting place of those companions by whose sides they so nobly fought, and, lingering over the graves after the crowd had dispersed, slowly went away, strengthened in their faith in a nation's gratitude.

CORRESPONDENCE.

GETTYSBURG, *August* 17, 1863.

To His Excellency, A. G. CURTIN,
Governor of Pennsylvania:

SIR:—By virtue of the authority reposed in me by your Excellency, I have invited the coöperation of the several loyal States having soldier-dead on the battle field around this place, in the noble project of removing their remains from their present exposed and imperfectly buried condition, on the fields for miles around, to a cemetery.

The chief executives of fifteen out of the seventeen States have already responded, in most instances, pledging their States to unite in the movement; in a few instances, highly approving of the project, and stipulating to urge upon the Legislatures to make appropriations to defray their proportionate share of expense.

I have, also, at your request, selected and purchased the grounds for this Cemetery, the land to be paid for by, and the title to be made to, the State of Pennsylvania, and to be held in perpetuity, devoted to the object for which it was purchased.

The grounds embrace about seventeen acres on Cemetery Hill, fronting on the Baltimore turnpike, and extending to the Taneytown road. It is the ground which formed the apex of our triangular line of battle, and the key to our line of defences. It embraces the highest point on Cemetery Hill, and overlooks the whole battle field. It is the spot which should be specially consecrated to this sacred purpose. It was here that such immense quantities of our artillery were massed, and during Thursday and Friday of the battle, from this most important point on the field, dealt out death and destruction to the Rebel army in every direction of their advance.

I have been in conference, at different times, with agents sent here by the Governors of several of the States, and we have arranged details for carrying out this sacred work. I herewith enclose you a copy of the proposed arrangement of details, a copy of which I have also sent the chief executive of each State having dead here.

I have, also, at your suggestion, cordially tendered to each State the privilege, if they desire, of joining in the title to the land.

I think it would be showing only a proper respect for the health of this community not to commence the exhuming of the dead, and removal to the Cemetery, until the month of November; and in the meantime the grounds should be artistically laid out, and consecrated by appropriate ceremonies.

I am, with great respect,

Your Excellency's obedient servant,

DAVID WILLS.

PENNSYLVANIA, EXECUTIVE CHAMBER,
HARRISBURG, *August* 31, 1863.

DEAR SIR:—Yours of the 26th instant was duly received, and ought to have been answered sooner, but you know how I am pressed.

I am much pleased with the details for the Cemetery which you have so thoughtfully suggested, and will be glad, so far as is in my power, to hasten their consummation on the part of Pennsylvania.

It is of course probable that our sister States, joining with us in this hallowed undertaking, may desire to make some alterations and modifications of your proposed plan of purchasing and managing these sacred grounds, and it is my wish that you give to their views the most careful and respectful consideration. Pennsylvania will be so highly honored by the possession within her limits of this Soldiers' mausoleum, and so much distinguished among the other States by their contributions in aid of so glorious a monument to patriotism and humanity, that it becomes her duty, as it is her melancholy pleasure, to yield, in every reasonable way, to the wishes, and suggestions, of the States who join with her in dedicating a portion of her territory to the solemn uses of a National sepulchre.

The proper consecration of the grounds must claim our early attention; and, as soon as we can do so, our fellow-purchasers should be invited to join with us in the performance of suitable ceremonies on the occasion.

I am, very respectfully,

Your obedient servant,

A. G. CURTIN.

DAVID WILLS, Esq.

GETTYSBURG, PA., *September* 23, 1863.

HON. EDWARD EVERETT:

SIR:—The several States having soldiers in the army of the Potomac, who fell at the battle of Gettysburg, in July last, gallantly fighting for the Union, have made arrangements here for the exhuming of all their dead, and their removal and decent burial in a Cemetery selected for that purpose, on a prominent part of the battle field.

The design is to bury all in common, marking with headstones, with the proper inscription, the known dead, and to erect a suitable monument to the memory of all these brave men, who have thus sacrificed their lives on the altar of their country.

The burial ground will be consecrated to this sacred and holy purpose on Thursday, the 23d day of October next, with appropriate ceremonies; and the several States interested, have united in the selection of you to deliver the oration on that solemn occasion. I am therefore instructed, by the Governors of the different States interested in this project, to invite you cordially to join with them in the ceremonies, and to deliver the oration for the occasion.

Hoping to have an early, and favorable reply from you,

I remain, sir, your most obedient servant,

DAVID WILLS,

Agent for the Governor of Pennsylvania.

BOSTON, *September* 26, 1863.

MY DEAR SIR :—I have received your favor of the 23d instant, inviting me, on behalf of the Governors of the States interested in the preparation of a Cemetery for the soldiers who fell in the great battles of July last, to deliver an address at the consecration. I feel much complimented by this request, and would cheerfully undertake the performance of a duty at once so interesting and honorable. It is, however, wholly out of my power to make the requisite preparation by the 23d of October. I am under engagements which will occupy all my time from Monday next to the 12th of October, and, indeed, it is doubtful whether, during the whole month of October, I shall have a day at my command.

The occasion is one of great importance, not to be dismissed with a few sentimental or patriotic commonplaces. It will demand as full a narrative of the events of the three important days as the limits of the hour will admit, and some appropriate discussion of the political character of the great struggle, of which the battle of Gettysburg is one of the most momentous incidents. As it will take me two days to reach Gettysburg, and it will be highly desirable that I should have at least one day to survey the battle field, I cannot safely name an earlier time than the 19th of November.

Should such a postponement of the day first proposed be advisable, it will give me great pleasure to accept the invitation.

I remain, dear sir, with much respect,

Very truly yours,

EDWARD EVERETT.

DAVID WILLS, Esq.,

Agent for the National Cemetery.

NOTE.—In compliance with Mr. EVERETT's suggestions, as expressed in the foregoing letter, Thursday, the 19th of November, was appointed for the ceremonial of the consecration.

GETTYSBURG, *November* 25, 1863.

Hon. EDWARD EVERETT:

DEAR SIR:—On behalf of the Governors of the several States interested in the National Cemetery, I request of you for publication a copy of your Address delivered at the consecration of the grounds on Thursday, the 19th of this month, the proceeds of the sale to be added to the fund for the erection of a monument to the memory of the heroes whose remains are deposited in the Cemetery.

In performing this official duty, allow me as a citizen of Gettysburg, and in behalf of my fellow citizens, to express our peculiar satisfaction at that part of your Address, which is devoted to a narrative of the all-important events, that have at once raised this place into permanent importance and celebrity. Knowing as we do that you used great diligence and care to procure as accurate an account as possible of the movements of the two armies in this vicinity, and their positions in the battle on the different days, we regard that portion of your Address as very important and valuable. Whilst its delivery commanded the closest attention of the vast assembly who listened to it—thus giving evidence of their intense interest and entire appreciation—this portion of the Oration, preserved in an authentic form, will descend to posterity as a production of permanent historical value.

Allow me, also, to express my gratification at the tribute paid by you to Major General REYNOLDS, in ascribing "to his forethought and self-sacrifice the triumph of the two succeeding days." In that well-deserved tribute the historian, who shall do justice to the battle of Gettysburg, will undoubtedly concur, pointing to him as the individual to whom our glorious success was in a great degree due. He was in the advance on the extreme left of the army of the Potomac, and in command of the First Army Corps. On Wednesday morning, July 1st, when pressing his corps forward to meet and retard the progress of the enemy, whose position and movements were beginning to be developed to him, he told one of his aides, as they approached Gettysburg and examined the face of the country, that Cemetery Hill must be held for our army at all hazards; that he would advance his corps rapidly to Seminary Ridge, west of the town, and temporarily occupy that position; that he would there engage the enemy, who was advancing, and delay his further progress, so as to give time for the whole of the army of the Potomac to concentrate on Cemetery Hill and the ridges running out either way from it; that, if pressed too hard, he would gradually fall back, contesting the ground step by step, and, if necessary to delay the enemy, would fight from house to house, through the town. He fell, the victim of a rebel sharpshooter, so soon in the action of Wednesday morning, as he was carrying out these designs, that but few persons are cognizant of his real plans. When the facts are fully made known, history and an impartial world will accord to him the highest praise. His great foresight and brave conduct on that occasion will forever endear him to those who love to worship at the shrine of true patriotism. He was truly a soldier—always with his men in the camp and in the field, sharing their hardships, toils and dangers. He loved his profession, and devoted himself exclusively to it; and in the vigor of manhood he nobly laid down his life, a sacrifice on his country's altar, on the soil of his native State, at the head of his brave corps, that the rest of the army of the Potomac might the more successfully reach the position of his own selection for its defence. This place of his choice proved to be the true position on which to meet and check the onward march of the rebellious invaders.

Not doubting that you will take an interest in this confirmation of the estimate placed by you on General Reynolds's services,

I remain, dear sir,

Yours, with great respect,

DAVID WILLS.

Boston, *December* 14, 1863.

My Dear Sir:—I have this day received your letter of the 25th of November, requesting, on behalf of the Governors of the several States interested in the National Cemetery, a copy, for publication in a permanent form, of the Address delivered by me at the consecration. I shall have great pleasure in complying with this request, the rather as it is proposed that the proceeds of the publication shall be added to the fund for the erection of a monument to the memory of the brave men whose remains are deposited in the Cemetery.

You will be pleased to accept my thanks for the obliging manner in which you speak of the historical portion of my Address. It was, of course, impossible to compress within so small a compass a narrative of the three eventful days, which should do exact justice to every incident or every individual. On some points, as in most narratives of battles, the printed accounts, and even the official reports, differ. In revising my Address for publication in this form, I shall correct one or two slight errors of the first draught, and take advantage of sources of information not originally accessible.

I am much gratified with your concurrence with me in the estimate I had formed of the character of General REYNOLDS, and of his very important services in determining the entire fortunes of this ever memorable battle.

I remain, dear sir, with great regard,

Very truly yours,

EDWARD EVERETT.

DAVID WILLS, Esq.,

Agent for the National Cemetery.

HEAD-QUARTERS ARMY OF THE POTOMAC,
November 13, 1863.

DAVID WILLS, Esq.,

Agent for the Governor of Pennsylvania, etc.:

SIR:—I have the honor to acknowledge the invitation which, on behalf of the Governor of Pennsylvania and other States interested, you extend to me and the officers and men of my command, to be present on the 19th instant at the consecration of the burial place of those who fell on the field of Gettysburg.

It seems almost unnecessary for me to say that none can have a deeper interest in your good work than comrades in arms, bound in close ties of long association and mutual confidence and support with those to whom you are paying this last tribute of respect; nor could the presence of any be more appropriate than that of those who stood side by side in the struggle, shared the peril, and the vacant places in whose ranks bear sad testimony to the loss they have sustained. But this army has duties to perform which will not admit of its being represented on the occasion; and it only remains for me in its name, with deep and grateful feelings, to thank you and those you represent for your tender care of its heroic dead, and for your patriotic zeal, which, in honoring the martyr, gives a fresh incentive to all who do battle for the maintenance of the integrity of the government.

I am, very respectfully,

Your obedient servant,

GEORGE G. MEADE,

Major General Commanding.

NEW YORK, *November* 19, 1863.

DAVID WILLS, Esq., *Agent, etc.:*

DEAR SIR:—I have had the honor to receive your invitation, on the part of the Governors of the loyal States, to be present at the consecration of the Military Cemetery at Gettysburg this day.

Besides the determination, on account of infirmities, never again to participate in any public meeting or entertainment, I was too sick at the time to do more than write a short telegram in reply to His Excellency, Governor CURTIN.

Having long lived with, and participated in the hardships and dangers of, our soldiers, I can never fail to honor

"the brave who sink to rest,
By all their country's wishes blest."

None deserve this tribute from their countrymen, more than those who have fallen in defence of the Constitution, and the Union of the thirty-four United States.

I remain yours,

Most respectfully,

WINFIELD SCOTT.

BORDENTOWN, N. J., *November* 21, 1863.

MY DEAR SIR:—I regret extremely, that, in consequence of the invitation you did me the honor to send me, remaining for several days among the advertised letters in the Philadelphia post office, I was not able to accept the same by appearing in person at the interesting consecration of the National Cemetery, at Gettysburg, on the nineteenth of this month.

On an occasion so solemn, awakening every patriotic emotion of the human heart, I cannot but deplore that I was not able to be present, to shed a tear over the remains of these gallant men, who gave back their lives to their God, in defence of their country.

Accept for yourself, my dear sir, and be pleased to present to the committee, my thanks for your kind invitation, and believe me, with great respect,

Your obedient servant,

CHARLES STEWART.

To DAVID WILLS, Esq., *Agent, etc.*

TREASURY DEPARTMENT, *November* 16, 1863.

DEAR SIR:—It disappoints me greatly to find that imperative public duties make it impossible for me to be present at the consecration of the grounds, selected as the last resting place of the soldiers, who fell in battle for their country at Gettysburg. It consoles me to think what tears of mingled grief and triumph will fall upon their graves, and what benedictions of the country, saved by their heroism, will make their memories sacred among men.

Very respectfully yours,

S. P. CHASE.

DAVID WILLS, Esq.,
Agent for the Governors of the States.

In the afternoon of the 18th, the President and the distinguished personages accompanying him, arrived at Gettysburg, by a special train. In the course of the evening, the President and Secretary of State were serenaded, and the following remarks were made by Mr. SEWARD, in response to the call:—

FELLOW CITIZENS:—I am now sixty years old and upwards; I have been in public life practically forty years of that time, and yet this is the first time that ever any people, or community, so near to the border of Maryland, was found willing to listen to my voice; and the reason was that I saw, forty years ago, that slavery was opening before this people a graveyard that was to be filled with brothers falling in mutual political combat. I knew that the cause that was hurrying the Union into this dreadful strife was slavery; and when, during all the intervening period, I elevated my voice, it was to warn the people to remove that cause while they could, by constitutional means, and so avert the catastrophe of civil war which has fallen upon the nation. I am thankful that you are willing to hear me at last. I thank my God that I believe this strife is going to end in the removal of that evil, which ought to have been removed by deliberate councils and peaceful means. (Good.) I thank my God for the hope that this is the last fratricidal war which will fall upon the country which is vouchsafed to us by Heaven,—the richest, the broadest, the most beautiful, the most magnificent, and capable of a great destiny, that has ever been given to any part of the human race. (Applause.) And I thank him for the hope that when that cause is removed, simply by the operation of abolishing it, as the origin and agent of the treason that is without justification, and without parallel, we shall thenceforth be united, be only one country, having only one hope, one ambition and one destiny. (Applause.) To-morrow, at least, we shall feel that we are not enemies, but that we are friends and brothers, that this Union is a reality, and we shall mourn together for the evil wrought by this rebellion. We are now near the graves of the misguided, whom we have consigned to their last resting place, with pity for their errors, and with the same heart full of grief with which we mourn over a brother by whose hand, raised in defence of his government, that misguided brother perished.

When we part to-morrow night, let us remember that we owe it to our country and to mankind that this war shall have for its conclusion the establishing of the principle of democratic government—the simple principle that whatever party, whatever portion of the community, prevails by constitutional suffrage in an election, that party is to be respected and maintained in power until it shall give place, on another trial and another verdict, to a different portion of the people. If you do not do this, you are drifting at once and irresistibly to the very verge of universal, cheerless and hopeless anarchy. But with that principle this government of ours—the purest, the best, the wisest, and the happiest in the world—must be, and, so far as we are concerned, practically will be, immortal. (Cheers.) Fellow citizens, good-night.

ORDER OF PROCESSION

FOR THE

CONSECRATION OF THE NATIONAL CEMETERY AT GETTYSBURG, PA.,

ON THE 19TH OF NOVEMBER, 1863.

Military, under command of Major General COUCH.

Major General MEADE and Staff, and the Officers and Soldiers of the Army of the Potomac.

Officers of the Navy and Marine Corps of the United States.

Aids. CHIEF MARSHAL. Aids.

PRESIDENT OF THE UNITED STATES.

Members of the Cabinet.

Assistant Secretaries of the several Executive Departments.

General-in chief of the Army, and Staff.

Lieutenant General SCOTT and Rear-Admiral STEWART.

Judges of the United States Supreme Court.

Hon. EDWARD EVERETT, Orator of the Day, and the Chaplain.

Governors of the States, and their Staffs.

Commissioners of the States on the Inauguration of the Cemetery.

Bearers with the Flags of the States.

VICE PRESIDENT OF THE UNITED STATES and Speaker of the House of Representatives.

Members of the two houses of Congress.

Officers of the two houses of Congress.

Mayors of Cities.

Gettysburg Committee of Arrangements.

Officers and members of the United States Sanitary Commission.

Committees of different Religious Bodies.

United States Military Telegraphic Corps.

Officers and representatives of Adams Express Company.

Officers of different Telegraph Companies.

Hospital Corps of the Army.

Soldiers' Relief Associations.

Knights Templar.

Masonic Fraternity.

Independent Order of Odd Fellows.
Other Benevolent Associations.
Literary, Scientific and Industrial Associations.
The Press.
Officers and Members of Loyal Leagues.
Fire Companies.
Citizens of the State of Pennsylvania.
Citizens of other States.
Citizens of the District of Columbia.
Citizens of the several Territories.

PROGRAMME OF ARRANGEMENTS,

AND ORDER OF EXERCISES FOR THE CONSECRATION OF THE NATIONAL CEMETERY, AT GETTYSBURG, ON THE 19TH OF NOVEMBER, 1863.

The military will form in Gettysburg at nine o'clock, A. M., on Carlisle street, north of the square, its right resting on the square, opposite M'Clellan's hotel, under the direction of Major General COUCH.

The State Marshals and Chief Marshal's aids will assemble in the public square at the same hour.

All civic bodies, except the citizens of States, will assemble, according to the foregoing printed programme, on York street, at the same hour.

The delegation of Pennsylvania citizens will form on Chambersburg street, its right resting on the square; and the other citizen delegations, in their order, will form on the same street, in rear of the Pennsylvania delegation.

The Marshals of the States are charged with the duty of forming their several delegations so that they will assume their appropriate positions when the main procession moves.

The head of the column will move at precisely ten o'clock, A. M.

The route will be up Baltimore street to the Emmitsburg road, thence to the junction of the Taneytown road, thence, by the latter road, to the Cemetery, where the military will form in line, as the General in command may order, for the purpose of saluting the President of the United States.

The military will then close up and occupy the space on the left of the stand.

The civic procession will advance and occupy the area in front of the stand, the military leaving sufficient space between them and the line of graves for the civic procession to pass.

The ladies will occupy the right of the stand, and it is desirable that they be upon the ground as early as ten o'clock, A. M.

The exercises will take place as soon as the military and civic bodies are in position, as follows:

Music, by BIRGFIELD'S Band.

Prayer, by Rev. T. H. STOCKTON, D. D.

Music, by the Marine Band.

Oration, by Hon. EDWARD EVERETT.

Music, Hymn composed by B. B. French, Esq.

Dedicatory Remarks, by the President of the United States.

Dirge, sung by Choir selected for the occasion.

Benediction, by Rev. H. L. Baugher, D. D.

After the benediction the procession will be dismissed, and the State Marshals and special aids to the Chief Marshal, will form on Baltimore street, and return to the court house in Gettysburg, where a meeting of the Marshals will be held.

An appropriate salute will be fired in Gettysburg on the day of the celebration, under the direction of Major General Couch.

PRAYER OF REV. DR. STOCKTON.

O God our Father, for the sake of Thy Son our Saviour, inspire us with Thy Spirit, and sanctify us to the right fulfilment of the duties of this occasion.

We come to dedicate this new historic centre as a National Cemetery. If all departments of the one government which Thou hast ordained over our Union, and of the many governments which Thou has subordinated to our Union, be here represented—if all classes, relations, and interests of our blended brotherhood of people stand severally and thoroughly apparent in Thy presence—we trust that it is because Thou hast called us, that Thy blessing awaits us, and that Thy designs may be embodied in practical results of incalculable and imperishable good.

And, so, with Thy holy Apostle, and with the Church of all lands and ages, we unite in the ascription, "Blessed be God, even the Father of our Lord Jesus Christ, the Father of mercies, and the God of all comfort, who comforteth us in all our tribulation, that we may be able to comfort them which are in any trouble, by the comfort wherewith we ourselves are comforted of God."

In emulation of all angels, in fellowship with all saints, and in sympathy with all sufferers, in remembrance of Thy works, in reverence of Thy ways, and in accordance with Thy word, we laud and magnify Thine infinite perfections, Thy creative glory, Thy redeeming grace, Thy providential goodness, and the progressively richer and fairer developments of Thy supreme, universal and everlasting administration.

In behalf of all humanity, whose ideal is divine, whose first memory is Thine image lost, and whose last hope is Thine image restored, and especially of our own nation, whose history has been so favored, whose position is so peerless, whose mission is so sublime, and whose future is so attractive, we thank Thee for the unspeakable patience of Thy compassion and the exceeding greatness of Thy loving kindness. In contemplation of Eden, Calvary, and Heaven, of Christ in the Garden, on the Cross, and on the Throne; nay, more, of Christ as coming again in all-subduing power and glory, we gratefully prolong our homage. By this Altar of Sacrifice; on this Field of Deliverance, on this Mount of Salvation, within the fiery and bloody line of these "munitions of rocks," looking back to the dark days of fear and trembling, and to the rapture of relief that came after, we multiply our thanksgivings, and confess our obligations to renew and perfect our personal and social consecration to Thy service and glory.

Oh, had it not been for God! For lo! our enemies, they came unresisted, multitudinous, mighty, flushed with victory, and sure of success. They exulted on our mountains, they revelled in our valleys; they feasted, they rested; they slept, they awaked, they grew stronger, prouder, bolder, every day; they spread abroad, they concentrated here; they looked beyond this horizan to the stores of wealth, to the haunts of pleasure, and to the seats of power in our capital and chief cities. They prepared to cast a chain of Slavery around the form of Freedom, binding life and death together forever. Their premature triumph was the mockery of God and man. One more victory, and all was theirs! But behind these hills was heard the feebler march of a smaller, but still pursuing host. Onward they hurried, day and night, for God and their country. Foot-sore, wayworn, hungry, thirsty, faint—but not in heart—they came to dare all, to bear all, and to do all that is possible to heroes. And Thou didst sustain them! At first they met the blast on the plain, and bent before it like the trees in a storm. But then, led by Thy hand to these hills, they took their stand upon the rocks and remained as firm and immovable as they. In vain were they assaulted. All art, all violence, all desperation, failed to dislodge them.—Baffled, bruised, broken, their enemies recoiled, retired, and disappeared. Glory to God for this rescue! But oh, the slain! In the freshness and fulness of their young and manly life, with such sweet memories of father and mother, brother and sister, wife and children, maiden and friends, they died for us. From the coasts beneath the Eastern star, from the shores of Northern lakes and rivers, from the flowers of Western prairies, and from the homes of the Midway and Border, they came here to die for us and for mankind. Alas, how little we can do for them! We come with the humility of prayer, with the pathetic eloquence of venerable wisdom, with the tender beauty of poetry, with the plaintive harmony of music, with the honest tribute of our Chief Magistrate, and with all this honorable attendance; but our best hope is in thy blessing, O Lord, our God! O Father, bless us! Bless the bereaved, whether present or absent; bless our sick and wounded soldiers and sailors; bless all our rulers and people; bless our army and navy; bless the efforts for the suppression of the rebellion; and bless all the associations of this day and place and scene forever. As the trees are not dead, though their foliage is gone, so our heroes are not dead, though their forms have fallen. In their proper personality they are all with Thee. And the spirit of their example is here. It fills the air; it fills our hearts. And, long as time shall last, it will hover in the skies and rest on this landscape; and the pilgrims of our own land, and from all lands, will thrill with its inspiration, and increase and confirm their devotion to liberty, religion, and God.

Our Father, who art in Heaven, Hallowed be thy name. Thy kingdom come. Thy will be done on earth as it is in Heaven. Give us this day our daily bread. And forgive us our debts, as we forgive our debtors. Lead us not into temptation, but deliver us from evil. For Thine is the kingdom, the power, and the glory, forever. *Amen.*

ADDRESS OF HON. EDWARD EVERETT.

Standing beneath this serene sky, overlooking these broad fields now reposing from the labors of the waning year, the mighty Alleghenies dimly towering before us, the graves of our brethern beneath our feet, it is with hesitation that I raise my poor voice to break the eloquent silence of God and Nature. But the duty to which you have called me must be performed;—grant me, I pray you, your indulgence and your sympathy.

It was appointed by law in Athens, that the obsequies of the citizens who fell in battle should be performed at the public expense, and in the most honorable manner. Their bones were carefully gathered up from the funeral pyre, where their bodies were consumed, and brought home to the city. There, for three days before the interment, they lay in state, beneath tents of honor, to receive the votive offerings of friends and relatives,—flowers, weapons, precious ornaments, painted vases, (wonders of art, which after two thousand years adorn the museums of modern Europe,)—the last tributes of surviving affection. Ten coffins of funeral cypress received the honorable deposit, one for each of the tribes of the city, and an eleventh in memory of the unrecognized, but not therefore unhonored, dead, and of those whose remains could not be recovered. On the fourth day the mournful procession was formed; mothers, wives, sisters, daughters led the way, and to them it was permitted by the simplicity of ancient manners to utter aloud their lamentations for the beloved and the lost; the male relatives and friends of the deceased followed; citizens and strangers closed the train. Thus marshalled, they moved to the place of interment in that famous Ceramicus, the most beautiful suburb of Athens, which had been adorned by Cimon, the son of Miltiades, with walks and fountains and columns,—whose groves were filled with altars, shrines, and temples,—whose gardens were kept forever green by the streams from the neighboring hills, and shaded with the trees sacred to Minerva and coeval with the foundation of the city,—whose circuit enclosed

> "the olive Grove of Academe,
> Plato's retirement, where the Attic bird
> Trilled his thick-warbled note the summer long,"—

whose pathways gleamed with the monuments of the illustrious dead, the work of the most consummate masters that ever gave life to marble. There, beneath the overarching plane-trees, upon a lofty stage erected for the purpose, it was ordained that a funeral oration should be pronounced by some citizen of Athens, in the presence of the assembled multitude.

Such were the tokens of respect required to be paid at Athens to the memory of those who had fallen in the cause of their country. For those alone who fell at Marathon a special honor was reserved. As the battle fought upon that immortal field was distinguished from all others in Grecian history for its influence over the fortunes of Hellas,—as it depended upon the event of that day whether Greece should live, a glory and a light to all coming time, or should expire, like the meteor of a moment; so the honors awarded to its martyr-heroes were such as were bestowed by Athens on no other occasion. They alone of all her sons were entombed upon the spot which they had forever rendered famous. Their names were inscribed upon ten pillars, erected upon the monumental tumulus which covered their ashes,(where after six hundred years, they were read by the traveler Pausanias,) and although the columns, beneath the hand of time and barbaric violence, have long since disappeared, the venerable mound still marks the spot where they fought and fell,—

> "That battle-field where Persia's victim horde
> First bowed beneath the brunt of Hellas' sword."

And shall I, fellow citizens, who, after an interval of twenty-three centuries, a youthful prilgrim from the world unknown to ancient Greece, have wandered over that illustrious plain, ready to put off the shoes from off my feet, as one that stands on holy ground,—who have gazed with respectful emotion on the mound which still protects the dust of those who rolled back the tide of Persian invasion, and rescued the land of popular liberty, of letters, and of arts, from the ruthless foe,—stand unmoved over the graves of our dear brethern, who so lately, on three of those all-important days which decide a nation's history,—days on whose issue it depended whether this august republican Union, founded by some of the wisest statesmen that ever lived, cemented with the blood of some of the purest patriots that ever died, should perish or endure,—rolled back the tide of an invasion, not less unprovoked, not less ruthless, than that which came to plant the dark banner of Asiatic despotism and slavery on the free soil of Greece ? Heaven forbid! And could I prove so insensible to every prompting of patriotic duty and affection, not only would you, fellow citizens, gathered many of you from distant States, who have come to take part in these pious offices of gratitude—you, respected fathers, brethern, matrons, sisters, who surround me—cry out for shame, but the forms of brave and patriotic men who fill these honored graves would heave with indignation beneath the sod.

We have assembled, friends, fellow citizens, at the invitation of the Executive of the great central State of Pennsylvania, seconded by the Governors of seventeen other loyal States of the Union, to pay the last tribute of respect to the brave men, who, in the hard fought battles of the first, second and third days of July last, laid down their lives for the country on these hill sides and the plains before us, and whose remains have been gathered into the Cemetery which we consecrate this day. As my eye ranges over the fields whose sods were so lately moistened by the blood of gallant and loyal men, I feel, as never before, how truly it was said of old, that it is sweet and becoming to die for one's country. I feel as never before, how justly, from the dawn of history to the present time, men have paid the homage of their gratitude and admiration to the memory of those who nobly sacrificed their lives, that their fellow men may live in safety and in honor. And if this tribute were ever due, when, to whom, could it be more justly paid than to those whose last resting place we this day commend to the blessing of Heaven and of men?

For consider, my friends, what would have been the consequences to the country, to yourselves, and to all you hold dear, if those who sleep beneath our feet, and their gallant comrades who survive to serve their country on other fields of danger, had failed in their duty on those memorable days. Consider what, at this moment, would be the condition of the United States, if that noble army of the Potomac, instead of gallantly and for the second time beating back the tide of invasion from Maryland and Pennsylvania, had been itself driven from these well contested heights, thrown back in confusion on Baltimore, or trampled down, discomfited, scattered to the four winds. What, in that sad event, would not have been the fate of the Monumental city, of Harrisburg, of Philadelphia, of Washington, the capital of the Union, each and every one of which would have lain at the mercy of the enemy, accordingly as it might have pleased him, spurred by passion, flushed with victory, and confident of continued success, to direct his course?

For this we must bear in mind, it is one of the great lessons of the war, indeed of every war, that it is impossible for a people without military organization, inhabiting the cities, towns, and villages of an open country, including, of course, the natural proportion of non-combatants of either sex, and of every age, to withstand the inroad of a veteran army. What defence can be made by the inhabitants of villages mostly built of wood, of cities unprotected by walls, nay, by a population of men, however hightoned and resolute, whose aged parents demand their care, whose wives and children are clustering about them, against the charge of the war-horse whose neck is clothed with thunder—against flying artillery and batteries of rifled cannon planted on every commanding eminence—against the onset of trained veterans led by skilful chiefs? No, my friends, army must be met by army, battery by battery, squadron by squadron; and the shock of organized thousands must be encountered by the firm breasts and valiant arms of other thousands, as well organized and as skilfully led. It is no reproach, therefore, to the unarmed population of the country to say, that we owe it to the brave men who sleep in their beds of honor before us, and to their gallant surviving associates, not merely that your fertile fields, my friends of Pennsylvania and Maryland, were redeemed from the presence of the invader, but that your beautiful capitals were not given up to threatened plunder, perhaps laid in ashes, Washington seized by the enemy, and a blow struck at the heart of the nation.

Who that hears me has forgotten the thrill of joy that ran through the country on the 4th of July—auspicious day for the glorious tidings, and rendered still more so by the simultaneous fall of Vicksburg—when the telegraph flashed through the land the assurance from the President of the United States that the army of the Potomac, under General MEADE, had again smitten the invader? Sure I am, that, with the ascriptions of praise that rose to Heaven from twenty millions of freemen, with the acknowledgments that breathed from patriotic lips throughout the length and breadth of America, to the surviving officers and men who had rendered the country this inestimable service, there beat in every loyal bosom a throb of tender and sorrowful gratitude to the martyrs who had fallen on the sternly contested field. Let a nation's fervent thanks make some amends for the toils and sufferings of those who survive. Would that the heartfelt tribute could penetrate these honored graves!

In order that we may comprehend, to their full extent, our obligations to the martyrs and surviving heroes of the army of the Potomac, let us contemplate for a few moments the train of events, which culminated in the battles of the first days of July. Of this stupendous rebellion, planned, as its originators boast, more than thirty years ago, matured and prepared for during an entire generation, finally commenced because, for the first time since the adoption of the Constitution, an election of President had been effected without the votes of the South, (which retained, however, the control of the two other branches of the government,) the occupation of the national capital, with the seizure of the public archives and of the treaties with foreign powers, was an essential feature. This was, in substance, within my personal knowledge, admitted, in the winter of 1860–61, by one of the most influential leaders of the rebellion; and it was fondly thought that this object could be effected by a bold and sudden movement on the 4th of March, 1861. There is abundant proof, also, that a darker project was contemplated, if not by the responsible chiefs of the rebellion, yet by nameless ruffians, willing to play a subsidary and murderous part in the treasonable drama. It was accordingly maintained by the Rebel emissaries in England, in the circles to which they found access, that the new American Minister ought not, when he arrived, to be received as the envoy of the

United States, inasmuch as before that time Washington would be captured, and the capital of the nation and the archives and muniments of the government would be in the possession of the Confederates. In full accordance also with this threat, it was declared, by the Rebel Secretary of War, at Montgomery, in the presence of his Chief and of his colleagues, and of five thousand hearers, while the tidings of the assault on Sumter were traveling over the wires on that fatal 12th of April, 1861, that before the end of May "the flag which then flaunted the breeze," as he expressed it, "would float over the dome of the Capitol at Washington."

At the time this threat was made, the rebellion was confined to the cotton-growing States, and it was well understood by them, that the only hope of drawing any of the other slaveholding States into the conspiracy, was in bringing about a conflict of arms, and "firing the heart of the South" by the effusion of blood. This was declared by the Charleston press, to be the object for which Sumter was to be assaulted; and the emissaries sent from Richmond, to urge on the unhallowed work, gave the promise, that, with the first drop of blood that should be shed, Virginia would place herself by the side of South Carolina.

In pursuance of this orignal plan of the leaders of the rebellion, the capture of Washington has been continually had in view, not merely for the sake of its public buildings, as the capital of the Confederacy, but as the necessary preliminary to the absorption of the border States, and for the moral effect in the eyes of Europe of possessing the metropolis of the Union.

I allude to these facts, not perhaps enough borne in mind, as a sufficient refutation of the pretence, on the part of the Rebels, that the war is one of self-defence, waged for the right of self-government. It is in reality, a war originally levied by ambitious men in the cotton-growing States, for the purpose of drawing the slaveholding border States into the vortex of the conspiracy, first by sympathy—which, in the case of South-Eastern Virginia, North Carolina, part of Tennessee and Arkansas, succeeded—and then by force and for the purpose of subjugating Maryland, Western Virginia, Kentucky, Eastern Tennessee and Missouri; and it is a most extraordinary fact, considering the clamors of the Rebel chiefs on the subject of invasion, that not a soldier of the United States has entered the States last named, except to defend their Union-loving inhabitants from the armies and guerillas of the Rebels.

In conformity with these designs on the city of Washington, and notwithstanding the disastrous results of the invasion of 1862, it was determined by the Rebel Government last summer to resume the offensive in that direction. Unable to force the passage of the Rappahannock, where General HOOKER, notwithstanding the reverse at Chancellorsville, in May, was strongly posted, the Confederate general resorted to strategy. He had two objects in view. The first was by a rapid movement northward, and by manœuvering with a portion of his army on the east side of the Blue Ridge, to tempt HOOKER from his base of operations, thus leading him to uncover the approaches to Washington, to throw it open to a raid by STUART's cavalry, and to enable LEE himself to cross the Potomac in the neighborhood of Poolesville and thus fall upon the capital. This plan of operations was wholly frustrated. The design of the Rebel general was promptly discovered by General HOOKER, and, moving with great rapidity from Fredericksburg, he preserved unbroken the inner line, and stationed the various corps of his army at all the points protecting the approach to Washington, from Centreville up to Leesburg. From this vantage-ground the Rebel general in vain attempted to draw him. In the mean time, by the vigorous operations of PLEASANTON's cavalry, the cavalry of STUART, though greatly superior in numbers, was so crippled as to be disabled from performing the part assigned it in the campaign. In this manner, General LEE's first object, namely, the defeat of HOOKER's army on the south of the Potomac and a direct march on Washington, was baffled.

The second part of the Confederate plan, which is supposed to have been undertaken in opposition to the views of General LEE, was to turn the demonstration northward into a real invasion of Maryland and Pennsylvania, in the hope, that, in this way, General HOOKER would be drawn to a distance from the capital, and that some opportunity would occur of taking him at disadvantage, and, after defeating his army, of making a descent upon Baltimore and Washington. This part of General LEE's plan, which was substantially the repetition of that of 1862, was not less signally defeated, with what honor to the arms of the Union the heights on which we are this day assembled will forever attest.

Much time had been uselessly consumed by the Rebel general in his unavailing attempts to out-manœuvre General HOOKER. Although General LEE broke up from Fredericksburg on the 3d of June, it was not till the 24th that the main body of his army entered Maryland. Instead of crossing the Potomac, as he had intended, east of the Blue Ridge, he was compelled to do it at Shepherdstown and Williamsport, thus materially deranging his entire plan of campaign north of the river. STUART, who had been sent with his cavalry to the east of the Blue Ridge, to guard the passes of the mountains, to mask the movements of LEE, and to harass the Union general in crossing the river, having been severely handled by PLEASANTON at Beverly Ford, Aldie, and Upperville, instead of being able to retard General HOOKER's advance, was driven himself away from his connection with the army of LEE, and cut off for a fortnight from all communication with it—a circumstance to which General LEE, in his report, alludes more than once, with evident displeasnre. Let us now rapidly glance at the incidents of the eventful campaign.

A detachment from EWELL's corps, under JENKINS, had penetrated, on the 15th of June, as far as Chambersburg. This movement was intended at first merely as a demonstration, and as a marauding expedition for supplies. It had, however, the salutary effect of alarming the country; and vigorous preparations were made, not only by the General Government, but here in Pennsylvania and in the sister States, to repel the inroad. After two days passed at Chambersburg, JENKINS, anxious for his communications with EWELL, fell back with his plunder to Hagerstown. Here he remained for several days, and then having swept the recesses of the Cumberland valley, came down upon the eastern flank of the South mountain, and pushed his marauding parties as far as Waynesboro'. On the 22d, the remainder of EWELL's corps crossed the river and moved up the valley. They were followed on the 24th by LONGSTREET and HILL, who crossed at Williamsport and Sheperdstown, and pushing up the valley, encamped at Chambersburg on the 27th. In this way the whole rebel army, estimated at 90,000 infantry, upwards of 10,000 cavalry, and 4,000 or 5,000 artillery, making a total of 105,000 of all arms, was concentrated in Pennsylvania.

Up to this time no report of HOOKER's movements had been received by General LEE, who, having been deprived of his cavalry, had no means of obtaining information. Rightly judging, however, that no time would be lost by the Union army in the pursuit, in order to detain it on the eastern side of the mountains in Maryland and Pennsylvania, and thus preserve his communications by the way of Williamsport, he had, before his own arrival at Chambersburg, directed EWELL to send detachments from his corps to Carlisle and York. The latter detachment, under EARLY, passed through this place on the 26th of June. You need not, fellow citizens of Gettysburg, that I should recall to you those moments of alarm and distress, precursors as they were of the more trying scenes which were so soon to follow.

As soon as Gen. HOOKER preceived that the advance of the Confederates into the Cumberland valley was not a mere feint to draw him away from Washington, he moved rapidly in pursuit. Attempts, as we have seen, were made to harass and retard his passage across the Potomac. These attempts were not only altogether unsuccessful, but were so unskilfully made as to place the entire Federal army between the cavalry of STUART and the army of LEE. While the latter was massed in the Cumberland valley, STUART was east of the mountains, with HOOKER's army between, and GREGG's cavalry in close pursuit. STUART was accordingly compelled to force a march northward, which was destitute of strategical character, and which deprived his chief of all means of obtaining intelligence.

Not a moment had been lost by General HOOKER in the pursuit of LEE. The day after the Rebel army entered Maryland, the Union army crossed the Potomac at Edward's Ferry, and by the 28th of June lay between Harper's Ferry and Frederick. The force of the enemy on that day was partly at Chambersburg, and partly moving on the Cashtown road in the direction of Gettysburg, while the detachments from EWELL'S corps, of which mention has been made, had reached the Susquehanna opposite Harrisburg and Columbia. That a great battle must soon be fought, no one could doubt; but in the apparent and perhaps real absence of plan on the part of LEE, it was impossible to foretell the precise scene of the encounter. Wherever fought, consequences the most momentous hung upon the result.

In this critical and anxious state of affairs, General HOOKER was relieved, and General MEADE was summoned to the chief command of the army. It appears to my unmilitary judgment to reflect the highest credit upon him, upon his predecessor, and upon the corps commanders of the army of the Potomac, that a change could take place in the chief command of so large a force on the eve of a general battle—the various corps necessarily moving on lines somewhat divergent, and all in ignorance of the enemy's intended point of concentration—and that not an hour's hesitation should ensue in the advance of any portion of the entire army.

Having assumed the chief command on the 28th, General MEADE directed his left wing, under REYNOLDS, upon Emmitsburg, and his right upon New Windsor, leaving General FRENCH with 11,000 men to protect the Baltimore and Ohio railroad, and convoy the public property from Harper's Ferry to Washington. BUFORD'S cavalry was then at this place, and KILPATRICK'S at Hanover, where he encountered and defeated the rear of STUART'S cavalry, who was roving the country in search of the main army of LEE. On the Rebel side, HILL had reached Fayetteville on the Cashtown road on the 28th, and was followed on the same road by LONGSTREET on the 29th. The eastern side of the mountain, as seen from Gettysburg, was lighted up at night by the camp-fires of the enemy's advance, and the country swarmed with his foraging parties. It was now too evident to be questioned, that the thunder-cloud, so long gathering blackness, would soon burst on some part of the devoted vicinity of Gettysburg.

The 30th of June was a day of important preparation. At half-past eleven o'clock in the morning, General BUFORD passed through Gettysburg, upon a reconnoissance in force, with his cavalry, upon the Chambersburg road. The information obtained by him was immediately communicated to General REYNOLDS, who was, in consequence, directed to occupy Gettysburg. That gallant officer accordingly, with the First Corps, marched from Emmitsburg to within six or seven miles of this place, and encamped on the right bank of Marsh's creek. Our right wing, meantime, was moved to

Manchester. On the same day the corps of HILL and LONGSTREET were pushed still further forward on the Chambersburg road, and distributed in the vicinity of Marsh's creek, while a reconnoissance was made by the Confederate General PETTIGREW up to a very short distance from this place.—Thus at nightfall, on the 30th of June, the greater part of the Rebel force was concentrated in the immediate vicinity of two corps of the Union army, the former refreshed by two days passed in comparative repose and deliberate preparation for the encounter, the latter separated by a march of one or two days from their supporting corps, and doubtful at what precise point they were to expect an attack.

And now the momentous day, a day to be forever remembered in the annals of the country, arrived. Early in the morning, on the 1st of July, the conflict began. I need not say that it would be impossible for me to comprise, within the limits of the hour, such a narrative as would do anything like full justice to the all-important events of these three great days, or to the merit of the brave officers and men, of every rank, of every arm of the service, and of every loyal State, who bore their part in the tremendous struggle—alike those who nobly sacrificed their lives for their country, and those who survive, many of them scarred with honorable wounds, the objects of our admiration and gratitude. The astonishingly minute, accurate, and graphic accounts contained in the journals of the day, prepared from personal observation by reporters who witnessed the scenes, and often shared the perils which they describe, and the highly valuable "notes" of Professor JACOBS, of the University in this place, to which I am greatly indebted, will abundantly supply the deficiency of my necessarily too condensed statement.*

---

* Besides the sources of information mentioned in the text, I have been kindly favored with a memorandum of the operations of the three days, drawn up for me by direction of Major General MEADE, (anticipating the promulgation of his official report,) by one of his aids, Colonel THEODORE LYMAN, from whom, also, I have received other important communications relative to the campaign. I have received very valuable documents relative to the battle from Major General HALLECK, Commander-in Chief of the army, and have been much assisted in drawing up the sketch of the campaign, by the detailed reports, kindly transmitted to me in manuscript from the Adjutant General's office, of the movements of every corps of the army, for each day, after the breaking up from Fredericksburg commenced. I have derived much assistance from Colonel JOHN B. BACHELDER's oral explanations of his beautiful and minute drawing (about to be engraved) of the field of the three days' struggle. With the information derived from these sources, I have compared the statements in General LEE's official report of the campaign, dated 31st July, 1863, a well-written article, purporting to be an account of the three days' battle, in the *Richmond Enquirer* of the 22d of July, and the article on "The Battle of Gettysburg and the Campaign of Pennsylvania," by an officer, apparently a colonel in the British army, in *Blackwood's Magazine* for September. The value of the information contained in this last essay may be seen by comparing the remark under date 27th June, that "private property is to

General REYNOLDS, on arriving at Gettysburg, in the morning of the 1st, found BUFORD with his cavalry warmly engaged with the enemy, whom he held most gallantly in check. Hastening himself to the front, General REYNOLDS directed his men to be moved over the fields from the Emmitsburg road, in front of M'MILLAN's and Dr. SCHMUCKER'S, under cover of the Seminary Ridge. Without a moment's hesitation, he attacked the enemy, at the same time sending orders to the Eleventh Corps (General HOWARD's) to advance as promptly as possible. General REYNOLDS immediately found himself engaged with a force which greatly outnumbered his own, and had scarcely made his dispositions for the action when he fell, mortally wounded, at the head of his advance. The command of the First Corps devolved on General DOUBLEDAY, and that of the field on General HOWARD, who arrived at 11.30, with SCHURZ's and BARLOW's divisions of the Eleventh Corps, he latter of whom received a severe wound. Thus strengthened, the advantage of the battle was for some time on our side. The attacks of the Rebels were vigorously repulsed by WADSWORTH's division of the First Corps, and a large number of prisoners, including General ARCHER, were captured. At length, however, the continued reinforcement of the Confederates from the main body in the neighborhood, and by the divisions of RODES and EARLY, coming down by separate lines from Heidlersberg and taking post on our extreme right, turned the fortunes of the day. Our army, after contesting the ground for five hours, was obliged to yield to the enemy, whose force outnumbered them two to one; and toward the close of the afternoon General HOWARD deemed it prudent to withdraw the two corps to the heights where we are now assembled. The greater part of the First Corps passed through the outskirts of the town, and reached the hill without serious loss or molestation. The Eleventh Corps and portions of the First, not being

be rigidly protected," with the statement in the next sentence but one, that "all the cattle and farm horses having been seized by EWELL, farm labor had come to a complete stand still." He, also, under date of 4th July, speaks of LEE's retreat being encumbered by "EWELL's *immense train of plunder.*" This writer informs us, that, on the evening of the 4th of July, he heard "reports coming in from the different *Generals*, that the enemy [MEADE's army] was *retiring*, and had been doing so all day long." At a consultation at head-quarters on the 6th, between Generals LEE, LONGSTREET, HILL, and WILCOX, this writer was told by some one, whose name he prudently leaves in blank, that the army had no intention, at present, of retreating for good, and that some of the enemy's dispatches had been intercepted, in which the following words occur: "The noble, but unfortunate army of the Potomac has again been obliged to retreat before superior numbers!" He does not appear to be aware, that in recording these wretched expedients, resorted to in order to keep up the spirits of LEE's army, he furnishes the most complete refutation of his own account of its good condition. I much regret that General MEADE's official report was not published in season to enable me to take full advantage of it, in preparing the brief sketch of the battles of the three days contained in this address. It reached me but the morning before it was sent to the press.

aware that the enemy had already entered the town from the north, attempted to force their way through Washington and Baltimore streets, which, in the crowd and confusion of the scene, they did with a heavy loss in prisoners.

General HOWARD was not unprepared for this turn in the fortunes of the day. He had, in the course of the morning, caused Cemetery Hill to be occupied by General STEINWEHR, with the second division of the Eleventh Corps. About the time of the withdrawal of our troops to the hill, General HANCOCK arrived, having been sent by General MEADE, on hearing of the death of REYNOLDS, to assume the command of the field till he himself could reach the front. In conjunction with General HOWARD, General HANCOCK immediately proceeded to post the troops and to repel an attack on our right flank. This attack was feebly made and promptly repulsed. At nightfall, our troops on the hill, who had so gallantly sustained themselves during the toil and peril of the day, were cheered by the arrival of General SLOCUM with the Twelfth Corps and of General SICKLES with a part of the Third.

Such was the fortunes of the first day, commencing with decided success to our arms, followed by a check, but ending in the occupation of this all-important position. To you, fellow citizens of Gettysburg, I need not attempt to portray the anxieties of the ensuing night. Witnessing, as you had done with sorrow, the withdrawal of our army through your streets, with a considerable loss of prisoners—mourning as you did over the brave men who had fallen—shocked with the wide-spread desolation around you, of which the wanton burning of the Harman House had given the signal—ignorant of the near approach of General MEADE, you passed the weary hours of the night in painful expectation.

Long before the dawn of the 2d of July, the new Commander-in-Chief had reached the ever-memorable field of service and glory. Having received intelligence of the events in progress, and informed by the reports of Generals HANCOCK and HOWARD of the favorable character of the positions, he determined to give battle to the enemy at this point. He accordingly directed the remaining corps of the army to concentrate at Gettysburg with all possible expedition, and breaking up his head-quarters at Taneytown at ten P. M., he arrived at the front at one o'clock in the morning of the 2d of July. Few were the moments given to sleep, during the rapid watches of that brief midsummer's night, by officers or men, though half of our troops were exhausted by the conflict of the day, and the residue wearied by the forced marches which had brought them to the rescue. The full moon, veiled by thin clouds, shone down that night on a strangely unwonted scene. The silence of the grave-yard was broken by the heavy tramp of armed men, by the neigh of the war-horse, the harsh rattle of the wheels of artillery hurrying to their stations, and all the indescribable tumult of preparation. The various corps of the army, as they arrived, were moved to their positions,

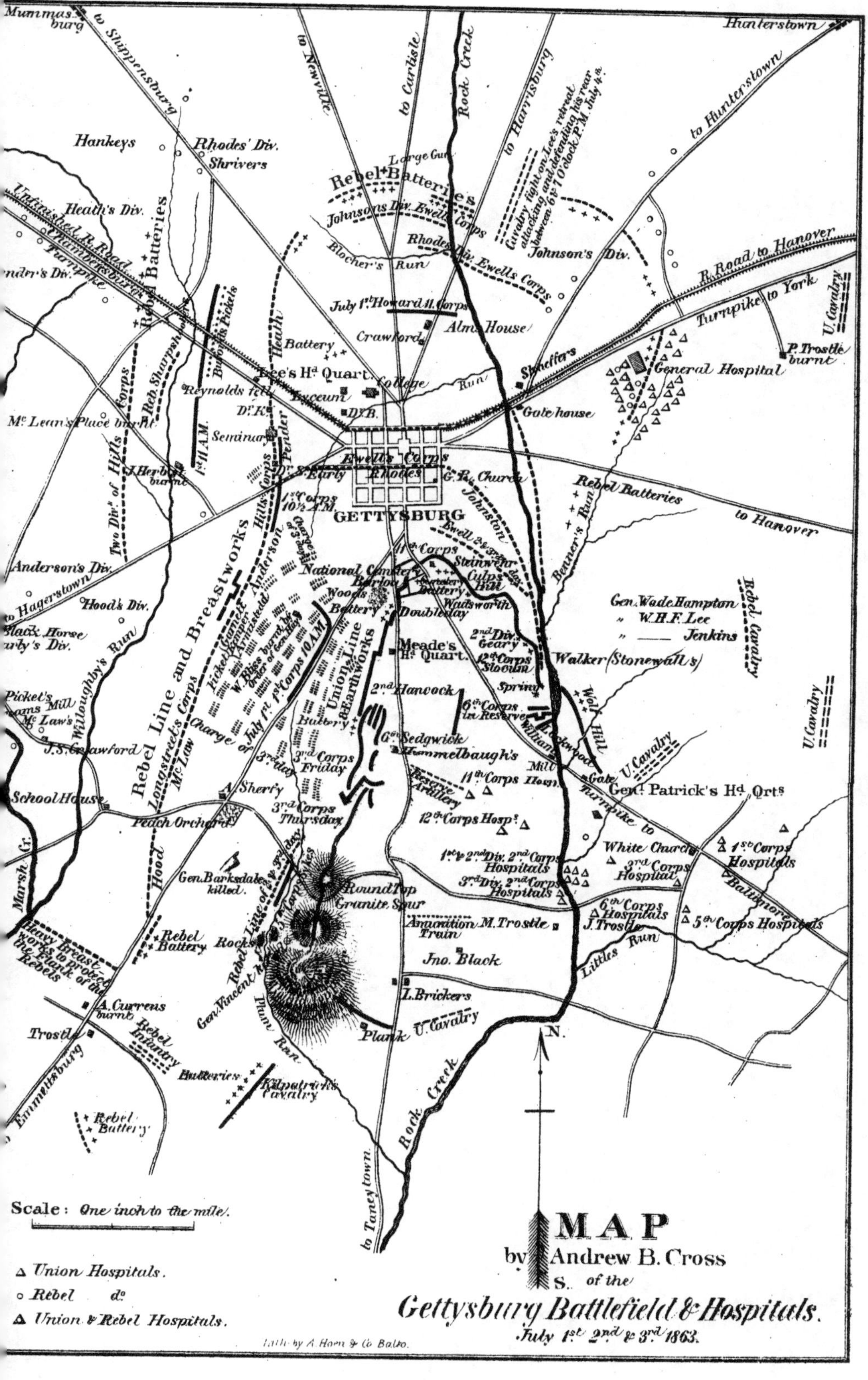
Mummasburg
to Shippensburg
to Newville
to Carlisle
Rock Creek
to Harrisburg
Hunterstown
to Hunterstown
Hankeys
Rhodes' Div.
Shrivers
Large Gun
Rebel Batteries
Johnsons Div. Ewells Corps
Cavalry fight on Lee's retreat attacking and defending his rear between 6 & 7 O'clock P.M. July 4th.
Heath's Div.
Unfinished R. Road
Chambersburg Turnpike
Rebel Batteries
Rhodes Div. Ewells Corps
Blocher's Run
Johnson's Div.
R. Road to Hanover
Turnpike to York
U. Cavalry
July 1st Howard 11. Corps
Crawford
Alms House
Heath
Battery
Buford's Pickets
Reb. Sharpshooters
Lee's Hd. Quart.
College
Run
Sheffers
General Hospital
P. Trostle burnt
Reynolds fell
Lyceum
Dr. K.
Dr. B.
Gate house
Mc Lean's Place burnt
Seminary
1st H.A.M.
Pender
Ewell's Corps
Rhodes
Early
G. R. Church
J. Herbst burnt
Two Div. of Hills Corps
Hills Corps
1st Corps 10½ A.M.
GETTYSBURG
Johnston
Rebel Batteries
Benner's Run
to Hanover
Rebel Line and Breastworks
Anderson
Ewell 2 & 3 day
11th Corps
Steinwehr
Culps Hill
National Cemetery
Barlow
Anderson's Div.
to Hagerstown
Hood's Div.
Woods
Battery
Doubleday
Wadsworth
Gen. Wade Hampton
" W.H.F. Lee
" —— Jenkins
Rebel Cavalry
Black Horse
Early's Div.
Willoughby's Run
Pickett
Garnett
Kemper
Armistead
W. Bliss burnt by order of Gen. Hays
1st Corps 10 A.M.
July 1st
Union Line & Earthworks
Meade's Hd. Quart.
2nd Div. Geary
12th Corps Slocum
Walker (Stonewall's)
Spring
Wolf Hill
Pickets
Mc Laws
Longstreet's Corps
Charge
2nd Hancock
6th Corps in Reserve
Battery
G. Sedgwick
Hummelbaugh's
J.S. Crawford
Mc Law
3rd day
3rd Corps Friday
Reserve Artillery
11th Corps
Mill
Hosp.
U. Cavalry
Gate
Gen. Patrick's Hd. Qrts.
U. Cavalry
School House
A. Sherfy
Peach Orchard
3rd Corps Thursday
12th Corps Hosp.
Turnpike to
White Church
1st Corps Hospitals
Marsh Cr.
Hood
Gen. Barksdale killed
Round Top
Granite Spur
1st & 2nd Div. 2nd Corps Hospitals
3rd Div. 2nd Corps Hospitals
3rd Corps Hospital
Baltimore
Heavy Breast works to protect the Flank of the Rebels
Rebel Battery
Rocks
Rebel Line of 2nd & 3rd day
Ammunition Train
M. Trostle
6th Corps Hospitals
J. Trostle
5th Corps Hospitals
Littles Run
Jno. Black
Gen. Vincent killed
A. Currens burnt
L. Brickers
Trostle
Rebel Infantry
Plum Run
Plank
U. Cavalry
N.
to Emmettsburg
Batteries
Kilpatrick's Cavalry
Rebel Battery
Rock Creek
to Taneytown
Scale: One inch to the mile.
△ Union Hospitals.
○ Rebel do.
▲ Union & Rebel Hospitals.
MAP
by Andrew B. Cross
of the
Gettysburg Battlefield & Hospitals.
July 1st 2nd & 3rd 1863.
Lith. by A. Hoen & Co. Balto.

on the spot where we are assembled and the ridges that extend south-east and south-west; batteries were planted and breastworks thrown up. The Second and Fifth Corps, with the rest of the Third, had reached the ground by seven o'clock, A. M.; but it was not till two o'clock in the afternoon that SEDGWICK arrived with the Sixth Corps. He had marched thirty-four miles since nine o'clock on the evening before. It was only on his arrival that the Union army approached an equality of numbers with that of the Rebels, who were posted upon the opposite and parallel ridge, distant from a mile to a mile and a half, overlapping our position on either wing, and probably exceeding by ten thousand the army of General MEADE.*

And here I cannot but remark on the providential inaction of the Rebel army. Had the contest been renewed by it at daylight on the 2d of July, with the First and Eleventh Corps exhausted by the battle and the retreat, the Third and Twelfth weary from their forced march, and the Second, Fifth and Sixth not yet arrived, nothing but a miracle could have saved the army from a great disaster. Instead of this, the day dawned, the sun rose, the cool hours of the morning passed, the forenoon and a considerable part of the afternoon wore away, without the slightest aggressive movement on the part of the enemy. Thus time was given for half of our forces to arrive and take their place in the lines, while the rest of the army enjoyed a much needed half day's repose.

At length, between three and four o'clock in the afternoon, the work of death began. A signal gun from the hostile batteries was followed by a tremendous cannonade along the Rebel lines, and this by a heavy advance of infantry, brigade after brigade, commencing on the enemy's right against the left of our army, and so onward to the left centre. A forward movement of General SICKLES, to gain a commanding position from which to repel the Rebel attack, drew upon him a destructive fire from the enemy's batteries, and a furious assault from LONGSTREET'S and HILL'S advancing troops. After a brave resistance on the part of his corps, he was forced back, himself falling severely wounded. This was the critical moment of the second day; but the Fifth and part of the Sixth Corps, with portions of the First and Second, were promptly brought to the support of the Third. The struggle was fierce and murderous, but by sunset our success was decisive, and the enemy was driven back in confusion. The most important service was rendered towards the close of the day, in the memorable advance between

* In the Address as originally prepared, judging from the best sources of information then within my reach, I assumed the equality of the two armies on the 2d and 3d of July. Subsequent inquiry has led me to think that I underrated somewhat the strength of LEE'S force at Gettysburg, and I have corrected the text accordingly. General HALLECK, however, in his official report accompanying the President's messages, states the armies to have been equal.

Round Top and Little Round Top, by General CRAWFORD's division of the Fifth Corps, consisting of two brigades of the Pennsylvania Reserves, of which one company was from this town and neighborhood. The Rebel force was driven back with great loss in killed and prisoners. At eight o'clock in the evening a desperate attempt was made by the enemy to storm the position of the Eleventh Corps on Cemetery Hill; but here, too, after a terrible conflict, he was repulsed with immense loss. EWELL, on our extreme right, which had been weakened by the withdrawal of the troops sent over to support our left, had succeeded in gaining a foothold within a portion of our lines, near Spangler's spring. This was the only advantage obtained by the Rebels to compensate them for the disasters of the day, and of this, as we shall see, they were soon deprived.

Such was the result of the second act of this eventful drama,—a day hard fought, and at one moment anxious, but, with the exception of the slight reverse just named, crowned with dearly earned but uniform success to our arms, auspicious of a glorious termination of the final struggle. On these good omens the night fell.

In the course of the night, General GEARY returned to his position on the right, from which he had hastened the day before to strengthen the Third Corps. He immediately engaged the enemy, and, after a sharp and decisive action, drove them out of our lines, recovering the ground which had been lost on the preceding day. A spirited contest was kept up all the morning on this part of the line; but General GEARY, reinforced by WHEATON's brigade of the Sixth Corps, maintained his position, and inflicted very severe losses on the Rebels.

Such was the cheering commencement of the third day's work, and with it ended all serious attempts of the enemy on our right. As on the preceding day, his efforts were now mainly directed against our left centre and left wing. From eleven till half-past one o'clock, all was still—a solemn pause of preparation, as if both armies were nerving themselves for the supreme effort. At length the awful silence, more terrible than the wildest tumult of battle, was broken by the roar of two hundred and fifty pieces of artillery from the opposite ridges, joining in a cannonade of unsurpassed violence—the Rebel batteries along two-thirds of their line pouring their fire upon Cemetery Hill, and the centre and left wing of our army. Having attempted in this way for two hours, but without success, to shake the steadiness of our lines, the enemy rallied his forces for a last grand assault. Their attack was principally directed against the position of our Second Corps. Successive lines of Rebel infantry moved forward with equal spirit and steadiness from their cover on the wooded crest of Seminary Ridge, crossing the intervening plain, and, supported right and left by their choicest brigades, charged furiously up to our batteries. Our own brave troops of the Second Corps, supported by DOUBLEDAY's division and STANNARD's brigade of the First, received the shock with firmness; the ground on both sides was long and fiercely contested, and was covered with the killed and the wounded; the tide of battle flowed and ebbed across the plain, till, after "a determined and gallant struggle;" as it is pronounced by General LEE, the Rebel advance, consisting of two-thirds of HILL's corps and the whole of LONGSTREET's—including PICKETT's division, the *elite* of his corps, which had not yet been under fire, and was now depended upon to decide the fortune of this last eventful day—was driven back with prodigious slaughter, discomfitted and broken. While these events were in progress at our left centre, the enemy was driven, with a considerable loss of prisoners, from a strong position on our extreme left, from which he was annoying our force on Little Round Top. In the terrific assault on our centre, Generals HANCOCK and GIBBON were wounded. In the Rebel army, Generals ARMISTEAD, KEMPER, PETTIGREW and TRIMBLE were wounded, the first named mortally, the latter also made prisoner, General GARNETT was killed, and thirty-five hundred officers and men made prisoners.

These were the expiring agonies of the three days' conflict, and with them the battle ceased. It was fought by the Union army with courage and skill, from the first cavalry skirmish on Wednesday morning to the fearful route of the enemy on Friday afternoon, by every arm and every rank of the service, by officers and men, by cavalry, artillery, and infantry. The superiority of numbers was with the enemy, who were led by the ablest commanders in their service; and if the Union force had the advantage of a strong position, the Confederates had that of choosing time and place, the prestige of former victories over the army of the Potomac, and of the success of the first day. Victory does not always fall to the lot of those who deserve it; but that so decisive a triumph, under circumstances like these, was gained by our troops, I would ascribe, under Providence, to the spirit of exalted patriotism that animated them, and the consciousness that they were fighting in a righteous cause.

All hope of defeating our army, and securing what General LEE calls "the valuable results" of such an achievement, having vanished, he thought only of rescuing from destruction the remains of his shattered forces. In killed, wounded and missing, he had, as far as can be ascertained, suffered a loss of about 37,000 men—rather more than a third of the army with which he is supposed to have marched into Pennsylvania. Perceiving that his only safety was in rapid retreat, he commenced withdrawing his troops at daybreak on the 4th, throwing up field works in front of our left, which, assuming the appearance of a new position, were intended probably to protect the rear of his army in their retreat. That day—sad celebration of the 4th of July for an army of Americans—was passed by him in hurrying off his trains. By nightfall, the main army was in full retreat upon the Cashtown and Fairfield roads, and it moved with such precipitation, that, short as the nights were, by day-light the following morning, notwithstanding a heavy rain, the rear guard had left its position. The struggle of the last two days resembled, in many respects, the battle of Waterloo; and if, in the evening of the third day, General MEADE, like the Duke of WELLINGTON, had had the assistance of a powerful auxiliary army to take up the pursuit, the route of the Rebels would have been as complete as that of NAPOLEON.

Owing to the circumstances just named, the intentions of the enemy were not apparent on the 4th. The moment his retreat was discovered, the following morning, he was pursued by our cavalry on the Cashtown road and through the Emmitsburg and Monterey passes, and by SEDGWICK's corps on the Fairfield road. His rear guard was briskly attacked at Fairfield; a great number of wagons and ambulances were captured in the passes of the mountains; the country swarmed with his stragglers, and his wounded were literally emptied from the vehicles containing them into the farm houses on the road. General LEE, in his report, makes repeated mention of the Union prisoners whom he conveyed into Virginia, somewhat overstating their number. He states, also, that "such of his wounded as were in a condition to be removed" were forwarded to Williamsport. He does not mention that the number of his wounded *not* removed, and left to the Christian care of the victors, was 7,540, not one of whom failed of any attention which it was possible, under the circumstances of the case, to afford them, not one of whom, certainly, has been put upon Libby prison fare—lingering death by starvation. Heaven forbid, however, that we should claim any merit for the exercise of common humanity.

Under the protection of the mountain ridge, whose narrow passes are easily held even by a retreating army, General LEE reached Williamsport in safety, and took up a strong position opposite to that place. General MEADE necessarily pursued with the main army by a flank movement through Middletown, Turner's Pass, having been secured by General FRENCH. Passing through the South mountain, the Union army came up with that of the Rebels on the 12th, and found it securely posted on the heights of Marsh run. The position was reconnoitred, and preparations made for an attack on the 13th. The depth of the river, swollen by the recent rains, authorized the expectation that the enemy would be brought to a general engagement the following day. An advance was accordingly made by General MEADE on the morning of the 14th; but it was soon found that the Rebels had escaped in the night, with such haste that EWELL's corps forded the river where the water was breast-high. The cavalry, which had rendered the most important services during the three days, and in harassing the enemy's retreat, was now sent in pursuit, and captured two guns and a large number of prisoners. In an action which took place at Falling Waters, Gen. PETTIGREW was mortally wounded. General MEADE, in further pursuit of the Rebels, crossed the Potomac at Berlin. Thus again covering the approaches to Washington, he compelled the enemy to pass the Blue Ridge at one of the upper gaps; and in about six weeks from the commencement of the campaign, General LEE found himself again on the south side of the Rappahannock, with the probable loss of about a third part of his army.

Such, most inadequately recounted, is the history of the ever-memorable three days, and of the events immediately preceding and following. It has been pretended, in order to diminish the magnitude of this disaster to the Rebel cause, that it was merely the repulse of an attack on a strongly defended position. The tremendous losses on both sides are a sufficient answer to this misrepresentation, and attest the courage and obstinacy with which the three days' battle was waged. Few of the great conflicts of modern times have cost victors and vanquished so great a sacrifice. On the Union side there fell, in the whole campaign, of generals killed, REYNOLDS, WEED and ZOOK, and wounded, BARLOW, BARNES, BUTTERFIELD, DOUBLEDAY, GIBBON, GRAHAM, HANCOCK, SICKLES and WARREN; while of officers below the rank of General, and men, there were 2,834 killed, 13,709 wounded, and 6,643 missing. On the Confederate side, there were killed on the field or mortally wounded, Generals ARMISTEAD, BARKSDALE, GARNETT, PENDER, PETTIGREW and SEMMES, and wounded, HETH, HOOD, JOHNSON, KEMPER, KIMBALL and TRIMBLE. Of officers below the rank of general, and men, there were taken prisoners, including the wounded, 13,621, an amount ascertained officially. Of the wounded in a condition to be removed, of the killed and the missing, the enemy has made no return. They are estimated, from the best data which the nature of the case admits, at 23,000. General MEADE also captured 3 cannon, and 41 standards; and 24,978 small arms were collected on the battle-field.

I must leave to others, who can do it from personal observation, to describe the mournful spectacle presented by these hill-sides and plains at the close of the terrible conflict. It was a saying of the Duke of WELLINGTON, that next to a defeat, the saddest thing was a victory. The horrors of the battle field, after the contest is over, the sights and sounds of woe,—let me throw a pall over the scene, which no words can adequately depict to those who have not witnessed it, on which no one who has witnessed it, and who has a heart in his bosom, can bear to dwell. One drop of balm alone, one drop of heavenly, life-giving balm, mingles in this bitter cup of misery. Scarcely has the cannon ceased to roar, when the brethren and sisters of Christian benevolence, ministers of compassion, angles of pity, hasten to the field and the hospital, to moisten the parched tongue, to bind the ghastly wounds, to soothe the parting agonies alike of friend and foe, and to catch the last whispered messages of love from dying lips. "Carry this miniature back to my dear wife, but do not take it from my bosom till I am gone." "Tell my little sister not to grieve for me; I am willing to die for my country." "Oh, that my mother were here!" When, since AARON stood between the living and the dead, was there ever so gracious a ministry as this? It has been said that it is characteristic of Americans to treat women with a deference not paid to them in any other country. I will not undertake to say whether this is so; but I will say, that, since this terrible war has been waged, the women of the loyal States, if never before, have entitled themselves to our highest admiration and gratitude,—alike those who at home, often with fingers unused to the toil, often bowed beneath their own domestic cares, have performed an amount of daily labor not exceeded by those who work for their daily bread, and those who, in the hospital and the tents of the Sanitary and Christian Commissions, have rendered services which millions could not buy. Happily, the labor and the service are their own reward. Thousands of matrons and thousands of maidens have experienced a delight in these homely toils and services, compared with which the pleasures of the ball room and the opera house are tame and unsatisfactory. This, on earth, is reward enough, but a richer is in store for them. Yes, brothers, sisters of charity, while you bind up the wounds of the poor sufferers—the humblest, perhaps, that have shed their blood for the country—forget not WHO it is that will hereafter say to you, "Inasmuch as ye have done it unto one of the least of these my BRETHREN, ye have done it unto me."

And now, friends, fellow citizens, as we stand among these honored graves, the momentous question presents itself: Which of the two parties to the war is responsible for all this suffering, for this dreadful sacrifice of life, the lawful and constitutional government of the United States, or the ambitious men who have rebelled against it? I say "rebelled" against it, although Earl RUSSELL, the British Secretary of State for Foreign Affairs, in his recent temperate and conciliatory speech in Scotland, seems to intimate that no prejudice ought to attach to that word, inasmuch as our English forefathers rebelled against CHARLES I. and JAMES II., and our American fathers rebelled against GEORGE III. These, certainly, are venerable precedents, but they prove only that it is just and proper to rebel against oppressive governments. They do not prove that it was just and proper for the son of JAMES II. to rebel against GEORGE I., or his grandson CHARLES EDWARD to rebel against GEORGE II.; nor, as it seems to me, ought these dynastic struggles, little better than family quarrels, to be compared with this monstrous conspiracy against the American Union. These precedents do not prove that it was just and proper for the "disappointed great men" of the cotton-growing States to rebel against "the most beneficent government of which history gives us any account," as the Vice President of the Confederacy, in November, 1860, charged them with doing. They do not create a presumption even in favor of the disloyal slaveholders of the South, who, living under a government of which Mr. JEFFERSON DAVIS, in the session of 1860–61, said that it "was the best government ever instituted by man, unexceptionably administered, and under which the people have been prosperous beyond comparison with any other people whose career has been recorded in history," rebelled against it because their aspiring politicians, himself among the rest, were in danger of losing their monopoly of its offices.—What would have been thought by an impartial posterity of the American rebellion against GEORGE III., if the colonists had at all times been more than equally represented in parliament, and JAMES OTIS, and PATRICK HENRY, and WASHINGTON, and FRANKLIN, and the ADAMSES, and HANCOCK, and JEFFERSON, and men of their stamp, had for two generations enjoyed the confidence of the sovereign and administered the government of the empire? What would have been thought of the rebellion against CHARLES I., if CROMWELL, and the men of his school, had been the responsible advisers of that prince from his accession to the throne, and then, on account of a partial change in the ministry, had brought his head to the block, and involved the country in a desolating war, for the sake of dismembering it and establishing a new government south of the Trent? What would have been thought of the Whigs of 1688, if they had themselves composed the cabinet of JAMES II., and been the advisers of the measures and the promoters of the policy which drove him into exile? The Puritans of 1640, and the Whigs of 1688, rebelled against arbitrary power in order to establish constitutional liberty. If they had risen against CHARLES and JAMES because those monarchs favored equal rights, and in order themselves, "for the first time in the history of the world," to establish an oligarchy "founded on the corner-stone of slavery," they would truly have furnished a precedent for the Rebels of the South, but their cause would not have been sustained by the eloquence of PYM, or of SOMERS, nor sealed with the blood of HAMPDEN or RUSSELL.

I call the war which the Confederates are waging against the Union a "rebellion," because it is one, and in grave matters it is best to call things by their right names. I speak of it as a crime, because the Constitution of the United States so regards it, and puts "rebellion" on a par with "invasion." The Constitution and law not only of England, but of every civilized country, regard them in the same light; or rather they consider the rebel in arms as far worse than the alien enemy. To levy war against the United States is the constitutional definition of treason, and that crime is by every civilized government regarded as the highest which citizen or subject can commit. Not content with the sanctions of human justice, of all the crimes against the law of the land it is singled out for the denunciations of religion. The litanies of every church in Christendom whose ritual embraces that office, as far as I am aware, from the metropolitan cathedrals of Europe to the humblest missionary chapel in the islands of the sea, concur with the Church of England in imploring the Sovereign of the Universe, by the most awful adjurations which the heart of man can conceive or his tongue utter, to deliver us from "sedition, privy conspiracy and rebellion." And reason good; for while a rebellion against tyranny—a rebellion designed, after prostrating arbitrary power, to establish free government on the basis of justice and truth—is an enterprise on which good men and angels may look with complacency, an unprovoked rebellion of ambitious men against a beneficent government, for the purpose—the avowed purpose—of establishing, extending and perpetuating any form of injustice and wrong, is an imitation on earth of that first foul revolt of "the Infernal Serpent," against which the Supreme Majesty of Heaven sent forth the armed myriads of his angels, and clothed the right arm of his Son with the three-bolted thunders of omnipotence.

Lord BACON, in "the true marshalling of the sovereign degrees of honor," assigns the first place to "the *Conditores Imperiorum*, founders of States and Commonwealths;" and, truly, to build up from the discordant elements of our nature, the passions, the interests and the opinions of the individual man, the rivalries of family, clan and tribe, the influences of climate and geographical position, the accidents of peace and war accumulated for ages—to build up from these oftentimes warring elements a well-compacted, prosperous and powerful State, if it were to be accomplished by one effort or in one generation, would require a more than mortal skill. To contribute in some notable degree to this, the greatest work of man, by wise and patriotic council in peace and loyal heroism in war, is as high as human merit can well rise, and far more than to any of those to whom BACON assigns this highest place of honor, whose names can hardly be repeated without a wondering smile—ROMULUS, CYRUS, CÆSAR, OTTOMAN, ISMAEL—is it due to our WASHINGTON, as the founder of the American Union. But if to achieve or help to achieve this greatest work of man's wisdom and virtue gives title to a place among the chief benefactors, rightful heirs of the benedictions, of mankind, by equal reason shall the bold, bad men who seek to undo the noble work, *Eversores Imperiorum*, destroyers of States, who for base and selfish ends rebel against beneficent governments, seek to overturn wise constitutions, to lay powerful republican Unions at the foot of foreign thrones, to bring on civil and foreign war, anarchy at home, dictation abroad, desolation, ruin—by equal reason, I say, yes, a thousandfold stronger shall they inherit the execrations of the ages.

But to hide the deformity of the crime under the cloak of that sophistry which strives to make the worse appear the better reason, we are told by the leaders of the Rebellion that in our complex system of government the seperate States are "sovereigns," and that the central power is only an "agency" established by these sovereigns to manage certain little affairs—such, forsooth, as Peace, War, Army, Navy, Finance, Territory, and Relations with the native tribes—which they could not so conveniently administer themselves. It happens, unfortunately for this theory, that the Federal Constitution (which has been adopted by the people of every State of the Union as much as their own State constitutions have been adopted, and is declared to be paramount to them) nowhere recognizes the States as "sovereigns"—in fact, that, by their names, it does not recognize them at all; while the authority established by that instrument is recognized, in its text, not as an "agency," but as "the Government of the United States." By that Constitution, moreover, which purports in its preamble to be ordained and established by "the People of the United States," it is expressly provided, that "the members of the State legislatures, and all executive and judicial officers, shall be bound by oath or affirmation to support the Constitution." Now it is a common thing, under all governments, for an agent to be bound by oath to be faithful to his sovereign; but I never heard before of sovereigns being bound by oath to be faithful to their agency.

Certainly I do not deny that the separate States are clothed with sovereign powers for the administration of local affairs. It is one of the most beautiful features of our mixed system of government; but it is equally true, that, in adopting the Federal Constitution, the States abdicated, by express renunciation, all the most important functions of national sovereignty, and, by one comprehensive, self-denying clause, gave up all right to contravene the Constitution of the United States. Specifically, and by enumeration, they renounced all the most important prerogatives of independent States for peace and for war,—the right to keep troops or ships of war in time of peace, or to engage in war unless actually invaded; to enter into compact with another State or a foreign power; to lay any duty on tonnage, or any impost on exports or imports, without the consent of Congress; to enter into any treaty, alliance, or confederation; to grant letters of marque and reprisal, and to emit bills of credit—while all these powers and many others are exprersly vested in the General Government. To ascribe to political communities, thus limited in their jurisdiction—who cannot even establish a post office on their own soil—the character of independent sovereignty, and to reduce a national organization, clothed with all the transcendent powers of government, to the name and condition of an "agency" of the States, proves nothing but that the logic of secession is on a par with its loyalty and patriotism.

Oh, but "the reserved rights!" And what of the reserved rights? The tenth amendment of the Constitution, supposed to provide for "reserved rights," is constantly misquoted. By that amendment, "the *powers* not delegated to the United States by the Constitution, nor prohibited by it to the States, are reserved to the States respectively, or to the people." The "powers" reserved must of course be such as could have been, but were not delegated to the United States,—could have been, but were not prohibited to the States; but to speak of the *right* of an *individual* State to secede, as a *power* that could have been, though it was not delegated to the *United States*, is simple nonsense.

But waiving this obvious absurdity, can it need a serious argument to prove that there can be no State right to enter into a new confederation reserved under a constitution which expressly prohibits a State to "enter into any treaty, alliance, or confederation," or any "agreement or compact with another State or a foreign power?" To say that the State may, by enacting the preliminary farce of secession, acquire the right to do the prohibited things—to say, for instance, that though the States, in forming the Constitution, delegated to the United States and prohibited to themselves the power of declaring war, there was by implication reserved to each State the right of seceding and then declaring war; that, though they expressly prohibited to the States and delegated to the United States the entire treaty-making power, they reserved by implication (for an express reservation is not pretended) to the individual States, to Florida, for instance, the right to secede, and then to make a treaty with Spain retroceding that Spanish colony, and thus surrendering to a foreign power the key to the Gulf of Mexico,—to maintain propositions like these, with whatever affected seriousness it is done, appears to me egregious trifling.

Pardon me, my friends, for dwelling on these wretched sophistries. But it is these which conducted the armed hosts of rebellion to your doors on the terrible and glorious days of July, and which have brought upon the whole land the scourge of an aggressive and wicked war—a war which can have no other termination compatible with the permanent safety and welfare of the country but the complete destruction of the military power of the enemy. I have, on other occasions, attempted to show that to yield to his demands and acknowledge his independence, thus resolving the Union at once into two hostile governments, with a certainty of further disintegration, would annihilate the strength and the influence of the country as a member of the family of nations; afford to foreign powers the opportunity and the temptation for humiliating and disastrous interference in our affairs; wrest from the Middle and Western States some of their great natural outlets to the sea and of their most important lines of internal communication; deprive the commerce and navigation of the country of two-thirds of our sea coast and of the fortresses which protect it; not only so, but would enable each individual State—some of them with a white population equal to a good sized Northern county—or rather the dominant party in each State, to cede its territory, its harbors, its fortresses, the mouths of its rivers, to any foreign power. It cannot be that the people of the loyal States—that twenty-two millions of brave and prosperous freemen—will, for the temptation of a brief truce in an eternal border war, consent to this hideous national suicide.

Do not think that I exaggerate the consequences of yielding to the demands of the leaders of the rebellion. I understate them. They require of us not only all the sacrifices I have named, not only the cession to them, a foreign and hostile power, of all the territory of the United States at present occupied by the Rebel forces, but the abandonment to them of the vast regions we have rescued from their grasp—of Maryland, of a part of Eastern Virginia and the whole of Western Virginia; the sea coast of North and South Carolina, Georgia, and Florida; Kentucky, Tennessee, and Missouri; Arkansas, and the larger portion of Mississippi, Louisiana, and Texas—in most of which, with the exception of lawless guerillas, there is not a Rebel in arms, in all of which the great majority of the people are loyal to the Union. We must give back, too, the helpless colored population, thousands of whom are perilling their lives in the ranks of our armies, to a bondage rendered tenfold more bitter by the momentary enjoyment of freedom. Finally, we must surrender every man in the Southern country, white or black, who has moved a finger or spoken a word for the restoration of the Union, to a reign of terror as remorseless as that of Robespierre, which has been the chief instrument by which the Rebellion has been organized and sustained, and which has already filled the prisons of the South with noble men, whose only crime is that they are not the worst of criminals. The South is full of such men. I do not believe there has been a day since the election of President LINCOLN, when, if an ordinance of secession could have been fairly submitted, after a free discussion, to the mass of the people in any single Southern State, a majority of ballots would have been given in its favor. No, not in South Carolina. It is not possible that the majority of the people, even of that State, if permitted, without fear or favor, to give a ballot on the question, would have abandoned a leader like PETIGRU, and all the memories of the GADSDENS, the RUTLEDGES, and the COTESWORTH PINCKNEYS of the revolutionary and constitutional age, to follow the agitators of the present day.

Nor must we be deterred from the vigorous prosecution of the war by the suggestion, continually thrown out by the Rebels and those who sympathize with them, that, however it might have been at an earlier stage, there has been engendered by the operations of the war a state of exasperation and bitterness which, independent of all reference to the original nature of the matters in controversy, will forever prevent the restoration of the Union, and the return of harmony between the two great sections of the country. This opinion I take to be entirely without foundation.

No man can deplore more than I do the miseries of every kind unavoidably incident to war. Who could stand on this spot and call to mind the scenes of the first days of July with any other feeling? A sad foreboding of what would ensue, if war should break out between North and South, has haunted me through life, and led me, perhaps too long, to tread in the path of hopeless compromise, in the fond endeavor to conciliate those who were predetermined not to be conciliated. But it is not true, as is pretended by the Rebels and their sympathizers, that the war has been carried on by the United States without entire regard to those temperaments which are enjoined by the law of nations, by our modern civilization, and by the spirit of Christianity. It would be quite easy to point out, in the recent military history of the leading European powers, acts of violence and cruelty, in the prosecution of their wars, to which no parallel can be found among us. In fact, when we consider the peculiar bitterness with which civil wars are almost invariably waged, we may justly boast of the manner in which the United States have carried on the contest. It is of course impossible to prevent the lawless acts of stragglers and deserters, or the occasional unwarrantable proceedings of subordinates on distant stations; but I do not believe there is, in all history, the record of a civil war of such gigantic dimensions where so little has been done in the spirit of vindictiveness as in this war, by the Government and commanders of the United States; and this notwithstanding the provocation given by the Rebel Government by assuming the responsibility of wretches like Quantrell, refusing quarter to colored troops and scourging and selling into slavery free colored men from the North who fall into their hands, by covering the sea with pirates, refusing a just exchange of prisoners, while they crowd their armies with paroled prisoners not exchanged, and starving prisoners of war to death.

In the next place, if there are any present who believe that, in addition to the effect of the military operations of the war, the confiscation acts and emancipation proclamations have embittered the Rebels beyond the possibility of reconciliation, I would request them to reflect that the tone of the Rebel leaders and Rebel press was just as bitter in the first months of the war, nay, before a gun was fired, as it is now. There were speeches made in Congress in the very last session before the outbreak of the Rebellion, so ferocious as to show that their authors were under the influence of a real frenzy. At the present day, if there is any discrimination made by the Confederate press in the affected scorn, hatred and contumely with which every shade of opinion and sentiment in the loyal States is treated, the bitterest contempt is bestowed upon those at the North who still speak the language of compromise, and who condemn those measures of the administration which are alleged to have rendered the return of peace hopeless.

No, my friends, that gracious Providence which overrules all things for the best, "from seeming evil still educing good," has so constituted our natures, that the violent excitement of the passions in one direction is generally followed by a reaction in an opposite direction, and the sooner for the violence. If it were not so—if injuries inflicted and retaliated of necessity led to new retaliations, with forever accumulating compound interest of revenge, then the world, thousands of years ago, would have been turned into an earthly hell, and the nations of the earth would have been resolved into clans of furies and demons, each forever warring with his neighbor. But it is not so; all history teaches a different lesson. The Wars of the Roses in England lasted an entire generation, from the battle of St. Albans in 1455 to that of Bosworth Field in 1485. Speaking of the former, HUME says: "This was the first blood spilt in that fatal quarrel, which was not finished in less than a course of thirty years; which was signalized by twelve pitched battles: which opened a scene of extraordinary fierceness and cruelty; is computed to have cost the lives of eighty princes of the blood; and almost entirely annihilated the ancient nobility of England. The strong attachments which, at that time, men of the same kindred bore to each other, and the vindictive spirit which was considered a point of honor, rendered the great families implacable in their resentments, and widened every moment the breach between the parties." Such was the state of things in England under which an entire generation grew up; but when Henry VII., in whom the titles of the two Houses were united, went up to London after the battle of Bosworth Field, to mount the throne, he was everywhere received with joyous acclamations, "as one ordained and sent from heaven to put an end to the dissensions" which had so long afflicted the country.

The great rebellion of England of the seventeenth century, after long and angry premonitions, may be said to have begun with the calling of the Long Parliament in 1640, and to have ended with the return of Charles II., in 1660—twenty years of discord, conflict and civil war; of confiscation, plunder, havoc; a proud hereditary peerage trampled in the dust; a national church overturned, its clergy beggared, its most eminent prelate put to death; a military despotism established on the ruins of a monarchy which had subsisted seven hundred years, and the legitimate sovereign brought to the block; the great families which adhered to the king proscribed, impoverished, ruined; prisoners of war—a fate worse than starvation in Libby—sold to slavery in the West Indies; in a word, everything that can embitter and madden contending factions. Such was the state of things for twenty years; and yet, by no gentle transition, but suddenly, and "when the restoration of affairs appeared most hopeless," the son of the beheaded sovereign was brought back to his father's blood-stained throne, with such "unexpressible and universal joy" as led the merry monarch to exclaim, "he doubted it had been his own fault he had been absent so long, for he saw nobody who did not protest he had ever wished for his return." "In this wonderful manner," says CLARENDON, "and with this incredible expedition did God put an end to a rebellion that had raged near twenty years, and had been carried on with all the horrid circumstances of murder, devastation and parracide that fire and sword, in the hands of the most wicked men in the world," (it is a royalist that is speaking,) "could be instruments of, almost to the desolation of two kingdoms, and the exceeding defacing and deforming of the third. . . . . By these remarkable steps did the merciful hand of God, in this short space of time, not only bind up and heal all those wounds, but even made the scar as undiscernable as, in respect of the deepness, was possible, which was a glorious addition to the deliverance."

In Germany, the wars of the Reformation and of CHARLES V., in the sixteenth century, the Thirty Years' war in the seventeenth century, the Seven Years' war in the eighteenth century, not to speak of other less celebrated contests, entailed upon that country all the miseries of intestine strife for more than three centuries. At the close of the last named war—which was the shortest of all, and waged in the most civilized age—"an officer," says ARCHENHOLZ, "rode through seven villages in Hesse, and found in them but one human being." More than three hundred principalities, comprehended in the Empire, fermented with the fierce passions of proud and petty States; at the commencement of this period the castles of robber counts frowned upon every hill-top; a dreadful secret tribunal, whose seat no one knew, whose power none could escape, froze the hearts of men with terror throughout the land; religious hatred mingled its bitter poison in the seething caldron of provincial animosity; but of all these deadly enmities between the States of Germany scarcely the memory remains. There are controversies in that country, at the present day, but they grow mainly out of the rivalry of the two leading powers. There is no country in the world in which the sentiment of national brotherhood is stronger.

In Italy, on the breaking up of the Roman Empire, society might be said to be resolved into its original elements—into hostile atoms, whose only movement was that of mutual repulsion. Ruthless barbarians had destroyed the old organizations, and covered the land with a merciless feudalism. As the new civilization grew up, under the wing of the church, the noble families and the walled towns fell madly into conflict with each other; the secular feud of Pope and Emperor scourged the land; province against province, city against city, street against street, waged remorseless war with each other from father to son, till DANTE was able to fill his imaginary hell with the real demons of Italian history. So ferocious had the factions become, that the great poet-exile himself, the glory of his native city and of his native language, was, by a decree of the municipality, condemned to be burned alive if found in the city of Florence. But these deadly feuds and hatred yielded to political influences, as the hostile cities were grouped into States under stable governments; the lingering traditions of the ancient animosities gradually died away, and now Tuscan and Lombard, Sardinian and Neapolitan, as if to shame the degenerate sons of America, are joining in one cry for a united Italy.

In France, not to go back to the civil wars of the League, in the sixteenth century, and of the Fronde, in the seventeenth; not to speak of the dreadful scenes throughout the kingdom, which followed the revocation of the edict of Nantes; we have, in the great revolution which commenced at the close of the last century, seen the blood-hounds of civil strife let loose as rarely before in the history of the world. The reign of terror established at Paris stretched its bloody Briarean arms to every city and village in the land, and if the most deadly feuds which ever divided a people had the power to cause permanent alienation and hatred, this surely was the occasion. But far otherwise the fact. In seven years from the fall of ROBESPIERRE, the strong arm of the youthful conquerer brought order out of this chaos of crime and woe; Jacobins whose hands were scarcely cleansed from the best blood of France met the returning emigrants, whose estates they had confiscated and whose kindred they had dragged to the guillotine, in the Imperial antechambers; and when, after another turn of the wheel of fortune, LOUIS XVIII. was restored to his throne, he took the regicide FOUCHE, who had voted for his brother's death, to his cabinet and confidence.

The people of loyal America will never ask you, sir, to take to your confidence or admit again to a share in the government the hard-hearted men whose cruel lust of power has brought this desolating war upon the land, but there is no personal bitterness felt even against them. They may live, if they can bear to live after wantonly causing the death of so many thousands of their fellow-men; they may live in safe obscurity beneath the shelter of the government they have sought to overthrow, or they may fly to the protection of the governments of Europe—some of them are already there, seeking, happily in vain, to obtain the aid of foreign powers in furtherance of their own treason. There let them stay. The humblest dead soldier, that lies cold and stiff in his grave before us, is an object of envy beneath the clods that cover him, in comparison with the living man, I care not with what trumpery credentials he may be furnished, who is willing to grovel at the foot of a foreign throne for assistance in compassing the ruin of his country.

But the hour is coming and now is, when the power of the leaders of the

Rebellion to delude and inflame must cease. There is no bitterness on the part of the masses. The people of the South are not going to wage an eternal war, for the wretched pretext by which this Rebellion is sought to be justified. The bonds that unite us as one people—a substantial community of origin, language, belief, and law, (the four great ties that hold the societies of men together;) common national and political interests; a common history; a common pride in a glorious ancestry; a common interest in this great heritage of blessings; the very geographical features of the country; the mighty rivers that cross the lines of climate and thus facilitate the interchange of natural and industrial products, while the wonder-working arm of the engineer has levelled the mountain-walls which separate the East and West, compelling your own Alleghenies, my Maryland and Pennsylvania friends, to open wide their everlasting doors to the chariot-wheels of traffic and travel; these bonds of union are of perennial force and energy, while the causes of alienation are imaginary, factitious, and transient. The heart of the people, North and South, is for the Union. Indications, too plain to be mistaken, announce the fact, both in the East and the West of the States in rebellion. In North Carolina and Arkansas the fatal charm at length is broken. At Raleigh and Little Rock the lips of honest and brave men are unsealed, and an independent press is unlimbering its artillery. When its rifled cannon shall begin to roar, the hosts of treasonable sophistry—the mad delusions of the day—will fly like the Rebel army through the passes of yonder mountain. The weary masses of the people are yearning to see the dear old flag again floating upon their capitols, and they sigh for the return of the peace, prosperity, and happiness, which they enjoyed under a government whose power was felt only in its blessings.

And now, friends, fellow citizens of Gettysburg and Pennsylvania, and you from remoter States, let me again, as we part, invoke your benediction on these honored graves. You feel, though the occasion is mournful, that it is good to be here. You feel that it was greatly auspicious for the cause of the country, that the men of the East and the men of the West, the men of nineteen sister States, stood side by side, on the perilous ridges of the battle. You now feel it a new bond of union, that they shall lie side by side, till the clarion, louder than that which marshalled them to the combat, shall awake their slumbers. God bless the Union; it is dearer to us for the blood of brave men which has been shed in its defence. The spots on which they stood and fell; these pleasant heights; the fertile plain beneath them; the thriving village whose streets so lately rang with the strange din of war; the fields beyond the ridge, where the noble REYNOLDS held the advancing foe at bay, and, while he gave up his own life, assured by his forethought and self-sacrifice the triumph of the two succeeding days; the little streams which wind through the hills, on whose banks in after-times the wondering ploughmen will turn up, with the rude weapons of savage warfare, the fearful missiles of modern artillery; Seminary Ridge, the Peach Orchard, Cemetery, Culp, and Wolf Hill, Round Top, Little Round Top, humble names, henceforwarded dear and famous—no lapse of time, no distance of space, shall cause you to be forgotten. "The whole earth," said PERICLES, as he stood over the remains of his fellow citizens, who had fallen in the first year of the Peloponnesian war, "the whole earth is the sepulchre of illustrious men." All time, he might have added, is the millennium of their glory. Surely I would do no injustice to the other noble achievements of the war, which have reflected such honor on both arms of the service, and have entitled the armies and the navy of the United States, their officers and men, to the warmest thanks and the richest rewards which a grateful people can pay. But they, I am sure, will join us in saying, as we bid farewell to the dust of these martyr-heroes, that wheresoever throughout the civilized world the accounts of this great warfare are read, and down to the latest period of recorded time, in the glorious annals of our common country, there will be no brighter page than that which relates THE BATTLES OF GETTYSBURG.

HYMN

COMPOSED BY B. B. FRENCH, ESQ., AT GETTYSBURG.

'Tis holy ground—
This spot, where, in their graves,
We place our country's braves,
Who fell in Freedom's holy cause,
Fighting for liberties and laws;
Let tears abound.

Here let them rest;
And summer's heat and winter's cold
Shall glow and freeze above this mould—
A thousand years shall pass away—
A nation still shall mourn this clay,
Which now is blest.

Here, where they fell,
Oft shall the widow's tear be shed,
Oft shall fond parents mourn their dead;
The orphan here shall kneel and weep,
And maidens, where their lovers sleep,
Their woes shall tell.

Great God in Heaven!
Shall all this sacred blood be shed?
Shall we thus mourn our glorious dead?
Oh, shall the end be wrath and woe,
The knell of Freedom's overthrow,
A country riven?

It will not be!
We trust, O God! thy gracious power
To aid us in our darkest hour.
This be our prayer—"O Father! save
A people's freedom from its grave.
All praise to Thee!"

DEDICATORY ADDRESS

OF

PRESIDENT LINCOLN.

Fourscore and seven years ago our fathers brought forth upon this continent a new nation, conceived in Liberty, and dedicated to the proposition that all men are created equal.

Now we are engaged in a great civil war, testing whether that nation, or any nation so conceived and so dedicated, can long endure. We are met on a great battle-field of that war. We are met to dedicate a portion of it as the final resting-place of those who here gave their lives that that nation might live. It is altogether fitting and proper that we should do this.

But in a larger sense we cannot dedicate, we cannot consecrate, we cannot hallow this ground. The brave men, living and dead, who struggled here have consecrated it far above our power to add or detract. The world will little note nor long remember what we say here, but it can never forget what they did here. It is for us, the living, rather to be dedicated here to the unfinished work that they have thus far so nobly carried on. It is rather for us to be here dedicated to the great task remaining before us—that from these honored dead we take increased devotion to the cause for which they here gave the last full measure of devotion—that we here highly resolve that the dead shall not have died in vain; that the nation shall, under God, have a new birth of freedom, and that the government of the people, by the people, and for the people, shall not perish from the earth.

BENEDICTION

BY

REV. H. L. BAUGHER, D. D.,

PRESIDENT OF PENNSYLVANIA COLLEGE, GETTYSBURG.

O Thou King of kings and Lord of lords, God of the nations of the earth, who, by Thy kind providence hast permitted us to engage in these solemn services, grant us thy blessing.

Bless this consecrated ground, and these holy graves. Bless the President of these United States, and his Cabinet. Bless the Governors and the Representatives of the States here assembled with all needed grace to conduct the affairs committed into their hands, to the glory of thy name, and the greatest good of the people.

May this great nation be delivered from treason and rebellion at home, and from the power of enemies abroad. And now may the grace of our Lord Jesus Christ, the love of God our Heavenly Father, and the fellowship of the Holy Ghost, be with you all. *Amen.*

www.ingramcontent.com/pod-product-compliance
Lightning Source LLC
LaVergne TN
LVHW011208110826
845150LV00006B/1357

* 9 7 8 1 4 2 5 5 1 8 4 5 5 *